ARTIFICIAL INTELLIGENCE:
AN MIT PERSPECTIVE

ARTIFICIAL INTELLIGENCE: AN MIT PERSPECTIVE

Volume 2:

**Understanding Vision
Manipulation
Computer Design
Symbol Manipulation**

**Edited by
PATRICK HENRY WINSTON
and
RICHARD HENRY BROWN**

The MIT Press
Cambridge, Massachusetts, and London, England

PUBLISHER'S NOTE

The format is intended to reduce the cost of publishing certain works in book form and to shorten the gap between editorial preparation and final publication. Detailed editing and composition have been avoided by photographing the text of this book directly from the editors' computer-prepared material.

Q
335
.A7865.
vol. 2

Library of Congress Cataloging in Publication Data

Main entry under title:

Artificial intelligence, an MIT perspective.

(The MIT Press series in artificial intelligence)
Includes bibliographical references and indexes.
CONTENTS: v. 1. Expert problem solving, natural language understanding, intelligent computer coaches, representation and learning.--v. 2. Understanding vision, manipulation, computer design, symbol manipulation.
1. Artificial intelligence. I. Winston, Patrick Henry. II. Brown, Richard Henry. III. Series.
Q335.A7865   001.53'5   78-26640
ISBN 0-262-23096-8 (v. 1)
ISBN 0-262-23097-6 (v. 2)

VOLUME II

VOLUME I

SERIES FOREWORD

Artificial intelligence is the study of intelligence using the ideas and methods of computation. Unfortunately, a definition of intelligence seems impossible at the moment because intelligence appears to be an amalgam of so many information-processing and information-representation abilities.

Of course psychology, philosophy, linguistics, and related disciplines offer various perspectives and methodologies for studying intelligence. For the most part, however, the theories proposed in these fields are too incomplete and too vaguely stated to be realized in computational terms. Something more is needed, even though valuable ideas, relationships, and constraints can be gleaned from traditional studies of what are, after all, impressive existence proofs that intelligence is in fact possible.

Artificial intelligence offers a new perspective and a new methodology. Its central goal is to make computers intelligent, both to make them more useful and to understand the principles that make intelligence possible. That intelligent computers will be extremely useful is obvious. The more profound point is that artificial intelligence aims to understand intelligence using the ideas and methods of computation, thus offering a radically new and different basis for theory formation. Most of the people doing artificial intelligence believe that these theories will apply to any intelligent information processor, whether biological or solid state.

There are side effects that deserve attention, too. Any program that will successfully model even a small part of intelligence will be inherently massive and complex. Consequently, artificial intelligence continually confronts the limits of computer science technology. The problems encountered have been hard enough and interesting enough to seduce artificial intelligence people into working on them with enthusiasm. It is natural, then, that there has been a steady flow of ideas from artificial intelligence to computer science, and the flow shows no sign of abating.

The purpose of this MIT Press Series in Artificial Intelligence is to provide people in many areas, both professionals and students, with timely, detailed information about what is happening on the frontiers in research centers all over the world.

Appropriately, these first two volumes in the series are intended to be a representative compendium of recent work done at MIT in the Artificial Intelligence Laboratory, a major center for aritificial intelligence research. The broad range of the material suggests the nature of the field, and it reflects our speculation about the kind of material that the series will include as it develops.

Patrick Henry Winston
Mike Brady

Purpose and Structure

Our purpose in assembling this two volume collection is to introduce advanced topics in Artificial Intelligence and to characterize the MIT point of view. With this in mind, we have selected contributions meant to be representative of either the research area explored or the methodology employed. Certainly the volumes are not construed to be exhaustive or to be exclusive -- our choices were often dictated by nontechnical factors.

Some of the shorter selections appear in full in order to convey a feeling for the detail and precision required in implementing working programs. Usually, however, length considerations have forced considerable abridgment so as to avoid the bulk that would increase costs and discourage cover-to-cover reading. This necessarily means that the sections often describe *what* can be done but not much about *how.* Excited readers should think of the volumes as a collection of hors d'oeuvres to be followed by entrees accessible through the references.

The arrangement of sections into chapters was difficult since the topics are nonexclusive. The chapter on representation has a section oriented toward language, for example.

Each chapter is introduced by a short note that is intended to introduce terms that may be unfamiliar or to offer an historical context. Occasionally, further background will be needed to appreciate what is being said, and it would therefore be good to have a basic textbook on Artificial Intelligence at hand. Perhaps *Artificial Intelligence* by Winston would be a good choice. Several others are listed in the references.

Sources

With one exception, all of the sections originally appeared as publications of the MIT Artificial Intelligence Laboratory. The section by William A. Martin originally appeared as a publication of the MIT Laboratory for Computer Science. Several sections also appeared in various forms in published journals.   We are able to include them through the kind permission of the publishers indicated in the acknowledgements at the end of each section.

Sponsors

Nearly all of the research described in these volumes was supported by the Defense Advanced Research Projects Agency. Without their help and guidance, Artificial Intelligence today would be a speculation rather than a force.   Other sponsors have made it possible to do essential work in areas that lie outside of DARPA's interests. The Office of Naval Research has sponsored all recent work on manipulation and productivity technology at MIT. The National Science Foundation, similarly, has sponsored all recent work on expert problem solving in the domain of electronics engineering. The National Institute of Education has sponsored some of the work on natural language understanding. And work on the LISP machine was initiated with help from IBM.

Contributors

We particularly thank Karen Prendergast for her meticulous and skillful work on layout, most of the drawing, and final preparation of the manuscript for printing.

We thank the authors of the sections for their help in adapting their work for our purpose.

We thank Robert Sjoberg for his help in creating the type fonts used in these volumes.

We also thank Suzin Jabari, for early help with drawing, and the people who helped proofread and debug: Jon Doyle, Ken Forbus, Margareta Hornell, Karen Prendergast, and Carol Roberts.

Textbooks

Nils J. Nilsson, *Problem-Solving Methods in Artificial Intelligence*, McGraw-Hill Book Company, New York, 1971.

Phillip C. Jackson, *Introduction to Artificial Intelligence*, **Mason and Lipscomb**, New York, 1974.

Earl B. Hunt, *Artificial Intelligence*, **Academic Press, New York,** 1975.

Bertram Raphael, *The Thinking Computer*, **W. H. Freeman, San** Francisco, 1976.

Patrick H. Winston, *Artificial Intelligence* **Addison-Wesley,** Reading, Massachusetts, 1977.

ARTIFICIAL INTELLIGENCE: AN MIT PERSPECTIVE

UNDERSTANDING VISION

DAVID MARR
SHIMON ULLMAN
KENT STEVENS
BERTHOLD HORN
BRETT BACHMAN
ROBERT WOODHAM
MARK LAVIN

Section Contents

Understanding vision has been a driving passion of many researchers in Artificial Intelligence. In this chapter, it is pursued from two directions. First, we have the work led by Marr that is heavily influenced by a desire to understand biological systems as well as vision for its own sake:

- *Marr* introduces the chapter with an overview section describing the modules he feels are most important in the development of a general theory of vision.

- *Ullman* then illustrates the style championed by Marr in a section devoted to understanding how light sources can be detected in a scene. He concludes that it is necessary to compare certain intensity ratios with intensity derivative ratios.

- *Stevens* continues by applying the same methodology to the problem of inferring surface orientation from textures and surface contours.

Second, we have the work led by Horn that concentrates on understanding and exploiting how light is reflected from surfaces.

- *Horn and Bachman* demonstrate the power of the reflectance map approach to understanding reflected light by using it to generate synthetic aerial photographs of real images. Their method is a first step toward better crop prediction and change detection.

- *Woodham* then takes a theoretical perspective and marries reflectance map techniques to ideas about how local shape constraints can propagate to force global conclusions.

- *Lavin* concludes the chapter with a section emphasizing a different sort of constraint exploitation. He shows how a sequence of line drawings of hills can be used to make a map of the terrain involved and to locate the path of the image-making vehicle in the map.

Marr has a Global View of Vision Theory

Marr's section is itself a good introduction to his overall point of view. Here, we will confine ourselves to previewing and underscoring a few critical points. But first, there is the question of approach. Marr articulates clearly his firm belief that vision research must follow these steps:

■   First, a competence to be understood is observed and precisely described, normally by careful experiment with human subjects.

■   Second, representations are selected or invented that facilitate explicit description of the target processing products.

■   Third, the competence and the representations are combined into a well-defined computation problem to be solved.

■   Fourth, algorithms are devised that perform the desired computation.

■   And fifth, results are validated by some combination of computer implementation and psychophysical experimentation.

Importantly, it is wrong to begin with devotion to some particular type of algorithm with a view toward finding a problem that it will solve. Oddly, this key point seems difficult to fully appreciate. The tendency is to run before getting the

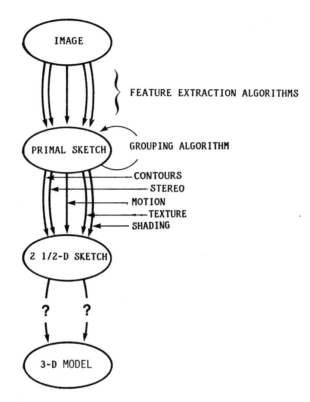

Figure 1. Marr's model of vision requires three levels of representation, each of which makes appropriate information explicit. The primal sketch makes information about intensity changes explicit, including the length, position, orientation, and contrast of line fragments; the 2 1/2 -D sketch makes information about surface orientation explicit.

ball.

At the highest level, observation of competences and definition of representations have led Marr to think in terms of the competences and representations suggested in figure 1. As shown, there are three levels of representation. The *primal sketch* makes information about intensity changes explicit, including the length, position, orientation, and contrast of line fragments. The *2 1/2-D* sketch makes information about surface orientation explicit. And the the *generalized-cone 3-D* model makes information about object shape explicit. Marr's section provides details about these representations and describes some of the competences required to deal with them. The sections by Ullman and Stevens provide more depth by way of close examination of particular competences and the algorithms that these competences engender.

Part of the motivation for these studies derives from a desire to understand biological vision, and another part has to do with making machines that see. In light of the desire to make machines that can see, it is natural to wonder if it would be sensible to copy neural mechanisms using what is known about human physiology. Regrettably, this is a bad idea. Knowing about human physiology cannot help much for the same reasons that knowing all about computer hardware does not help us make them intelligent.

This does not mean that attention paid to human vision is relevant only to the goal of understanding biological vision at some neural level. We firmly believe an understanding of the limits of biological vision cannot be ignored. We want systems whose strength will undoubtedly derive from many subsystems. Consequently, it is very useful to know how strong each subsystem must be to do its part of the total job. Such information helps establish what subsystems must compute and whether various subsystems can be built to operate at reasonable speed.

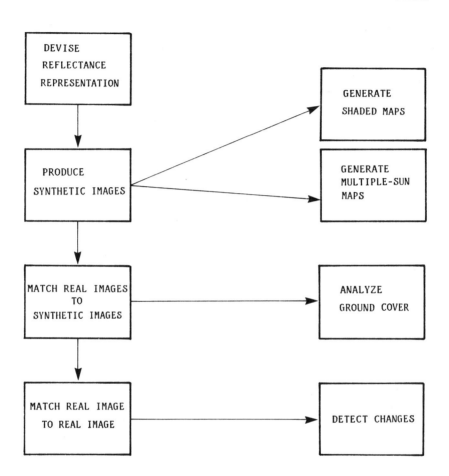

Figure 2. Roadmap for the development of a theory of image formation and exploitation. Applications of the theory appear to the right.

Horn Concentrates on Understanding Image Formation

Understanding an image implies a need to understand how light reflection depends on various combinations of surface material, surface orientation, and light-source position. Among the products are tools for dealing with the following needs:

■   Automated generation of shaded relief maps.

■   Generation of low-level, obliquely-viewed images.

■   Generation of special maps that bring out particular terrain features.

■   Classification of ground cover for crop prediction.

■   Matching images to terrain data for satellite navigation.

■   Making maps for automatic or semiautomatic change detection.

The roadmap for the theory development is shown in figure 2. As shown, the progression involves a number of key representations: the reflectance map, the digital terrain map, the synthetic image, the multiple-sun synthetic image, the albedo image, and the change-detection image. Since understanding reflectance maps is prerequisite to following Horn's section, we will now describe what is involved.

The purpose of the reflectance map is to make explicit the relationship among observed intensity, surface material, surface orientation, and light-source position. To see how, consider figure 3. All points (p, q) in the space correspond to surface orientations. For a given surface material and light-source position, a surface's orientation determines its reflected light intensity. By drawing lines through points representing orientations that have the same intensity, one has the

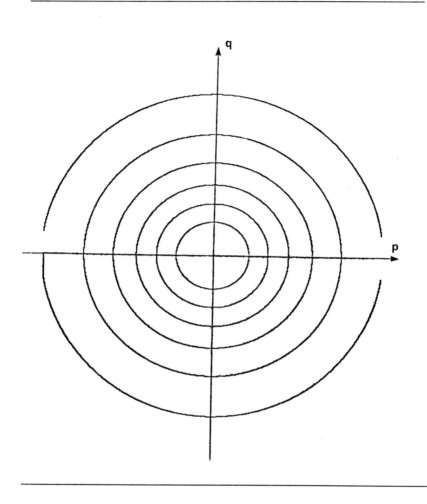

Figure 3. In the reflectance map each point represents some tilt of the viewed surface. For this particular map, the circular contours of constant reflectance suggest that the light source is behind the viewer and the viewed surface has normal reflectance properties.

isointensity lines shown.

The line-of-sight connecting the viewer with the surfaces viewed is assumed to be along the z-axis, and p and q are actually the partial derivatives of the surface z(x, y) with respect to x and y. Thus the point (0, 0) corresponds to a surface whose normal points directly at the viewer. A point (p, 0) indicates a surface that is tilted by rotation about the y-axis only.

The isointensity lines in the sample reflectance map are concentric circles because the surface material is assumed ordinary and the light source is assumed to be directly behind the viewer. These conditions assure that the amount of tilt, given by $p^2 + q^2$, is all that matters.

Using the same surface material but moving the light source off the z-axis gives the reflectance map shown in figure 4. The point (0, 0) no longer corresponds to the orientation of maximum intensity -- the p and q of maximum intensity now specify the surface orientation for which the surface normal points directly to the light source.

Figure 5 shows what a cone and a sphere look like when seen from above under both of the lighting conditions so far described by the two sample reflectance maps. It is clear that a poor choice can make understanding difficult -- there can be little or no impression of shape.

Once it is possible to predict intensities from material, orientation, and light-position information, it is then possible to produce synthetic high-altitude images. These are immediately useful for producing shaded relief maps. Appropriate combinations of ground cover and sun position can be used to give the user the best possible feel for the mountains and hills that constitute the terrain.

Interestingly, however, shaded relief maps need not conform to what might actually be observed. Horn has made images that correspond to terrain illuminated by three suns, one blue, one red, and one green. Such images give special insight into terrain properties at a glance. Slopes with exposure to the south, for example, are readily identified because of their red hue

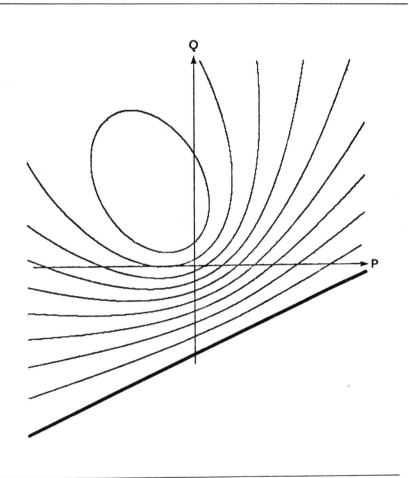

Figure 4. In this reflectance map, the contours of constant reflectance correspond to a normal surface material and a light source striking the viewed surface from the upper left (or from the northwest, thinking in map terms).

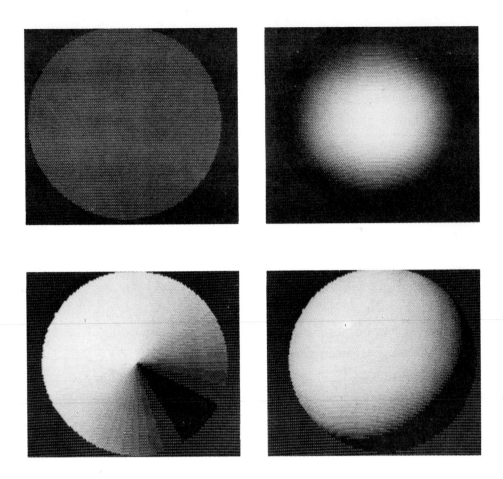

Figure 5. The impression of surface given by an image depends on the light source and surface material and these in turn are characterized by reflectance maps. The two images on the left are cones viewed from a line of sight through the tip and along the axis. The images on the right are both spheres. The upper cone-sphere pair was made by a program that assumed that the light source is behind the viewer. In the lower pair, the assumed light source was displaced. These situations correspond to the reflectance maps just shown in previous figures. In all cases the surface material was assumed to be a standard one with no special properties.

from the red, southern sun.

The thrust of Horn's section in this chapter, however, is to make images that match photographs as closely as possible with a view toward registering real aerial photographs with terrain models. Such matching is a vital first step toward improving the use of satellite images.

After a real aerial photograph is registered with a synthetic one produced from a terrain model, some areas will refuse to match well because the actual ground cover is not the one assumed in generating the synthetic image. Rather than an annoyance, we believe the discrepancies suggest a solution to the classification problem. Since registration evidently does not absolutely require ground cover information, it seems sensible to use differences between two registered images to estimate surface reflectance. Then the ratio of real to synthetic intensity can be used in terrain classification, particularly if it is calculated for each of the spectral bands recorded in LANDSAT images.

Horn defines an *albedo map* to be an image in which each point's intensity is the ratio of the intensity in the real image to the intensity in the synthetic image. In addition to use in classification, it seems likely that albedo maps will be useful in change detection. It would be nice if change could be detected by subtracting one image from another. Unfortunately, the changes in sun position from hour to hour and from day to day make this impossible by swamping changes caused by changes in the ground cover. Instead, Horn proposes to divide earlier and later real image intensities by the intensities predicted by the terrain model to give two registered albedo maps. Then, one albedo map is subtracted from the other, producing change that will correspond to ground-cover differences occurring between the earlier and later recording times.

For human use, the two albedo maps can be done in different colors and superimposed. The human analyst's eye is instantly drawn to places where changes have taken place because their hue will differ from the surrounding area.

Understanding Constraint Remains a Key Idea

Waltz' study of line-drawing interpretation made the idea of constraint propagation immensely popular. The idea is to first catalogue all possible ways various edge types can form junctions. Then the catalogue can be used to do analysis in much the same way that one solves jigsaw puzzles. Locally, things fit together in only a few ways. The fit constraints, taken together, make for extreme global constraint that usually enables unique global conclusions about edge types.

In Woodham's section, the idea of constraint propagation is combined with Horn's notions about reflectance maps. In the course of his discussion, Woodham probes the theory of reflectance constraints to provide solid, quantitative theory for the simultaneous use of multiple reflectance maps.

Loosely speaking, Lavin's section is also about constraint, this time in connection with motion vision and the use of multiple views of hills to establish constraint.

REPRESENTING AND COMPUTING VISUAL INFORMATION

DAVID MARR

Vision is the construction of efficient symbolic descriptions from images of the world. An important aspect of vision is the choice of representations for the different kinds of information in a visual scene. In the early stages of the analysis of an image, the representations used depend more on what it is possible to compute from an image than on what is ultimately desirable, but later representations can be more sensitive to the specific needs of recognition. David Marr surveys work in vision at MIT from a perspective in which the representational problems assume a primary importance. An overall framework is suggested for visual information processing which consists of three major levels of representations; the primal sketch, which makes explicit the intensity changes and local two-dimensional geometry of an image; the $2^1/_2$-D sketch, which is a viewer-centered representation of the depth, orientation and discontinuities of the visible surfaces; and the 3-D model representation, which allows an object-centered description of the three-dimensional structure and organization of a viewed shape.

Understanding information processing tasks and vision

Vision is an information processing task, and like any other, it needs understanding at two levels. The first, which I call the computational theory of an information processing task, is concerned with what is being computed and why; and the second level, that at which particular algorithms are designed, with how the computation is to be carried out [Marr and Poggio 1977a]. For example, the theory of the Fourier transform is a level 1 theory, and is expressed independently of ways of obtaining it (algorithms like the Fast Fourier Transform, or the parallel algorithms of coherent optics) that lie at level 2. Chomsky calls level 1 theories competence theories, and level 2 theories performance theories. The theory of a computation must precede the design of algorithms for carrying it out, because one cannot seriously contemplate designing an algorithm or a program until one knows precisely what it is meant to be doing.

I believe this point is worth emphasizing, because it is important to be clear about the level at which one is pursuing one's studies. For example, there has recently been much interest in so-called cooperative algorithms [Marr and Poggio 1976] or relaxation labelling [Rosenfeld, Hummel and Zucker 1976]. The attraction of this technique is that it allows one to write plausible constraints directly into an algorithm, but one must remember that such techniques amount to no more than a style of programming, and they lie at the second of the two levels. They have nothing to do with the theory of vision, whose business it is to derive the constraints and characterize the solutions that are consistent with them.

If one accepts in broad terms this statement of what it means to understand an information processing task, one can go on to ask about the particular theories that one needs to understand vision. Vision can be thought of as a *process*, that produces from images of the external world a description that is useful to the viewer and not cluttered by irrelevant information. These descriptions, in turn, are built or assembled from many different but fixed representations, each capturing some aspect of the visual scene. In this article, I shall try to present a summary of our work on vision at MIT seen from a perspective in which the representational problems assume a primary importance. I shall include summaries of our present ideas as well as of completed work.

The important point about a representation is that it makes certain information *explicit* (cf. the principle of explicit naming, [Marr 1976]). For example, at some point in the analysis of an image, the intensity changes present there need to be made explicit, so does the geometry -- of the image and of the viewed shape -- and so do other parameters like color, motion, position and binocular disparity. To understand vision thus requires that we first have some idea of which representations to use, and then we can proceed to analyze the computational problems that arise in obtaining and manipulating each representation. Clearly the choice of representation is crucial in any given instance, for an inappropriate choice can lead to unwieldy and inefficient computations. Fortunately, the human visual system offers a good example of an efficient vision processor, and therefore provides important clues to the representations that are most appropriate and likely to yield successful solutions.

This point of view places the nature of the representations at the center of attention, but it is important to remember that the limitations on the processes that create and use these representations are an important factor in determining their structure, because one of the constraints on vision is that the description ultimately produced be derivable from images. In general, the structure of a representation is determined at the lower levels mostly by what it is possible to compute, whereas later on they can afford to be influenced by what it is desirable to compute for the purposes of recognition.

Early processing problems

There are two important kinds of information contained in an intensity array, the intensity changes present there, and the local geometry of the image. The primal sketch [Marr 1976] is a primitive representation that allows this information to be made explicit. Following the clues available from neurophysiology [Hubel and Wiesel 1962], intensity changes are represented by blobs and by oriented elements that specify a position, a contrast, a spatial extent associated with the intensity change, a weak characterization of the type of intensity change involved, and a specification of points at which intensity changes cease (so-called termination points). The representation of local geometry makes explicit two-dimensional geometrical relations between significant items in an image. These include parallel relationships between nearby edges, and the relative positions and orientations of significant places in the image. These significant places are marked by "place-tokens," and they are defined in a variety of ways, by blobs or local patches of different intensity, by small lines, and by the ends of lines or bars. The local geometrical relations between place-tokens are represented by inserting virtual lines that join nearby place-tokens, thus making explicit the existence of a relation between the two tokens, their relative orientation, and the distance between them (figure 1).

The idea of place-tokens and of this way of representing geometrical relations arose from considering the computational problems that are posed by early visual processing, and one of the questions we have been asking is, can one find any psychophysical evidence that the human visual system makes use of a similar representation? We have recently obtained two results related to this point. Stevens [1978] has examined the perception of random-dot interference patterns (figure 2), constructed by superimposing two copies of a random dot pattern where one copy has undergone some composition of expansion, translation, or rotation transformations [Glass 1969]. He found that a simple algorithm suffices to account quantitatively for

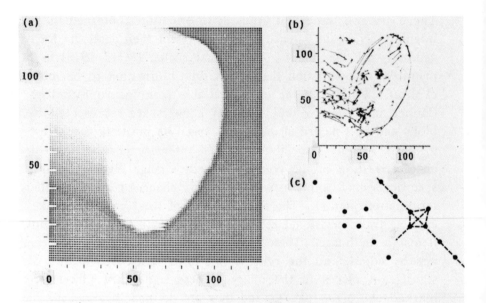

Figure 1. Primal Sketch. The primal sketch makes explicit information held in an intensity array. Changes in intensity are represented by oriented edge, line and bar elements, associated with which is a measure of the contrast and spatial extent of the intensity change. Local two-dimensional geometry of significant places in the image are marked by "place-tokens", which can be defined in a variety of ways, and the geometric relations between them are represented by inserting "virtual lines" between nearby tokens.

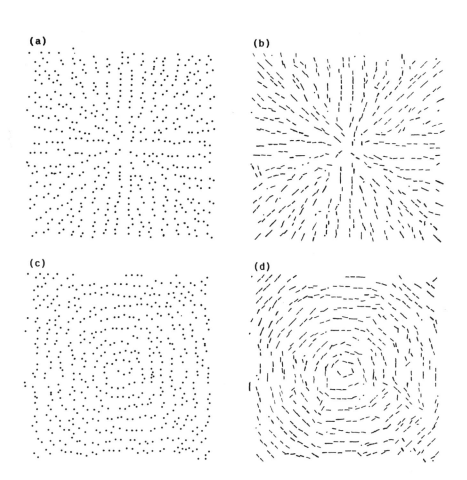

Figure 2. A and C are random-dot interference patterns of the kind described by Glass [1969]. B and D exhibit the results of running the algorithm described in the text and in Figure 3. The neighborhood radius was such that roughly 8 neighborhoods were included [Stevens 1977].

human performance on these patterns. The algorithm consists of three steps:

(1) Each dot defines a place-token. For example, some dots can be replaced by small lines or larger blobs without disrupting the subjective impression of flow.

(2) Virtual lines are inserted between nearby place-tokens, and the neighborhood in which the virtual lines are inserted depends in a predictable way on the density of the dots.

(3) The orientations of the virtual lines attached to all the points in each neighborhood are histogrammed, and locally parallel organization is found by searching for a peak in this histogram. The bucket width that best matches human performance is about 10 degrees.

The details of these steps are set out in figure 3. The interesting features of the algorithm are; (a) It is not iterative. Stevens could find no evidence that human performance rests on a cooperative algorithm, although this type of problem is ideal for that approach. (b) The algorithm is purely local. No global-to-local or top-down interactions are necessary to explain human performance. (c) What the algorithm finds is locally parallel organization. In this case, the organization lies in the virtual lines constructed between nearby dots, but locally parallel organization among the real edges and lines in an image also forms an important part of the structure of an image [Marr 1976].

The second study is one by Schatz [1977] on texture vision discrimination. Marr [1976] suggested that such discriminations could be carried out by first-order discriminations acting on the description in the primal sketch. Marr supposed that certain grouping processes were needed before the discriminations are made in order to account for the full range of human texture discrimination, but in a careful examination of the problem, Schatz found that many of the examples he constructed could be explained by assuming that the discriminations are made only on real edges or on virtual lines inserted between neighboring place-tokens. If this were generally true, it would stand in elegant relation to Julesz's [1975] conjecture, that a necessary condition for the discriminability of two textures is that their dipole statistics differ. This condition is known not to be sufficient, a state of affairs that one can view as implying that we have access to only a proper subset of all dipole statistics. It is possible that this proper subset consists only of real edges and of the virtual lines that join nearby place-tokens.

If one accepts that texture discrimination relies upon first-order discriminations of this type, it is natural to ask how sensitive are the particular discrimination functions that we can bring to bear on an image. Riley [1977] has found evidence that the available functions are extremely coarse. For example, figure 4 consists of a background in which the line segments have a random orientation, surrounding a square containing lines of only three orientations. Surprisingly, the square cannot be discerned without scrutiny. One interpretation of this and related findings is, that discriminations on orientations other than horizontal and vertical are made on the output of 5 channels, each nearly binary, and with an angular width of about 35 degrees -- in other words, only very little information is available about the distribution of orientations in an image. It appears that our discrimination ability is as poor or poorer for the other stimulus dimensions, for example intensity distribution [Riley 1977].

In another study concerned with what can be extracted from an image, Ullman [1976a] enquired about the possible physical basis for the subjective quality of fluorescence, which is normally associated with the presence of a light source. He noted that at a light source boundary, the ratio of intensity to intensity gradient changes sharply, whereas this is not true at reflectance boundaries unless the surface orientation changes sharply. He showed that, in the mini-world of Mondrians, the discriminant to which this leads predicts human performance satisfactorily.

Ken Forbus [1978] has extended this work to the

Figure 3. The algorithm for computing locally parallel structure has three fundamental steps. In the case of the Moire dot patterns, each dot contributes a place token. A virtual line represents the position, separation, and orientation between a pair of neighboring dots. To favor relatively nearer neighbors, relatively short virtual lines are emphasized. The second step is to histogram the orientations of the virtual lines that were constructed. For example, the neighbor D would contribute orientations AD, DF, DG, and DH to the histogram. The final step (after smoothing the histogram) is to determine the orientation at which the histogram peaks, and to select that virtual line (AB) closest to that orientation as the solution. [Stevens 1977]

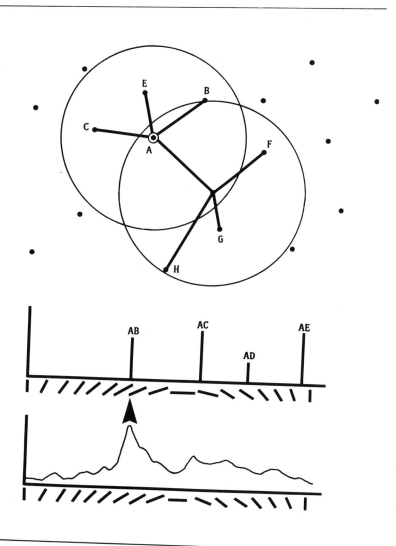

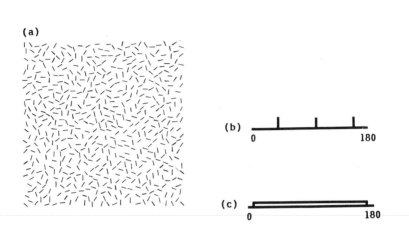

Figure 4. The pattern A contains two regions, one of whose line segments has the orientation distribution shown in B, and the other has the distribution C. Surprisingly, three orientations cannot be distinguished from a random orientation distribution.

detection of surface luster. Since glossiness is due to the specular component of a surface reflectivity function, one can treat the detection of gloss as essentially the detection of light sources that appear reflected in a surface (see [Beck 1974]), and this depends ultimately on the ability to detect light sources. Forbus divided the problem into three categories; (a) in which the specularity is too small to allow gradient measurements, (b) in which both intensity and gradient measurements are available, but the specularity is local (as it is for a curved surface or a point source), and (c) in which the surface is planar and the source is extended. He derived diagnostic criteria for each case.

Delimiting regions from a discriminant

Whenever a region is defined in an image by a predicate, for example by a difference in texture or brightness, one faces the problem of delimiting the region accurately. There are two approaches to designing algorithms for this problem; one is to use the predicate directly, deciding whether a given location lies within or without the region by testing some function of the predicate there. The second approach is to differentiate the predicate, defining the region by its boundaries rather than by properties of its interior.

The difficulties with the problem arise because one is usually ignorant beforehand of the scale at which significant predicate signals may be gathered. For example, suppose one wished to find the boundary between two regions that are distinguished by different densities of dots. Dot density has to be measured by selecting a neighborhood size and counting the number of dots that lie within it. If the neighborhood size is too large, one may not be able to resolve the regions. If it is so small as to contain zero, one or two dots, natural fluctuations may obscure any changes in density.

One solution to this problem is to make the measurements simultaneously at several neighborhood sizes, looking for agreement between the results obtained in those neighborhood sizes that lie just above the size at which random fluctuations appear. This technique can be applied to region finding or to boundary finding, and an example of the results is given in figure 5. The dot density here is not known *a priori.*

This issue is of considerable techical interest, but it is important not to lose sight of the underlying computational problem, which is what kind of boundary is to be found, and why? The techniques of O'Callaghan [1974] for example are designed to find boundaries in dot patterns so accurately that their positions are determined up to the decision about which dots it passes through. The justification for this type of study is that humans can assign boundaries this accurately, but the

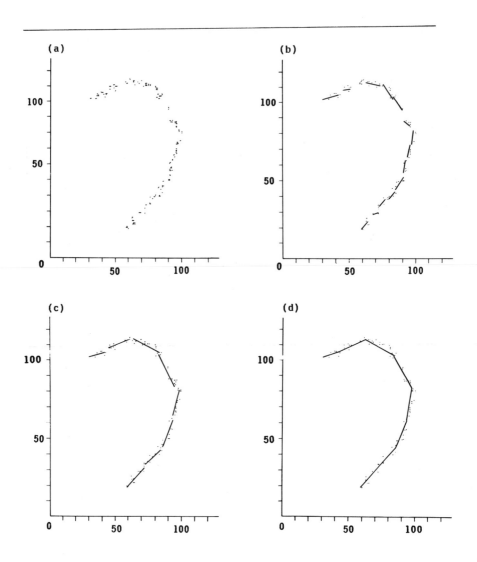

Figure 5. Finding a boundary from dot (or place-token) density changes. Once a rough assignment of boundary points has been made (*a*) local line-fitting (*b*) and grouping (*c* and *d*) techniques can recover a rough specification of the boundary quite easily.

difficulty lies in formulating a reasonable definition of what the boundary is.

This problem is a deep one, touching the heart of the question of what early vision is *for*. I shall return to it later in this essay, but it is perhaps worth remarking here that there seems to be a clear need for being able to do early visual processing roughly and fast as well as more slowly and accurately, which means having ways of handling rough descriptions of regions -- ways of characterizing their approximate extent and shape -- *before* characterizing their precise boundaries. Figure 6 contains one example of a region whose rough extent is clear, but whose exact boundary is not.

The motivation for wanting this is that rough descriptions are very useful during the early stages of building a shape description for recognition [Marr and Nishihara 1977]. For example a man often appears as a roughly vertical rectangle in an image, and this information is useful because it eliminates many other shapes from consideration quite early. Campbell [1977] has suggested that the extraction of rough descriptions from an image may depend on the ability to examine its lower spatial frequencies. Even if this is one of the available mechanisms it is unlikely to be the only one, because sparse line drawings can raise the same problems while having almost no power in their low frequencies. It may be that some notion of rough grouping applied to low resolution place-tokens set up by pieces of contour in the image provides a useful approach to this problem.

Lightness

Ever since Ernst Mach noticed the bands named after him, there has been considerable interest in the problem of computing perceived brightness. Of especial interest is the recent work of Land and McCann [1971] on the retinex theory (see also [Horn 1974]), which is concerned with the quantity they call lightness; and that of Colas-Baudelaire [1973] on the computation of

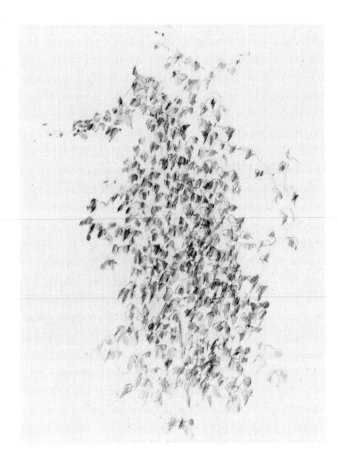

Figure 6. An example of a region whose rough boundary is clear, but whose exact boundary is not. (Drawing (c) K. Prendergast, 1977).

perceived brightness. Lightness is an approximation to reflectance that is obtained by filtering out slow intensity changes, the underlying idea being that these are usually due to the illuminant, not to changes in reflectance. The problem with this idea is of course that some slow changes in intensity are perceptually important (see [Horn 1977] for an analysis of shape from shading). The linear filter model of Colas-Baudelaire performs well on images in which there are no sharp changes in intensity, but the author found it difficult to extend his model to the more general case. The recent finding of Gilchrist [1977], that perceived depth influences perceived brightness, suggests that some aspects of the problem occur quite late -- in our terms, at the level of the $2^1/_2$-D sketch (see below).

Our own work on the brightness problem is probably not relevant to the perception of brightness, but it is interesting as a demonstration that the primal sketch loses very little information. Woodham and Marr (unpublished program) have written a program that inverts the primal sketch, so that its output is an intensity array. The basic idea is to scan outwards from edges, assigning a constant brightness to points along the scan lines, and arresting the scan when it encounters another edge. Figure 7 exhibits the results of running this program, showing the original image (7a), the primal sketch (7b), and the reconstructed intensity array (7c).

Structure from motion

I said earlier that, especially at the earlier stages of visual information processing, the representations and processes are determined more by what it is possible to compute from an image than by what is desirable. Examples are the problems associated with structure from motion, stereopsis, texture gradients, and shading.

Given a sequence of views of objects in motion, the human visual system is capable of interpreting the changing views in terms of the shapes of the viewed objects, and their motion in

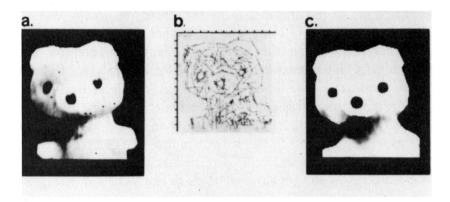

Figure 7. An image (*a*), the spatial components of its primal sketch (*b*), and a reconstruction of the image from the primal sketch (*c*). This shows that our current primal sketch programs lose little of the information in an image.

three-dimensional space. Even if each successive view is unrecognizable, the human observer easily perceives these views in terms of moving objects [Wallach and O'Connell 1953]. To answer the question of how a succession of images yields an interpretation in terms of three-dimensional structure in motion, Ullman [1977] divided the problem into two parts: (1) finding a correspondence between elements in successive views; and (2) determining the three-dimensional structures and their motion from the way corresponding elements move between views.

An important preliminary question about the correspondence problem concerns the level at which it takes place. Is it primarily a low-level relation, established between small and simple parts of the scenes and largely independent of

higher-level knowledge and three-dimensional interpretation?   Or
do higher level influences, like the interpretation of the whole of
a shape from one frame, play an important part in determining
the correspondence?

Ullman has assembled a considerable amount of evidence
that the former view is correct.   For example, figure 8 shows two
successive frames, one denoted with full lines and the other with
dotted lines.   If the whole pattern were being analyzed from one
frame, the shape of the wheel extracted, and used to match the
elements in the next frame, the observer presented with these
frames in rapid succession should perceive them as a whole wheel
rotating.   Notice however that the inner and outer parts of the
wheel have their closest neighbors in one direction, whereas the
center parts have theirs in the other;   because of this, if the
matching were done early and locally, the observer should see the
center part rotating one way, and the inner and outer rings
rotating the other (as shown with arrows in figure 8).   When
appropriately timed, this is in fact what happens.

Another line of evidence is the following.   The most
important factor in finding a correspondence between elements is
the distance the element moves from one view to the next.   But
is this distance an objective two-dimensional measurement or an
interpreted movement in three-dimensional space?   There is some
confusion in the literature about this point, since many studies
have assumed that correspondence strength is linked to the
smoothness of apparent motion [Kolers 1972], and this is
apparently more closely related to three- than to two-dimensional
distances.   Ullman [1977] has however shown that this assumption
is false, and that it is the two-dimensional distance alone that
determines the correspondence.

The second part of the problem is to determine the
three-dimensional structure once the correspondence between
successive views has been established.   Unless this problem is
constrained in some way, it cannot be solved, so one has to
search for reasonable assumptions on which to base the design of
one's algorithms.   (This state of affairs is a common one in the

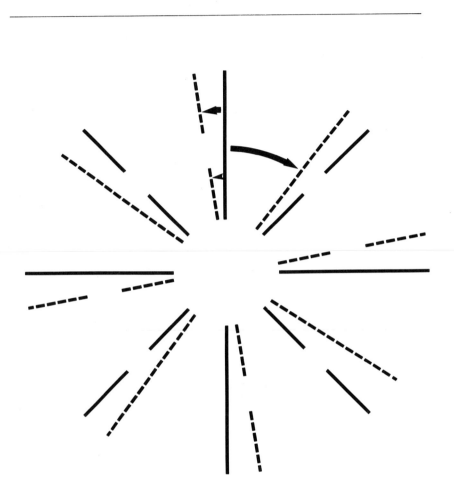

Figure 8. Evidence that the correspondence problem for apparent motion involves matching operations that act at a low level [Ullman 1977].

theory of visual processes, as we shall see when we discuss the problems of stereopsis, and shape from contour). Ullman suggested basing the interpretation on the following assumptions; (1) any two-dimensional transformation that has a unique interpretation as a rigid body moving in space should be interpreted as such an object in motion, and (2) that the imaging process is locally an orthogonal projection. He then showed that under orthogonal projection, three-dimensional shape and motion may be recovered from as little as three views each showing the image of the same five points, no four of which are coplanar. This result leads to algorithms capable of recovering shape and motion from scenes containing arbitrary objects in motion. The final question is whether the algorithms that humans employ to recover shape and motion rely on these same two assumptions, and this question is currently under investigation. The important point here is that for more human-like algorithms, the number of views can be traded off against the accuracy of the computation, decreasing the emphasis on the particular number "three."

Stereopsis

Ever since Julesz [1971] made the first random-dot stereogram, it has been clear that at least to a first approximation stereo vision can be regarded as a modular component of the human visual system. Marr [1974] and Marr and Poggio [1976] formulated the computational theory of the stereo matching problem in the following way:

(R1) Uniqueness. Each item from each image may be assigned at most one disparity value. This condition rests on the premise that the items to be matched correspond to physical marks on a surface, and so can be in only one place at a time.

(R2) Continuity. Disparity varies smoothly almost everywhere. This condition is a consequence of the cohesiveness of matter, and it states that only a relatively small fraction of the area of an image is composed of boundaries.

By representing these constraints geometrically, Marr and

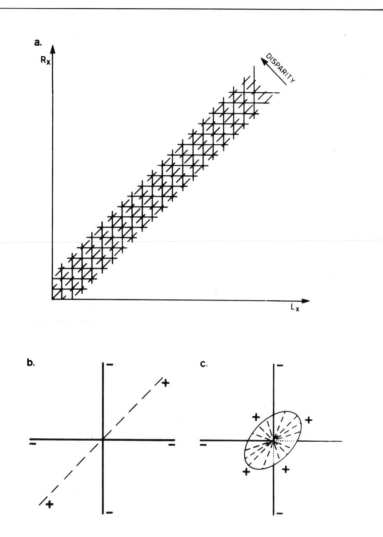

Figure 9. The structure of a network for implementing the algorithm described by equation 1. Such a network was used to solve the stereograms exhibited in figures 10 and 11. [Marr & Poggio 1976]

Poggio [1976] embodied them in a cooperative algorithm. In figure 9, *Lx* and *Rx* represent the positions of descriptive elements from the left and right views, and the horizontal and vertical lines indicate the range of disparity values that can be assigned to left-eye and right-eye elements. The uniqueness condition then corresponds to the assertion that only one disparity value may be "on" along each horizontal or vertical line. The continuity condition states that we seek solutions that tend to spread along the dotted diagonals, which are lines of constant disparity, and between adjacent diagonals. Figure 9b shows how this geometry appears at each intersection point. Figure 9c gives the corresponding local geometry when the images are two-dimensional rather than one. Figure 9a shows the explicit structure of the two rules *R1* and *R2* for the case of a one-dimensional image, and it also represents the structure of a network for implementing the algorithm described by equation 1 Solid lines represent "inhibitory" interactions, and dotted lines represent "excitatory" ones. 9b gives the local structure at each node of the network 9a. This algorithm may be extended to two-dimensional images, in which case each node in the corresponding network has the local structure shown in 9c. Such a network was used to solve the stereograms exhibited in figures 10 and figure 11.

It can be shown [Marr, Poggio and Palm 1977] that, if a network is created with the positive and negative connections shown in figure 9c, states of such a network that satisfy the constraints on the computation are stable, and that given suitable inputs, the network will converge to these stable states for a wide variety of the control parameters. Thus one can think of the network as defining an algorithm that operates on many input elements to produce a global organization *via* local but highly interactive constraints. Formally, the algorithm reads:

$$C_{xyd}^{(n-1)} = u \left\{ \sum_{x'y'd' \in S(xyd)} C_{xyd}^{(n)} - \epsilon \sum_{x'y'd' \in O(xyd)} C_{x'y'd'}^{(n)} + C_{xyd}^{(o)} \right\}$$

where $u(z) = 0$ if $z < \theta$, and $u(z) = 1$ otherwise; S and O are the circular and thick line neighborhoods of the cell C_{xyd} in figure 9c. This is an example of a "cooperative" algorithm [Marr and Poggio 1977a], and it exhibits typical non-linear cooperative phenomena like hysteresis, filling-in, and disorder-order transitions. Figures 10 and 11 illustrate two applications of the algorithm to random-dot stereograms.

In figure 10 the initial state of the network C_{xyd} is defined by the input such that a node takes the value 1 if it occurs at the intersection of a 1 in the left and right eyes (see figure -9), and it has value 0 otherwise. The network iterates on this initial state, and the parameters used here, as suggested by the combinatorial analysis, were $\theta = 3.0$, $\epsilon = 2.0$ and $M = 5$, where θ is the threshold and M is the diameter of the "excitatory" neighborhood illustrated in figure 9c. The stereograms themselves are labelled LEFT and RIGHT, the initial state of the network as 0, and the state after n iterations is marked as such. To understand how the figures represent states of the network, imagine looking at it from above. The different disparity layers in the network lie in parallel planes spread out horizontally, so that the viewer is looking down through them. In each plane, some nodes are on and some are off. Each of the seven layers in the network has been assigned a different gray level, so that a node that is switched on in the top layer (corresponding to a disparity of +3 pixels) contributes a dark point to the image, and one that is switched on in the lowest layer (disparity = -3) contributes a lighter point. Initially (iteration 0) the network is disorganized, but in the final state, stable order has been achieved (iteration 14), and the inverted wedding-cake structure has been found. The density of this stereogram is 50%.

The algorithm of equation 1 is capable of solving

Figure 10. This shows the results of applying the algorithm defined by equation 1 to a random-dot stereograms. **The density is 50%.** [Marr & Poggio 1976].

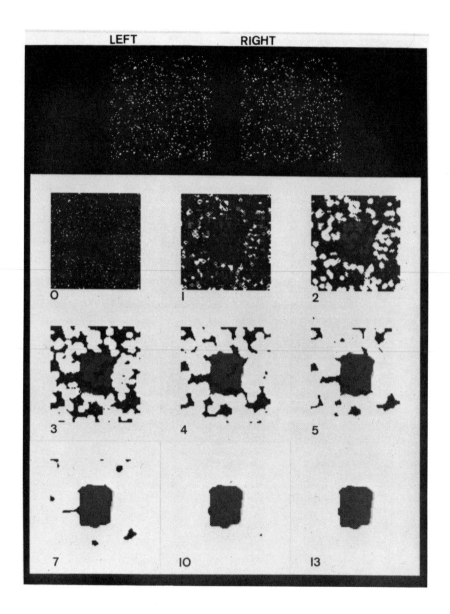

Figure 11. The algorithm of equation 1, with the parameter values used in Figure 10, but with less density. [Marr and Poggio 1976].

random-dot stereograms with densities from 50% down to less than 10%, as shown in figure 11. For this and smaller densities, the algorithm converges increasingly slowly. If a simple homeostatic mechanism is allowed to control the threshold θ as a function of the average activity (number of "on" cells) at each iteration, the algorithm can solve stereograms whose density is very low. In this example, the density is 5% and the central square has a disparity of +2 relative to the background. The algorithm "fills in" those areas where no dots are present, but it takes several more iterations to arrive near the solution than in cases where the density is 50%. When we look at a sparse stereogram, we perceive the shapes in it as cleaner than those found by the algorithm. This seems to be due to subjective contours that arise between dots that lie on shape boundaries.

There are a number of findings that cast doubt on the relevance of this algorithm to the question of how human stereo vision works. The most important of these findings are (a) the apparently crucial role played by eye-movements in human stereo vision (see especially [Richards 1977]); (b) our ability to tolerate up to 15% expansion of one image [Julesz 1971]; (c) our ability to tolerate the severe defocussing of one image [Julesz 1971]; (d) evidence that stereo detectors are organized into three "pools" (convergent, zero disparity, and divergent) and that this organization is important for stereo vision [Richards 1971]; and (e) our ability to perceive depth in rivalrous stereograms [Mayhew and Frisby 1976]. These difficulties led Marr and Poggio [1977b] to formulate a second stereo algorithm, designed specifically as a model for human stereopsis.

Our first stereo theory was inspired by Julesz's belief that stereoscopic fusion is a cooperative process -- a belief based primarily on the observation that it exhibits hysteresis. The main problem with the cooperative algorithm is that it apparently works too well in some ways (it performs better that humans do when eye-movements are eliminated), and not well enough in others (humans see depth in rivalrous stereograms). Our ability to fuse two images when one is blurred, the rivalrous stereogram results of Mayhew and Frisby [1976], and the recent results of Julesz and Miller [1976] on the existence of independent spatial-frequency-tuned channels in binocular fusion, suggest that several copies of the image, obtained by successively coarser filtering, are used during fusion, perhaps helping one another in a way similar to that in which local regions help each other in our cooperative algorithm.

The second idea was a notion that originated with Marr and Nishihara [1977] and about which I shall have more to say later, which is that one of the things early visual processing does is to construct a "depth map" of the surfaces round a viewer. In this map, each direction away from the viewer is associated with a distance (or some function of distance) and a surface orientation. We have christened the resulting data structure the $2^1/_2$-D sketch.

The important point here is that the $2^1/_2$-D sketch is in some sense a memory. This provided the key idea: Suppose that the hysteresis Julesz observed is not due to a cooperative process at all, but is in fact the result of using a memory buffer in which to store the depth map of the image as it is discovered. Then, the fusion process itself need not be cooperative, and in fact it would not even be necessary for the whole image ever to be fused everywhere provided that a depth map of the viewed surface were built and maintained in this intermediate memory. This idea leads to the following theory. (1) Each image is convolved with bar-shaped masks of various sizes, and matching takes place between peak mask values for disparities up to about twice the panel-width of the mask (see [Felton, Richards and Smith 1972]), for pairs of masks of the same size and polarity. (2) Wide masks can control vergence movements, thus causing small masks to come into correspondence. (3) When a correspondence is achieved, it is held and written down somewhere (e.g. in the $2^1/_2$-D sketch). (4) There is a backwards relation between the memory and the masks, perhaps simply through the control of eye-movements, that allows one to fuse any piece of a surface easily once its depth map has been established in the memory.

This theory leads to many experimental predictions, which are currently being tested.

Intermediate processing problems

We have discussed the types of information that need to be represented early in the processing of visual information, and we have examined the computational structure of some of the processes that can derive and maintain this information. We turn now to the question of what all this information is to be used for.

The current approach to machine vision assumes that the next step in visual processing consists of a process called *segmentation,* whose purpose is to divide the image into regions that are meaningful either in terms of physical objects or for the purpose at hand. Despite considerable efforts over a long period, the theory and practice of segmentation remain primitive, and once again I believe that the main reason lies in the failure to formulate precisely the goals of this stage of the processing. What for example is an object? Is a head one? Is it still one if it is attached to a body? What about a man on horseback?

These questions point to some of the difficulties one has when trying to formulate what should be recovered as a region from early visual processing. Furthermore, however one chooses to answer them, it is usually still impossible to recover the desired regions using only local grouping techniques acting on a representation like the primal sketch. Most images are too complex, and even the simplest images cannot often be segmented entirely at that level [Marr 1976].

Something additional is clearly needed, and one approach to the dilemma has been to invoke specialized knowledge about the nature of the scenes being viewed to aid segmentation of the image into regions that correspond roughly to the objects expected in the scene. Tenenbaum and Barrow [1976], for example, applied knowledge about several different types of scene to the segmentation of images of landscapes, an office, a room, and a compressor. Freuder [1976] used a similar approach to identify a hammer in a simple scene. If this approach were correct, it would mean that a central problem for vision is arranging for the right piece of specialized knowledge to be made available at the appropriate time during segmentation. Freuder's work, for example, was almost entirely devoted to the design of a heterarchical control system that made this possible. More recently, the constraint relaxation technique of Rosenfeld, Hummel and Zucker [1976] has attracted considerable attention for just this reason, that it appears to offer a technique whereby constraints drawn from disparate sources may be applied to the segmentation problem whilst incurring only minimal penalties in control. It is however difficult to analyze such algorithms rigorously even in very clearly defined situations [Marr, Poggio and Palm 1977], and in the naturally more diffuse circumstances that surround the segmentation problem, it may often be impossible.

Reformulating the problem

The basic problem seems to be how to formulate precisely the next stage of visual processing. Given a representation like the primal sketch, and the many possible boundary-defining processes that are naturally associated with it, which boundaries should one attend to and why? The segmentation approach fails because objects and desirable regions are not visually primitive constructions, and hence cannot be recovered reliably from the primal sketch or similar representation without additional specialized knowledge. If we are to succeed, we must discover precisely what information it is that needs to be made explicit at this stage, what, if any, additional knowledge it is appropriate to apply, and we must design a representation that matches these requirements.

In order to search for clues to a suitable representation, let us return to the physics of the situation. The primal sketch represents intensity changes and the local two-dimensional geometry of an image. The principle factors that determine these are (1) the illuminant, (2) surface reflectance, (3) the shape of the visible surface, and (4) the vantage point. The first two factors raise the difficult problems of color and brightness, and I shall not discuss them further. The third and fourth factors are independent of the first two (whether two shapes are the same does not depend upon their colors or on the lighting), and so may be treated separately.

I shall argue that, since most early visual processes extract information about the visible surface, it is these surfaces, their shape and disposition relative to the viewer, that need to be made explicit at this point in the processing. Furthermore, because surfaces exist in three-dimensional space, this imposes constraints on them that are general, and not confined to particular objects. It is these constraints that constitute the *a priori* knowledge that it is appropriate to bring to bear next.

One example of the exploitation of fairly general constraints was the work of Waltz [1975], who formulated the constraints that apply to images of polyhedra. The representation on which that work was based was line drawings, but these are not suitable for our needs here because part of the task we wish to carry out is the discovery of physical edges that are only weakly present or even absent in the primal sketch. The approach of Mackworth [1973] was closer to what we want, since it involved a primitive way of representing surfaces.

Part of our task in formulating the problem of intermediate vision is therefore the examination of ways of representing and reasoning about surfaces. We therefore start our enquiry by discussing the general nature of shape representations. What kinds are there, and how may one decide among them? Although it is difficult to formulate a completely general classification of shape representations, Marr and Nishihara [1977] attempted to set out the basic design choices that have to be made when a representation is formulated. They concluded that there are three characteristics of a shape representation that are largely responsible for determining the information that it makes explicit. The first is the type of *coordinate system* it uses, whether it is defined relative to the viewer or to the object being viewed; the second characteristic concerns the nature of the *shape primitives* used by the representation, that is, the elements whose positions the coordinate system is used to define. Are they two- or three-dimensional, in what sizes do they come, and how detailed are they? And the third characteristic is concerned with the organization a representation imposes on the information in a description; for example is the description modular or does it have little internal structure? We have two sources of information that can help us to formulate the important issues in intermediate visual information processing, firstly the computational problems that arise, and secondly, psychophysics.

Vision provides several sources of information about shape. The most direct are stereo and motion, but texture gradients in a single image are nearly as effective, and the theatrical techniques of facial make-up rely on the sensitivity of perceived shape to shading. It often happens that some parts of a scene are open to inspection by some of these techniques, and other parts by others. Yet different as the techniques are, they have two important characteristics in common. They rely on information from the image rather than on *a priori* knowledge about the shapes of the viewed objects; and the information they specify concerns the depth or surface orientation at arbitrary points in an image, rather than the depth or orientation associated with particular objects.

If one views a stereo pair of a complex surface, like a crumpled newspaper or the "leaves" cube of Ittelson (1960), one can easily state the surface orientation of any piece of the surface, and whether one piece is nearer to or further from the viewer than its neighbors. Nevertheless one's memory for the shape of the surface is poor, despite the vividness of its surface orientation during perception. Furthermore, if the surface contains elements nearly parallel to the line of sight, their apparent surface orientation when viewed monocularly can differ from the apparent surface orientation when viewed binocularly.

From these observations, one can perhaps draw some simple inferences.

■   There is at least one internal representation of the depth, or surface orientation, or both, associated with each surface point in a scene.

■   Because surface orientation can be associated with unfamiliar shapes, its representation probably precedes the decomposition of the scene into objects. (This point is particularly relevant to our discussion of intermediate visual information processing.)

■   Because the apparent orientation of a surface element can change, depending on whether it is viewed binocularly or monocularly, the representation of surface orientation is probably driven almost entirely by perceptual processes, and is influenced only slightly by specific knowledge of what the surface orientation actually is. Our ability to "perceive" the surface much better than we can "memorize" it may also be connected with this point.

In addition, it seems likely that the different sources of information can influence the *same* representation of surface orientation.

The computational problem

In order to make the most efficient use of these different and often complementary sources of information, they need to be combined in some way. The computational question is, how best to do this? The natural answer is to seek some representation of the visual scene that makes explicit just the information these processes can deliver.

Fortunately, the physical interpretation of the representation we seek is clear. All these processes deliver information about the depth or surface orientation associated with surfaces in an image, and these are well-defined physical quantities. We therefore seek a way of making this information explicit, of maintaining it in a consistent state, and perhaps also of incorporating into the representation any physical constraints that hold for the values that depth and surface orientation take over the kinds of surface that occur in the real world. Table 1 lists the type of information that the different early processes can extract from images. The interesting point here is that although processes like stereo and motion are in principle capable of delivering depth information directly, they are in practice more likely to deliver information about local *changes* in depth, for example by measuring local changes in disparity. Texture gradients and shading provide more direct information about surface orientation. In addition, occlusion, brightness, and size clues can deliver information about discontinuities in depth. It is for example amazing how clear an impression of depth can be obtained from a monocular image containing bright or dim rectangles of different sizes against a dark background. The main function of the representation we seek is therefore not only to make explicit information about depth, local surface orientation, and discontinuities in these quantities, but also to create and maintain a global representation of depth that is consistent with the local cues that these sources provide. We call such a representation the $2^1/_2$-D sketch, and the next section describes a particular candidate for it.

A possible form for the $2^1/_2$-D sketch

The example I give for the $2^1/_2$-D sketch is a viewer-centered representation, which uses surface primitives of one (small) size. It includes a representation of contours of surface discontinuity, and it has enough internal computational structure to maintain its descriptions of depth, surface orientation and surface

Table 1

The form in which various early visual processes deliver information about the changes in a scene.

r = depth
δr = small, local changes in depth
Δr = large changes in depth
$\underset{\sim}{s}$ = local surface orientation

Information source	Natural parameter
Stereo	Disparity, hence especially δr and Δr
Motion	r, hence δr, Δr
Shading	$\underset{\sim}{s}$
Texture gradients	$\underset{\sim}{s}$
Perspective cues	$\underset{\sim}{s}$
Occlusion	Δr

discontinuity in a consistent state. The representation itself has no additional internal structure.

Depth may be represented by a scalar quantity r, the distance from the viewer of a point on a surface. Surface discontinuities may be represented by oriented line elements. Surface orientation may be represented by a unit vector (x, y, z) in three-dimensional space. Following those who have used gradient space ([Huffman 1971] [Horn 1977]) we can rewrite this as $(p, q, 1)$, which can be represented as a vector (p, q) in two-dimensional space. In other words, surface orientation may be represented by covering an image with needles. The length of each needle defines the dip of the surface at that point, so that zero length corresponds to a surface that is perpendicular to the vector from the viewer to that point, and the length increases as the surface tilts away from the viewer. The orientation of the needle defines the direction of the surface's dip. Figure 12 illustrates this representation.

In principle, the relation between depth and surface orientation is straightforward -- one is simply the integral of the other, taken over regions bounded by surface discontinuities. It is therefore possible to devise a representation with intrinsic computational facilities that can maintain the two variables, of depth and surface orientation, in a consistent state. But note that, in any such scheme, *surface discontinuities* acquire a special status (as curves across which integration stops). Furthermore, if the representation is an active one, maintaining consistency through largely local operations, curves that mark surface discontinuities (e.g. contours that arise from occluding contours in the image) must be "filled in" completely, so that at no point along an object boundary can the integration leak across it. It is interesting that subjective contours have this property, and that they are closely related to subjective changes in brightness that are often associated with changes in perceived depth. If the human visual processor contains a representation that resembles the $2^1/_2$-D sketch, it would therefore be interesting to ask whether subjective contours occur within it. (See [Ullman 1976b]

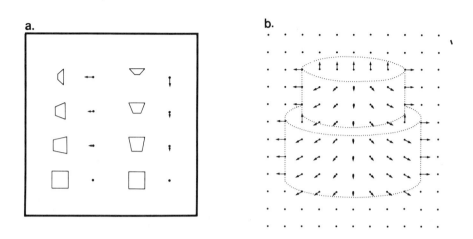

Figure 12. The $2^1/_2$-D sketch represents depth, contours of surface discontinuity, and the orientation of visible surfaces. A convenient representation of surface orientation is described in the text and illustrated here. The orientation of the needles is determined by the projection of the surface normal on the image plane, and the length of the needles represents the dip out of that plane (*a*). A typical $2^1/_2$-D sketch appears in *b*, although depth information is not represented in the figure.

for an analysis of the shape of curved subjective contours).

In summary, my argument is that the $2^1/_2$-D sketch is useful because it makes explicit information about the image in a form that is closely matched to what early visual processes can deliver. We can formulate the goals of intermediate visual processing as being primarily the construction of this representation, discovering for example what are the surface orientations in a scene, which of the contours in the primal sketch correspond to surface discontinuities and should therefore be represented in the $2^1/_2$-D sketch, and which contours are missing in the primal sketch and need to be inserted into the

$2^1/_2$-D sketch in order to bring it into a state that is consistent with the structure of three-dimensional space. This formulation avoids the difficulties associated with the terms "region" and "object," and allows one to ask precise questions about the computational structure of the $2^1/_2$-D sketch and of processes to create and maintain it. We are currently much occupied with these problems.

Later processing problems

The $2^1/_2$-D sketch is a poor representation for the purposes of recognition because it is unstable (in the sense of [Marr and Nishihara 1977]), it depends on the vantage point, and it fails to make explicit pieces of a shape (like an arm) that are larger that the primitive size. Except for the simplest of purposes, it is an inadequate vehicle for a visual system to convey information about shape to other processes, and so I turn now to representations that are more suitable for recognition tasks.

If one were to design a shape representation to suit the problems of recognition, one would naturally base it on an object-centered coordinate system. In addition, one would have to include shape primitives of many different sizes, so as to be able to make explicit shape characteristics that can range from a wart to an elephant. Marr and Nishihara [1977] discuss these questions in detail, and I shall not repeat their observations here. The deepest issues are those raised by having to define an object-based coordinate system. Since they are central to the problem of defining representations for use in later processing of visual information, I shall spend the remainder of the essay discussing this topic.

Marr and Nishihara [1977] pointed out that there are two types of object-centered coordinate system that one might attempt to define precisely. One refers all locations on an object to a single coordinate frame that embraces the entire object, and the other distributes the coordinate system, making it local to each articulated component or individual shape characteristic. **Marr** and Nishihara concluded that the second of these schemes is the more desirable, and they gave as an example the representation illustrated in figure 13. But with a representation of this kind, the most difficult questions begin after its internal structure has been defined. How can one define canonically the coordinate scheme for an arbitrary shape, and even more difficult, how can such a thing be found from an image *before* a description of the viewed shape has been computed? Some kind of answers to these questions must be found if the representation is to be used for recognition.

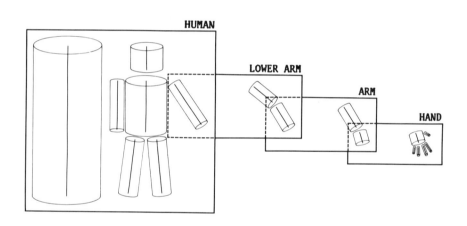

Figure 13. Organization of shape information in a 3-D model description. Each box corresponds to a 3-D model. Its model axis is on the left side, and the arrangement of its component axes are shown on the right side.

If the coordinate system used for a given shape is to be canonical, its definition must take advantage of any salient geometrical characteristics that the shape possesses. For example, if a shape has natural axes, distinguished by length or by symmetry, then they should be used. The coordinate system for a sausage should take advantage of its major axis, and for a face, of its axis of symmetry.

Highly symmetrical objects, like a sphere, square, or circular disc, will inevitably lead to ambiguities in the choice of coordinate systems. For a shape as regular as a sphere this poses no great problem, because its description in all reasonable systems is the same. One can even allow other factors, like the direction of motion or of spin, to influence the choice of coordinate frame. For other shapes, the existence of more than one possible choice probably means that one has to represent the object in several ways. This is acceptable provided that the number of ways is small. For example, there are four possible axes on which one might wish to base the coordinate system for representing a door, the midlines along its length, its width, its thickness, and to represent how the door opens, the axis of its hinges. For a typewriter, there are two choices at the top level; an axis parallel to its width, because that is usually its largest dimension, and the axis about which a typewriter is roughly symmetrical.

In general, if an axis can be distinguished in a shape, it can be used as the basis for a local coordinate system. One approach to the problem of defining object-centered coordinate systems is therefore to examine the class of shapes having an axis as an integral part of their structure. One such is the class of *generalized cones*. (A generalized cone is the surface swept out by moving a cross section of constant shape but smoothly varying size along an axis, as in figure 14).

Binford [1971] drew attention to this class of surfaces, suggesting that it might provide a convenient way of describing three-dimensional surfaces for the purposes of computer vision. I regard it as an important class not because the shapes themselves are easily decribable, but because the presence of an axis allows one to define a canonical local coordinate system. Fortunately many objects, especially those whose shape was achieved by

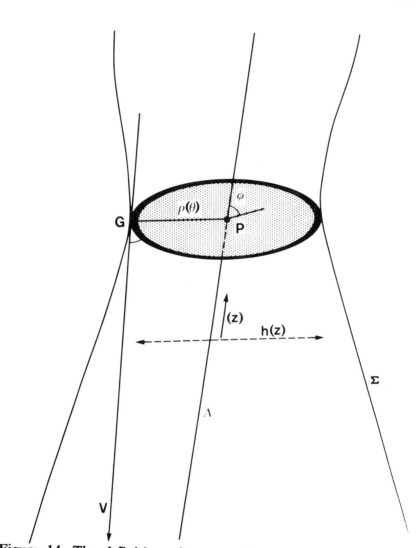

Figure 14. The definition of a generalized cone. A generalized cone is the surface generated by moving a smooth cross-section ρ along a straight axis $\wedge$. The cross-section may vary smoothly in size (as prescribed by the function $h(z)$), but its shape remains constant. The eccentricity of the cone is the angle ψ between its axis and a plane containing a cross-section.

Figure 15. These pipecleaner figures illustrate the point that a shape representation does not have to reproduce a shape's surface in order to describe it adequately for recognition; as we see here, animal shapes can be portrayed quite effectively by the arrangement and relative sizes of a small number of sticks. The simplicity of these descriptions is due to the correspondence between the sticks shown here and natural or canonical axes of the shapes described. To be useful for recognition, a shape representation must be based on characteristics that are uniquely defined by the shape and which can be derived reliably from images of it. [Marr & Nishihara 1977]

growth, are described quite naturally in terms of one or more generalized cones. The animal shapes in figure 15 provide some examples -- the individual sticks are simply axes of generalized cones that approximate the shapes of parts of these animals. Many artifacts can also be described in this way, like a car (a small box sitting atop and in the middle of a longer one), and a building (a box with a vertical axis).

It is important to remember that there exist surfaces that cannot conveniently be approximated by generalized cones, for example a cake that has been cut at its intersection with some arbitrary plane, or the surface formed by a crumpled newspaper. Cases like the cake can be dealt with by introducing suitable surface primitives that describe the plane of the cut, but the crumpled newspaper poses apparently intractable problems.

Even if a shape possesses a canonical coordinate system, one is still faced with the problem of finding it from an image. Blum [1973], Agin [1972] and Nevatia [1974] have addressed problems that are related to this question. Blum's sym-axis theory is an interesting one, because he specifies precisely what it is that is computed from a two-dimensional outline. Unfortunately, it is not clear that what this theory computes is in fact useful for shape recognition (see e.g. figure 16), and when applied to a three-dimensional shape, the sym-axis is in general a two-dimensional sheet, so it cannot easily be used to define an object-centered coordinate system. Agin's and Nevatia's work, on the other hand, concerns the analysis of a depth map. This is an important problem, and it would be interesting to see a careful analysis of the conditions under which their techniques will succeed.

Finding the natural coordinate system from an image

My own interest in the problem grew from the 3-D representation theory of Marr and Nishihara [1977], in particular from the question of how to interpret the outlines of objects as seen in a two-dimensional image. The rest of this essay

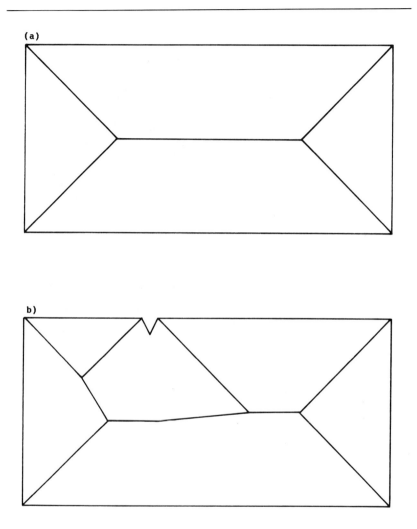

Figure 16. Blum's [1973] grassfire technique for recovering an axis from a silhouette is undesirably sensitive to small perturbations in the contour. *a* shows the Blum transform of a rectangle, and *b*, of a rectangle with a notch [Agin 1972].

Figure 17. "Rites of spring" by P. Picasso. We immediately interpret the silhouettes in terms of particular 3-D surfaces, despite the paucity of information in the image.

summarizes a recent article by Marr [1977a]. The starting point for this work was the observation that when one looks at the silhouettes in Picasso's work "Rites of Spring" (figure 17), one perceives them in terms of very particular three-dimensional shapes, some familiar, some less so. This is quite remarkable, because the silhouettes could in theory have been generated by an infinite variety of shapes which, from other viewpoints, have no discernable similarities to the shapes we perceive. One can perhaps attribute part of the phenomenon to a familiarity with the depicted shapes; but not all of it, because one can use the medium of a silhouette to convey a new shape, and because even with considerable effort it is difficult to imagine the more bizarre three-dimensional surfaces that could have given rise to the same silhouettes. The paradox is, that the bounding contours in figure 17 apparently tell us more than they should about the shape of the dark figures. For example, neighboring points on such a contour could in general arise from widely separated points on the original surface, but our perceptual interpretation usually ignores this possibility.

The first observation to be made here is that the occluding contours that bound these silhouettes are contours of surface discontinuity, that is precisely the contours with which the $2^1/_2$-D sketch is concerned. Second, because we can interpret the contours as three-dimensional shapes, implicit in the way we interpret them must lie some *a priori* assumptions that allow us to infer a shape from an outline. If a surface violates these assumptions, our analysis will be wrong, in the sense that the shape we assign to the contours will differ from the shape that actually caused them. An everyday example of this phenomenon is the shadowgraph, where the appropriate arrangement of one's hands can, to the surprise and delight of a child, produce the shadow of an apparently quite different shape, like a duck or a rabbit.

What assumptions is it reasonable to suppose that we make? In order to explain them, I need to define the four structures that appear in figure 18. These are (1) some three

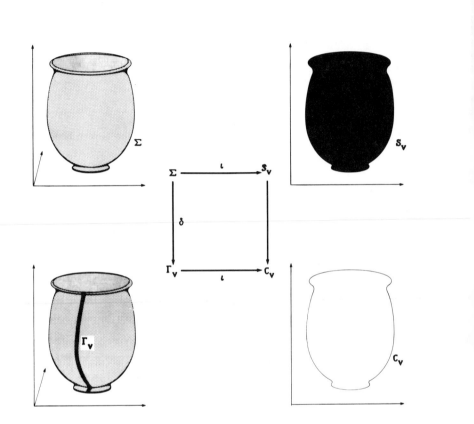

Figure 18. From viewpoint V, the three-dimensional surface Σ forms the silhouette S_V in the image *via* the imaging process ι. The boundary of S_V, obtained by the boundary operator ∂ is denoted by C_V and we call it the contour of Σ. The set of points on Σ that ι maps onto C_V we call the contour generator of C_V, and it is denoted by Γ_V The map from Σ to Γ_V induced by ∂ is denoted by δ. [Marr 1977].

dimensional surface Σ; (2) its image or silhouette S_V as seen from a viewpoint V; (3) the bounding contour C_V of S_V; and (4) the set of points on the surface Σ that project onto the contour C_V. We shall call this last set the *contour generator* of C_V, and we shall denote it by Γ_V.

If one is presented with a contour in an image, without any knowledge of the surface or perspective that caused it, there is very little information on which one can base one's analysis. The only obvious feature available is the distinction between convex and concave pieces of contour -- that is, the presence of inflection points. In order that inflection points be "reliable," one needs to make some assumptions about the way the contour was generated, and I chose the following restrictions:

R1: The surface Σ is smooth.

R2: Each point on the contour generator Γ_V projects to a different point on the contour C_V.

R3: Nearby points on the contour C_V arise from nearby points on the contour generator Γ_V.

R4: The contour generator Γ_V of C_V is planar.

The first restriction is only a technical one. The second and third say that each point on the contour in the image comes from one point on the surface (which is an assumption that facilitates the analysis but is not of fundamental importance), and that where the surface looks continuous in the image, it really is continuous in three dimensions. The fourth condition, together with the constraint that the imaging process be an orthogonal projection, is simply a necessary and sufficient condition that the difference between convex and concave contour segments reflects properties of the surface, rather than characteristics of the imaging process.

It turns out that the following theorem is true, and it is

a result that I found very surprising.

> *Theorem.* If *R1* is true, and *R2 - R4* hold for all distant
> viewing directions that lie in some plane, then the
> viewed surface is a generalized cone.

This means that if, for distant viewpoints whose viewing
directions lie parallel to some plane, a surface's shape can
successfully be inferred using only the convexities and concavities
of its bounding contours in an image, then that surface is a
generalized cone or is composed of several such cones. The
interesting thing about this result is that it implicates generalized
cones. We have already seen that the important thing about
these cones is that an axis forms an integral part of their
structure. But this is a feature of their three-dimensional
organization, and ought in some sense to be independent of the
issues raised by vision. What the theorem says is that there is a
natural link between generalized cones and the imaging process
itself. The combination of these two must mean, I think, that
generalized cones will play an intimate role in the development
of vision theory.

Interpreting the image of a single generalized cone

If we take this result at face value, we can now ask an obvious
question. Let us assume that our data consist of contours of
surface discontinuity in the image of a generalized cone, since
without this assumption we can deduce nothing. How may such
contours be interpreted? To specify a generalized cone, we have
to specify its axis $\wedge$, cross-section $\rho(\theta)$, and axial scaling function
$h(z)$ (figure 14); how can we discover these from an image?
The answer to this question is based on the notion of the
skeleton of a generalized cone. The skeleton is not a difficult
idea, since it is very like the set of lines a cartoonist draws to
convey the shape of a curved object. It consists of three classes
of contour: (a) the contours that occur in a generalized cone's

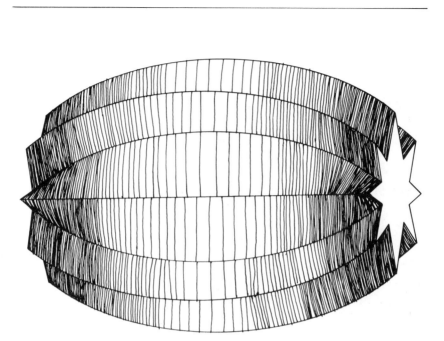

Figure 19. A sketch of a generalized cone showing its silhouette (the circumscribing contour), and its fluting (the contours spanning its length). The radial extremities of a generalized cone are illustrated in Figure 20.

silhouette; (b) the contours that arise from maxima and minima in a cone's axial scaling function (called the cone's *radial extremities*); and (c) contours that arise from maxima and minima in the cone's cross-section (its *fluting*). These categories are illustrated in figure 19.

The reason why the skeleton is a useful construct for recognition is that one can detect its presence in an image by the many relationships that exist among its parts. For example, radial extremities are all parallel to each other, and the silhouette

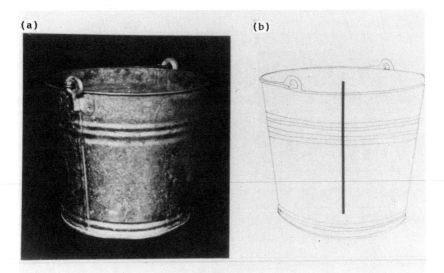

Figure 20. Methods based on the theory described here suffice to solve this image of a bucket. An axial symetry is established by its sides about the bucket's axis (shown thickened), and a parallel relationship holds between components of its radial extremity.

and fluting have a kind of symmetry about the image of the cone's axis. It turns out that one can use these relationships to set up constraints on a set of contours such that, if those constraints are all satisfied by a unique interpretation of the contours in the image, one can be reasonably certain that a skeleton has been found, and hence that the contours can be interpreted as arising from a generalized cone whose axis is then determined. The practical importance of this result is illustrated in figure 20, where one can see that the image of the "sides" is

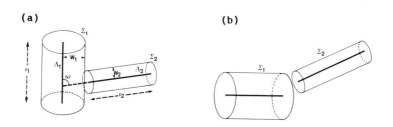

Figure 21. The two main types of joins between two generalized cones. *a* shows a side-to-end join, and *b* shows an end-to-end join.

symmetrical about the bucket's axis, and there is a clear parallel relationship between the image of the bucket's top, the corrugations in its side, and the visible part of its base (the bucket's radial extremities). These relations, of symmetries and parallelism, are preserved by an orthogonal projection. Hence provided that the contours are formed along a viewing direction that is not too close to the axis of the cone, these relations will still be present in the image. If the viewing direction lies so close to the cone's axis that its image is substantially foreshortened, these relationships will no longer be present, but it is part of the overall theory that such views have to be handled differently [Marr and Nishihara 1977].

Real-life objects are often approximately composed of several different cones, joined together in various ways (see figure 13), and we therefore have to study ways of decomposing a multiple cone into its components -- for example, a human body into arms, legs, torso and head. Marr [1977a] analyzed the two types of join shown in figure 21, giving criteria that define segmentation points on the contour produced by two joined cones. Figure 22 exhibits the segmentation points P and Q for the case in which two short cones are joined side-to-end. P. Vatan has written a computer program that can carry out this segmentation, and an example of its operation is illustrated in figure 23.   The initial outline in (a) was obtained by applying local grouping processes to the *primal sketch* of the image of a toy donkey [Marr 1976].   This outline was then smoothed and divided into convex and concave sections to get (b).   Next, strong segmentation points, like the deep concavity circled in (c), are identified and a set of heuristic rules are used to connect them with other points on the contour to get the segmentation shown in (d).   The component axes shown in (e) are then derived from these.   The resulting segments are checked to see that they obey the rules for images of generalized cones.   The boundaries must for example be symmetric about the axes, and in the case of side-to-end joins, the axis of the cone that is attached by its end must intersect the segmentation points that separate the two cones' contours.   In this example, most of the symmetry relations have degenerated into parallelism.   The thin lines in (f) indicate the position of the head, leg, and tail components along the torso axis, and the snout and ear components along the head axis.   (This algorithm is due to P. Vatan).

Some comments on the limitations of this theory

The results of this theory are limited in their scope to a particular class of views and surfaces, but on the other hand, they use only a limited kind of visual information, little more than occluding contours that are formed in an image by rays that graze a smooth surface.   Interestingly, these particular contours are unsuitable for use in stereopsis or structure-from-motion computations, because they are not formed from markings that define precise locations on the viewed surface.   Creases and folds on a surface also give rise to contours in an image, and these have yet to be studied in detail.   Information about shape from shading, texture, stereo or motion information has not yet been

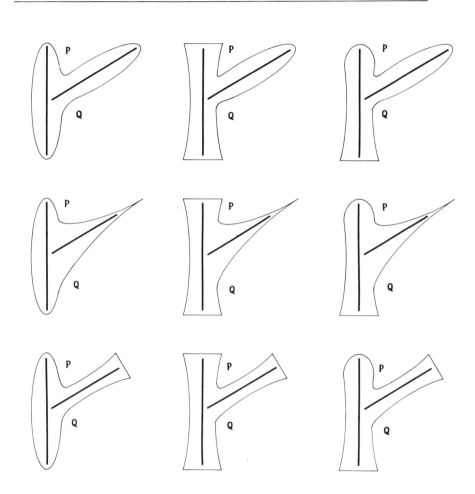

Figure 22. This figure illustrates the types of side-to-end join that can occur between two short generalized cones. In the first column, the left-hand cone is convex; in the center it is concave, and in the right it is convex on one side of the join and concave on the other. The other cone is convex in the top row, and concave in the other two. Segmentation depends upon finding the points P and Q, which are defined by theorem 7 of **Marr** [1977] and illustrated here for each case.

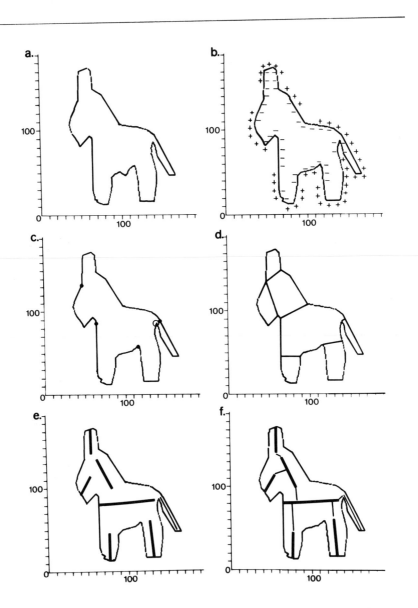

Figure 23. The occluding contours in an image can be used to locate the images of the natural axes of a shape composed of generalized cones [Marr 1977].

TABLE 2

A framework for the derivation of shape information from images.

IMAGE(S)

↓

PRIMAL
SKETCH(ES)

Describes the intensity changes present in an image, labels distinguished locations like termination points, and makes explicit local two-dimensional geometrical relations.

↓

2 1/2-D
SKETCH

Represents contours of surface discontinuity, and depth and orientation of visible surface elements, in a coordinate frame that is centered on the viewer.

↓

3-D MODEL
REPRESENTATION

Shape descriptions that include volumetric shape primitives of a variety of sizes, whose positions are defined using an object-centered coordinate system. This representation imposes considerable modular organization on its descriptions.

considered. By adding these other sources of information, I hope
that a set of methods can eventually be assembled that together
approach a comprehensive treatment of possible image
configurations.

Conclusion

I have tried to make three main points. The first is
methodological, namely that it is important to be very clear
about the nature of the understanding we seek [Marr and Poggio
1977a] [Marr 1977b]. The results we try to achieve should be
precise, at the level of what I called a computational theory, and
should deal with problems that can confidently be attributed to a
real aspect of vision, and not (for example) to an artifact of the
limitations of one's current vision program.

The second main point is that the critical issues for
vision seem to me to revolve around the nature of the
representations used - that is, the particular characteristics of the
world that are made explicit - and the nature of the processes
that recover these characteristics, create and maintain the
representations, and eventually read them. By analyzing the
spatial aspects of the problem of vision [Marr and Nishihara
1977], an overall framework for visual information processing is
suggested, that consists of three principal representations: (1)
the primal sketch, which makes explicit the intensity changes and
local two-dimensional geometry of an image; (2) the $2^1/_2$-D
sketch, which is a viewer-centered representation of the depth and
orientation of the visible surfaces and includes contours of
discontinuities in these quantities; and (3) the 3-D model
representation, whose important features are (a) that its
coordinate system is object-centered, (b) that it includes
volumetric primitives, that make explicit the space occupied by an
object and not just its visible surfaces, and (c) that primitives of
various sizes are included, arranged in a modular, hierarchical
organization.

The third main point concerns the study of processes for

recovering the various aspects of the physical characteristics of a scene from images of it. The critical act in formulating computational theories for such processes is the discovery of valid constraints on the way the world behaves that provide sufficient additional information to allow recovery of the desired characteristic. Several examples are already available, including Land and McCann [1971], which rests on the distinction between sharp and shallow intensity changes; stereopsis [Marr 1974] [Marr and Poggio 1976] [Marr and Poggio 1977b] which uses continuity and uniqueness; structure from visual motion [Ullman 1977], which uses rigidity; fluorescence [Ullman 1976a]; and shape from contour [Marr 1977a]. The discovery of constraints that are valid and sufficiently universal leads to results about vision that have the same quality of permanence as results in other branches of science [Marr 1977b].

　　　　Finally, once a computational theory for a process has been formulated, algorithms for implementing it may be designed, and their performance compared with that of the human visual processor. This allows two kinds of result. Firstly, if performance is essentially identical, one has good evidence that the constraints of the underlying computational theory are valid and may be implicit in the human processor; and secondly, if a process matches human performance, it is probably sufficiently powerful to form part of a general purpose vision machine.

References

G. J. Agin, *Representation and Description of Curved Objects*, Stanford AI Memo 173, 1972.

J. Beck, *Surface Color Perception*, Cornell University Press, 1974.

T. O. Binford, *Visual Perception by Computer*, presented to the IEEE Conference on Systems and Control, 1971.

H. Blum, "Biological Shape and Visual Science, (part 1)," *J.*

Theor. Biol. , *38,* 1973.

F. W. C. Campbell, "Sometimes a Biologist Has to Make a Noise Like a Mathematician," *NRP Bulletin on Neurophysiology and Psychophysics* (in press), 1977.

P. Colas-Baudelaire, *Digital Picture Processing and Psychophysics: a Study of Brightness Perception* Report No. UTEC-CSC-74-025, Department of Computer Science, University of Utah, 1973.

T. B. Felton, W. Richards, and R. A. Smith, Jr., "Disparity Processing of Spatial Frequencies in Man," *J. of Physiology*, 255, 1972.

K. Forbus, *Light Source Effects*, MIT AI Laboratory Memo 422, 1977.

E. C. Freuder, *A Computer Vision System for Visual Recognition Using Active Knowledge*, MIT AI Laboratory Technical Report 345, 1976.

L. Glass, "Moire Effect from Random Dots," *Nature, 243,* 1969.

A. L. Gilchrist, "Perceived Lightness Depends on Perceived Spatial Arrangement," *Science, 195,* 1977.

B. K. P. Horn, "Determining Lightness from an Image," *Computer Graphics and Image Processing, 3,* 1974.

B. K. P. Horn, "Understanding Image Intensities," *Artificial Intelligence,* 1977.

D. H. Hubel and T. N. Wiesel, "Receptive Fields, Binocular Interaction and Functional Architecture in the Cat's Visual Cortex," *J. Physiol., Lond. 160,* 1962.

D. A. Huffman, "Impossible Objects as Nonsense Sentences," in *Machine Intelligence 6*, R. Meltzer and D. Michie (eds.), The Edinburgh University Press, 1971.

W. H. Ittelson, *Visual Space Perception*, pp. 145-147, Springer, 1960.

B. Julesz, *Foundations of Cyclopean Perception*, The University of Chicago Press, 1971.

B. Julesz, "Experiments in the Visual Perception of Texture," *Scientific American 232*, 1975.

B. Julesz and J. E. Miller, "Independent Spatial-Frequency-Tuned Channels in Binocular Fusion and Rivalry," *Perception 4*, 1976.

P. A. Kolers, *Aspects of Motion Perception*, Pergamon Press, 1972.

E. H. Land, and J. J. McCann, "Lightness and Retinex Theory," *J. Opt. Soc. Am. 61*, 1971.

A. K. Mackworth, "Interpreting Pictures of Polyhedral Scenes." *Artificial Intelligence 4*, 1973.

D. Marr, *A Note on the Computation of Binocular Disparity in a Symbolic, Low-Level Visual Processor*, MIT AI Laboratory Memo 327, 1974.

D. Marr, "Early Processing of Visual Information," *Phil. Trans. Roy. Soc. B. 275*, 1976.

D. Marr, "Analysis of Occluding Contour," *Proc. Roy. Soc. B 197*, 1977a.

D. Marr, "Artificial Intelligence - a Personal View," *Artificial*

Intelligence 9, 1977b.

D. Marr and H. K. Nishihara, "Representation and Recognition of the Spatial Organization of Three-Dimensional Shapes," *Proc. Roy. Soc. B. 200,* 1977.

D. Marr and T. Poggio, "Cooperative Computation of Stereo Disparity," *Science 194,* 1976.

D. Marr and T. Poggio, "From Understanding Computation to Understanding Neural Circuitry," *Neurosciences Res. Prog. Bull. 15,* 1977a.

D. Marr and T. Poggio, "A Theory of Human Stereo Vision," MIT AI Laboratory Memo 451, 1977b.

D. Marr, T. Poggio, and G. Palm, "Analysis of a Cooperative Stereo Algorithm," *Biol. Cybernetics 28,* 1977.

J. E. W. Mayhew and J. P. Frisby, "Rivalrous Texture Stereograms," *Nature 264,* 1976.

R. Nevatia, *Structured Descriptions of Complex Curved Objects for Recognition and Visual Memory,* Stanford AI Memo 250, 1974.

J. F. O'Callaghan, "Computing the Perceptual Boundaries of Dot Patterns," *Computer Graphics and Image Processing 3,* 1974.

W. A. Richards, "Anomalous Stereoscopic Depth Perception," *J. Opt. Soc. Amer. 61,* 1971.

W. A. Richards, "Stereopsis With and Without Monocular Cues," *Vision Res.* 17, 1977.

M. Riley, *Discriminant Functions in Early Visual Processing,* (in preparation) 1977.

A. Rosenfeld, R. A. Hummel, and S. W. Zucker, "Scene Labelling by Relaxation Operations," *IEEE Transactions on Systems, Man and Cybernetics, SMC-6,* 420-433.

B. R. Schatz, "Computation of Texture Discrimination," *Proc. 5th Int. Joint Conf. Art. Intelligence,* 1977, also MIT AI Laboratory Memo 426, 1977.

K. A. Stevens, "Computation of Locally Parallel Structure," *Biol. Cybernetics 29* (also available as MIT AI Laboratory Memo 392), 1978.

J. M. Tenenbaum and H. G. Barrow, *Experiments in Interpretation-Guided Segmentation,* Stanford Research Institute Technical Note 123, 1976.

S. Ullman, "On Visual Detection of Light Sources," *Biol. Cybernetics 21,* 1976a.

S. Ullman, "Filling-in the Gaps: The Shape of Subjective Contours and a Model for their Generation," *Biol. Cybernetics 25,* 1976b.

S. Ullman, *The Interpretation of Visual Motion,* MIT PhD Thesis, 1977, to be published by MIT Press, 1978.

H. Wallach and D. N. O'Connell, "The Kinetic Depth Effect," *J. Exp. Psychol. 45,* 1953.

D. Waltz, "Understanding Line Drawings of Scenes with Shadows," in *The Psychology of Computer Vision,* P. H. Winston (ed.), McGraw-Hill, 1975.

The complete version of this paper appears as "Representing Visual Systems" *Lectures on Mathematics in the Life Sciences,*

VISUAL DETECTION OF LIGHT SOURCES

SHIMON ULLMAN

Human-level vision is the result of many cooperating computations, each of which must be thoroughly understood. Light-source detection is one such computation. Experiments show that humans are capable of detecting self-illuminating surfaces in their visual field and that this capacity is based, to a great extent, on immediate processing by the visual system, rather than on a higher-level analysis. This section by Shimon Ullman inquires into how this processing might happen and presents a method for accomplishing light source detection in the so-called Mondrian world. The method involves a comparison of changes in intensity and changes in the derivative of intensity at region boundaries. Ullman's complete PhD thesis, on the subject of motion vision analysis, is part of the MIT Press series in Artificial Intelligence.

The Detection Problem

How can people detect light sources in their visual field? The work described here addresses these questions from a computational point of view in a restricted domain, referred to here as the "Mondrian World."

There are many instances in which human beings exhibit the ability to correctly identify light sources in their visual field. For example, in most cases it is easy to tell whether a light bulb is turned on or off. A simple demonstration of this ability is the use of brake-lights in automobiles as a warning system. This is not to say that humans can always detect light sources correctly. On the contrary: we cannot detect a weak light source if the background is too bright, for example stars in daytime, while on the other hand, areas which are not actual light sources are sometimes perceived as such, as in the case of the retro-reflecting signs on the highways. However, the interesting point is not that we occasionally make erroneous judgments, but that in most situations we make the right ones.

Is this capacity based on a high-level analysis or on immediate perception? Does the perception of a shining lamp depend on the knowledge we have about it? To eliminate such possible uses of high-level knowledge the problem of detecting light sources was confined to "Achromatic Mondrians." By an Achromatic Mondrian I mean an array of rectangular shapes, of different sizes, and different levels of black, gray and white, as in figure 1. The term "Mondrians" for such arrays was used by E. Land and J. McCann, [Land 1971] because of their resemblance to the paintings by Piet Mondrian. These Mondrians serve to simplify the environment, especially by excluding colors, and by discarding both shadings and "fuzzy" light sources like, for example, an ordinary light bulb. (Evans [1974] has some work on the contribution of colors to the perception of fluorescence.)

Experiments

A Mondrian is composed of pieces of paper, glued together onto a white, translucent, background sheet. It is then placed on a thick piece of cardboard. By making a hole in the cardboard, and placing it above a fluorescent lamp, the area above the hole becomes a uniform light source. Figure 1 and figure 2 show typical Mondrians.

The following notation will be used: the light falling on a Mondrian is called the *illumination*, and is denoted by I; the *radiant area* in the Mondrian is denoted by A; and the light transmitted through it is called the *source-intensity*, and is denoted by L.

A subject is presented with a Mondrian, and asked whether he detects any light source in it, and if so, where. This procedure is repeated for different light source and illumination values, and for different Mondrians.

The key is under what conditions will the subject be able to detect light sources in the Mondrian, and by what possible methods can such a task be accomplished?

Results

Figure 3 summarizes the results of 140 measurements in a typical experiment. It depicts the degree to which the light source was perceivable, as a function of the light source intensity and the (immediate) background intensity. At a given illumination I, if we begin such a measurement with a very low source intensity and gradually increase it, at first, the source is not detectable. When it grows stronger there is a range of uncertainty, and then, finally, it becomes prominent. The range of uncertainty is bounded by two "thresholds": the lower threshold is the source intensity at which the subject suspects for the first time the presence of a light source; the upper threshold is the source intensity at which he becomes sure. This distinction is important when carrying out experiments with a "just noticeable" light

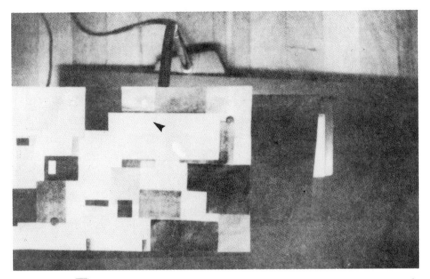

Figure 1. A Mondrian. The place of the light source is indicated by an arrow.

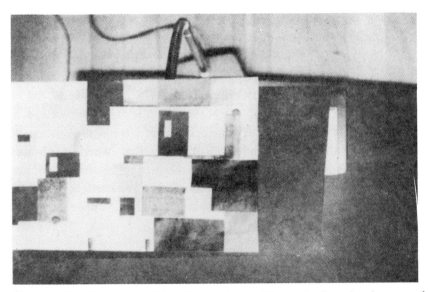

Figure 2. The same Mondrian, but with a darker background around the light source.

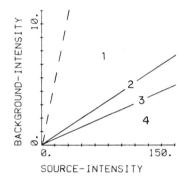

Figure 3. The detectability of a light source as a function of its intensity and the background intensity. The intensity units are 100 foot-lambert.

source, as it specifies the experimental condition more precisely. In this diagram, 1 means "undetectable," 2 to 3 is the range of uncertainty and 4 means that the light source was prominent. The main points to note at this stage are:

■ There is a linear dependence between the source intensity and the background intensity such that, when it obtains, the source is detectable. In the setting of this particular experiment the lower threshold was achieved at a source to background ratio of about 23, and the upper threshold at a ratio of about 35.

■ When the background is altered, the dependence remains linear, but the threshold values change. The dashed line in figure 3 represents the upper threshold in a different setting, where the (immediate) background reflectance was 10 times higher than that of the first experiment. The threshold values in this case were about 10 times lower. This last result means that light sources are sometimes conspicuous in scenes with relatively low contrasts. We shall return to the contrast issue in the next section where physical parameters, which may seem to underline the perception of fluorescence, are examined.

We proceed by examining the following six factors from the point of view of their relevance to light-sources detection.

- The highest intensity in the visual field.

- High absolute intensity value.

- Local contrast.

- Global contrast.

- Intensity compared with the average intensity in the scene.

- Lightness computation.

We shall conclude that even in the simple case of the Mondrian, these factors are not sufficient to account for the ability of human subjects to detect light sources in their visual field.

The highest intensity in the scene. A perceived light source is not necessarily associated with the highest light intensity in the field. Suppose, for example, that we create an illumination gradient, and at the place where the intensity is low, we place a weak light source. The intensities can be (and were) set in such a way, that the light source will be perceivable, while the intensity graph will look like that in figure 4: The intensity at B is *higher* than the intensity at A. It is, in fact, the highest intensity in the scene.

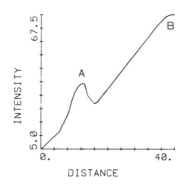

Figure 4. An intensity profile in the vicinity of a weak light source. Only A is perceived as a light source, although the intensity at B is higher.

Still, only A is perceived as a light source.

Thus, having the highest intensity in the scene is neither a necessary, nor is it, obviously, a sufficient condition, for being perceived as a light source.

High absolute intensity value. A light source is not necessarily associated with an area of high absolute intensity. Against a dark enough background a firefly is perceived as a light source, although the absolute light intensity coming from it is very low. Also, in the situation described above, where L was held constant and I increased, the total intensity coming from area A (the light source) *increased,* while at the same time it ceased to appear as a light source. The conclusion is that it was not the high intensity value at A that made it appear radiant. Rather, it seems that the major role was played by the ratio between the intensity at A and that of the surroundings.

Contrast. A variable that seems suitable to explain the dependence between source intensity and illumination is the contrast. The contrast between intensity I_1 and intensity I_2 is usually defined as $(I_1 - I_2) / (I_1 + I_2)$. As this contrast is a monotonic function of I_1/I_2, (assuming I_1/I_2 is positive) high contrast simply corresponds to I_1 being "many times" greater than I_2.

We can now try to explain the result mentioned in the last section in terms of contrast. Suppose we have an illumination $I = 100$ units on some arbitrary scale, $L = 100$ units, and instead of a Mondrian we have a uniform surface with reflectance $= 0.5$ (that is, it reflects 50% of the the incident light.) The light intensity coming from A will be 100 (source intensity) + 100 * 0.5 (reflection), that is, 150 units. From the surroundings, we get only the 50 units of reflected light, so that the ratio is 3:1, If the illumination is raised to 1000 units, the new intensities ratio between A and the surroundings will be only 6:5. Although the light intensity at A is higher this time, the contrast is much lower.

A plausible conclusion from the discussion so far is that whenever the contrast between a stimulus A and its surroundings exceeds a certain value, the former is perceived as a light source. There is a kind of rationale to such a conclusion: surfaces in nature do not usually have reflectivity values approaching the extremes of 100% or 0%. A very high contrast value is thus not likely to be achieved by reflectance changes alone; rather, it might indicate the presence of a light source.

The experimental data (figure 3) shows, however, the inadequacy of such a simple explanation. In the case of the dark background a contrast of 15 to 1 is still below the lower threshold, while with the light background a ratio of 4 to 1 is more than enough to make the light source prominent. Moreover, a contrast of 4 to 1 cannot serve as an indicator to the presence of a self-illuminating surface, since much higher contrasts are found in natural scenes with no light sources in them. Thus, the perception of a light source cannot be *identified* with a high enough contrast. While a high enough contrast seems, at least in the Mondrian world where shadows are excluded, sufficient to induce the perception of a light source, it is not a necessary condition. In other words, the presence of a light source can be "deduced" from factors other than contrast. Hence an attempt was made to find such a factor, or perhaps a computation, which the visual system can perform autonomously without resorting to high-level knowledge. What makes the question intriguing is the fact that there does not seem to be an obvious candidate for the task.

We proceed by discussing more of the immediate candidates for a solution, and show their inadequacy. They are: global as opposed to local contrast, average illumination, and lightness computation.

Global versus local contrast. Consider the situation in figure 1. The source intensity was set at the lower threshold. Figure 2 is of the same setting, only this time with a dark area surrounding the light source. The contrast between the source and its immediate surroundings was thus multiplied by 10. This change in contrast did not, however, make the light source more noticeable. The following claim can be raised: the change in contrast between figure 1 and figure 2 is only in the *immediate* contrast, that is, between the light source and its immediate surroundings. The *global* contrast, namely between the light source and the darkest area in the field, had not been effected. The experiment was repeated therefore, this time changing the global surroundings as well, and with similar results. Using the above distinction it can now be stated that light sources are sometimes detectable when both the global and the local contrasts were low, therefore *neither* is a necessary condition for the source detection.

Average illumination. Another factor that had been considered is the influence of changes in the average illumination. Will the thresholds of detection become lower, if we use, for example, a darker Mondrian (while maintaining both global and immediate contrasts fixed)? No such influence has been detected.

Lightness computation. Finally, let me turn to a brief analysis of the above results in terms of *lightness* to see whether this approach provides us with the key to the detection of low-contrast sources. The computation of lightness from intensities involves the separation of sharp intensity changes from gradual ones [Land 1971] [Horn 1974]. One might try to use this decomposition to explain the fact that A in figure 4 is perceived as a light source, although the intensity at B is higher: if the lightness contrast is computed instead of the intensity contrast, then area A obviously gets the highest value. Examination of the experimental data reveals, however, that the computation of contrast via lightness does not help solving the basic problem: high contrast is still not a necessary condition. The visual system somehow distinguishes between possible interpretations of the scene: a contrast created by light-and-dark surfaces on the one hand, and a contrast created by the presence of a light source on the other. To make the problem clearer, consider the following one-dimensional intensity array:

44 43 43 42 42 41 41 40 40 110 109 108 107 106 105 104 103 102 101 100
50 49 48 47 46

The corresponding lightness matrix discards slow changes and therefore will look like this:

30 30 30 30 30 30 30 30 30 100 100 100 100 100 100 100 100 100 100 100
50 50 50 50 50

In both cases, there is more than a single possible interpretation. One interpretation is that the areas simply have different reflectivities. Thus, the central area can be normalized to 1.0, and the left and right areas assigned the values of 0.3 and 0.5 respectively. A different interpretation is that the right area has a reflectivity of 1.0, the left 0.6, and the center is a light source.

To be sure, if we knew the real reflectance of one area, we could have determined (at least in the case of Mondrians) *all* the reflectance values in the picture, and then we could have also assigned the label "light source" to areas of reflectance greater than unity. The only trouble with this method is that there does not seem to exist a way of determining real reflectance values. Still, in many cases the visual system is able to make the right interpretation of the scene. In a picture rather similar to the array presented above, but with even less contrast, a light source had been perceived. That is, the visual system managed to somehow pick (correctly) the light-source interpretation. How can this be done? From now on we proceed along theoretical lines, searching for a method to accomplish the following task: given an array of light intensities obtained from some scene, find the light sources. It should be emphasized that the only information available for subsequent processing is this intensity array alone. Hence the method should be expressed only in terms of these measurements.

The Proposed Method

Roughly speaking, the proposed method is the following: given two adjacent areas, compute both their intensity-ratio and their gradient-ratio, and compare the two. If the ratios are not equal, one of the areas is a light source.

It is based on the following two observations:

- All that is needed for the detection of a light source, is the correct values of the reflectance *ratios* in the scene.

- In many cases this real reflectance ratio can be computed, even in the presence of a light source, by comparing *intensity gradients*.

First consider using the value of (r_0/r_1). The preceding discussion seemed to imply that a correct normalization of the reflectances is needed in order to detect light sources, by identifying them with areas of reflectance greater than 1. It turns out, however, that we do not need that much.

Consider two adjacent areas: area 0 and area 1, and suppose that we somehow know the reflectance ratio r_0/r_1. Assuming the illumination is a continuous function of the position, we can then determine whether one of the above areas is a light source. The continuity of I implies that the illumination on the two sides of the borderline between the areas is approximately equal, if the measurements are taken close enough to the borderline. From this equality it follows that if neither of the areas is a light source, the intensity ratio should equal the reflectance ratio. Hence, if the ratio values do not agree, we can deduce the presence of a light source and, as it turns out, we can also compute the actual source intensity.

As had been mentioned, the only values permitted in the computation are the intensity values at points in the visual field. The way used both by Land and Horn to determine reflectance ratios from these intensities is basically the following: find the points of sharp changes in the intensity distribution, like point A in figure 5. Then conclude that the ratio r_0/r_1 is equal to the ratio e_0/e_1 when e_0 is measured to the left of the "jump" A, and e_1 is measured to the right of it. This computation, however, presupposes the existence of no light sources in the picture. For otherwise it might be the case that, for example, $r_0 = r_1$, but there is a light source at area 0 which creates the intensity jump at A. That is to say, in order to compute the reflectances ratio we need first to discover the light sources, and in order to discover the light sources we need the reflectance ratios! But there is a way out of this circle. Suppose, (and this is usually the case), that the illumination is not absolutely uniform, but has a gradient which over some area is more or less linear, say a gradient of 100 intensity units to an inch. When such an illumination is reflected from a surface of reflectance K, not

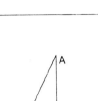

Figure 5. An intensity profile around the borderline between two surfaces. The reflectance at area 0 is twice the reflectance of 1. There is a change both in the intensity and in the gradient.

only is the overall intensity reduced by a factor of K, but the *gradient* will be K times the original as well.

In figure 5, the reflectances are taken to be 1/2 in area 0 and 1/4 in area 1. Note that not only is $I_A/I_B = 2$, but S_A/S_B also is equal to 2; where S_A is the slope of the intensity graph measured from A to the left, and S_B is the slope measured from B to the right. If we now add a uniform light source to area 0, the ratio I_A/I_B will change, but the ratio S_A/S_B will *remain the same*, and still equal to r_0/r_1. S_A and S_B can, of course, be computed from the intensity values alone.

Thus, we can use the gradient ratio to compute the reflectance ratio, and then use this ratio as shown in the preceding section to test for the presence of a light source. Next, I describe how the computation is actually implemented.

The Source Operator and its Implementation

First, we need to review the notation. I denotes the illumination; L, the source intensity (the source is assumed to be in area 0); S is the gradient; r denotes the reflectance; and e stands for the intensity of the light reaching the eye. Note that e is the only parameter we are allowed to measure. The discussion so far shows that from the obvious relation:

$$e_0 = (I_0 * r_0) + L$$

we can deduce that under "smooth" illumination:

$$L = e_0 - e_1 * (S_0/S_1)$$

if the points 0 and 1, where the measurements are taken, are close enough to each other. However, real-world measurements tend to look noisy -- we can no longer suppose that I_A is equal to I_B, as they are too far apart. Rather, $I_B = I_A + Kd$, where K is the intensity gradient in intensity units per unit distance, and d is the distance of B from A (positive if B is to the right of A). Starting with the first equation, we now get:

$$L = e_0 - r_0 * (I_1 + Kd) = e_0 - I_1 r_0 - r_0 Kd$$

$$= e_0 - e_1 * (r_0/r_1) - S_0 d \text{ (Since } r_0 K = S_0)$$

This last equation, with the slopes replacing the reflectances:

$$L = e_0 - e_1 * (S_0/S_1) - S_0 d$$

will be referred to as the "S-Operator"

It is a rather straightforward task to implement the S-Operator and run it on actual intensity arrays. The algorithm basically computes the S-Operator between each picture point and its left (or right) neighbour, though several details have to be added, mainly to cope with problems of noise and insufficient resolution.

Figure 6 shows the intensity distribution obtained from a scene which contained a light source to the right of point A. Figure 7 shows the corresponding output of the S-Operator, which was looking for the left borderline of a light source. As negative S-values are meaningless in the particular algorithm that had been used, the output can be taken as the positive value of the S-value, as in figure 8. The "source value" is the highest at the real source borderline. Its relative magnitude is sufficient to allow the setting of some threshold, above which an area can be labeled as a light source. In the general case, this threshold has to depend on the overall intensity. This dependence contributes to the fact that a light source, which is detectable at low illuminations, becomes undetectable at higher ones.

Suppose that the lower detection threshold is taken to be the computed reflected intensity. That is, L should exceed e_0, or roughly $e_1*(r_0/r_1)$ to become noticeable. This assumption implies that the contrast at the detection threshold will be somewhat higher than twice the value of (r_0/r_1), a value which is in agreement with the experimental results. This agreement suggests another interesting result. If r_1/r_0 is sufficiently greater than 2 it should be possible to perceive a light source at area 0 even when the intensity coming from this area is lower than the intensity of its surroundings. This prediction was tested and verified. For example, using $r_1 = 6r_0$ a light source at area 0 was perceivable when the intensity e_0 was only half the intensity e_1.

Humans possess the ability to detect self-illuminating surfaces in their visual field. This capacity is largely based on immediate perception. There does not, however, seem to exist any single, simple parameter responsible for the generation of this perception. Theoretical considerations suggest a possible way of accomplishing the source-detection task, based on simple intensity and gradient comparisons. It is not known whether this

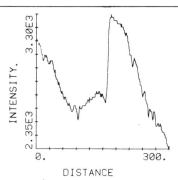

Figure 6. Intensity profile obtained from a scene with a light source. The intensity units are the Vidicon output units which are proportional to the total light flux per unit area.

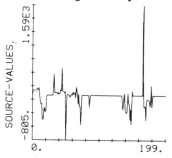

Figure 7. Output of the S-operator applied to the picture in Figure 6.

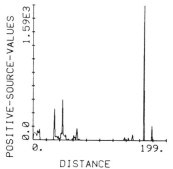

Figure 8. The positive part of 7. The highest S-value is obtained at the source borderline.

method is indeed used by the visual system. It was, however, successfully implemented on a computer system.

References

R. M. Evans, *The Perception of Color*, John Wiley and Sons, 1974.

Berthold K. P. Horn, "Determining Lightness from an Image," *Computer Graphics and Image Processing*, 3, 4 277-299, 1974.

E. H. Land and J. J. McCann, "Lightness Theory," *Journal of the Optical Society*, 61, 1-11,

The complete version of this paper appears in *Biol. Cybernetics*, Vol. 21, pp. 205-212, 1976.

REPRESENTING AND ANALYZING SURFACE ORIENTATION

KENT A. STEVENS

When we look at a surface, in addition to perceiving its color, texture, and other physical properties, we see it *in space*; that is, the surface appears three dimensional. This usually has been considered to be equivalent to our perceiving the distance to the surface. However, in this preview of his PhD thesis, Kent Stevens suggests that much of the impression of three-dimensionality may be due to *surface orientation*, which he has studied with particular attention to the problem of inferring surface orientation from a single image composed of contours or lines. The word *infer* is used because there is not sufficient information in the image to allow the visual system to merely "recover" or "extract" the surface orientation. Rather, the visual system must make implicit assumptions about the nature of the surfaces it sees. Stevens has found evidence for these computational assumptions that in turn suggest the form in which surface orientation is internally represented.

Theories of Surface Perception from Single Images

While a single image does not have a unique three-dimensional interpretation, it often presents a striking appearance of three-dimensionality. Observe the cube in figure 1. The vertices appear to differ in depth and one may make judgements about which vertex is closer. However, it is difficult to attribute any quantitative depth, either relative or absolute, to points on the cube. In contrast to the indeterminate depth, the surface orientation of the faces of the cube can be judged quantitatively with precision. From perceived surface orientation one may then deduce qualitative differences in depth between the vertices. For instance, the Necker cube "depth reversal" illusion may be understood as a reversal in surface orientation. This study investigates computational methods for describing the three-dimensional shape of a surface in terms of surface orientation. The description would be computed from information in a single image; motion and stereopsis are excluded. I suspect that much of the apparent three-dimensionality of single images is due to perceived surface orientation, although most theories of surface perception have, in effect, equated "apparent three-dimensionality" to "apparent depth". Three major theories have been developed in this regard.

Some investigators hypothesize that *depth cues* in the image are unconsciously interpreted in terms of prior visual experiences [Ittelson 1960]. For example, the size of the image of an object would be a cue to depth if the actual size of the object were known. Most of the depth cues require that objects be recognized prior to their interpretation in depth. Cues to surface orientation, *per se*, are not emphasized.

Another explanation for the three-dimensionality of a single image evolved from the Gestalt law of *Praegnanz* [Koffka 1935]. Three-dimensionality is believed to result from tendencies to minimize differences among angles and lengths. Hence, if for a given image there is a three-dimensional interpretation that is simpler, more regular, or more symmetric than the two-dimensional interpretation, then the image will be seen in depth. This theory postulates that "... the rules of perspective (or some approximation thereto) are implicit in an analog medium representing physical space, within which the representation of an object moves towards a stable state characterized by figural goodness or minimum complexity" [Attneave and Frost 1969].

Gibson introduced a stimulus-response theory of surface perception in which distance, surface orientation, and even size-constancy are "specified" by "higher-order variables" in the image [Gibson 1950]. While this appears similar to the depth cue theory, it was claimed that the visual input need not be interpreted, that the stimulus uniquely specifies the percept. When it was demonstrated that a single image is ambiguous in terms of three dimensional interpretations, Gibson then emphasized the role of the dynamic visual stimuli presented as one moves through the visual world. The single image was then labelled as "not ecological," that is, not naturally presented to the visual system. However, adopting this attitude leads one to ignore sources of spatial information that are available in the single image and avoids the issue of accounting for the vivid three-dimensionality that persists in spite of the vague depth.

The view taken by the present research is that while the depth cues in a single image are often weak, there are generally strong cues to surface orientation. The vivid impression of three-dimensionality in figure 1 derives largely from the perceived surface orientation; that is to say, the "three-dimensionality" is not just perceived depth. While it is well known that ellipses appear to be slanted circles, trapezoids appear as perspective rectangles, and that texture gradients suggest surfaces that appear to slant out of the image plane, the perception of surface orientation has not been systematically studied. Here a computational theory of surface perception is described that has the following basis:

- Surface orientation is analyzed to a large extent prior to object recognition.
- Surface orientation is represented explicitly in the visual system.
- The analysis of surface orientation involves implicit assumptions about the visible surfaces.
- The visual system performs two distinct types of analysis of surface orientation: orthographic analysis and perspective analysis.
- The analysis is performed when certain *triggering criteria* are met.

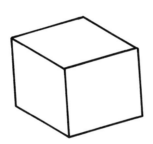

Figure 1. The reversals that we experience with the Necker cube can be understood in terms of ambiguity in surface orientation.

In the following, aspects of the evolving theory are presented.

Representing Local Surface Orientation

The spatial orientation of a point on a surface has only two degrees of freedom and thus can be considered as a point in a two-dimensional space. The primitive descriptor of surface orientation, therefore, can be thought of as a coordinate-pair for a point in this space. However the descriptor can have many forms depending both on the underlying space and on the choice of coordinate system imposed on that space. Since methods for inferring surface orientation are dependent on the form of the descriptor, it is important to make explicit our assumptions about the underlying representation of surface orientation. Although there are strong computational arguments for the human visual system having an explicit representation of surface orientation [Marr 1977], we know little about the form of that representation.

In the present study it is postulated that each element of the representation is composed of two orthogonal components, the *tilt* and *slant* of the surface at that point. To define these terms, consider the orthographic projection onto the image plane of a unit vector normal to a surface at a given point. The orientation of the projected vector corresponds to the tilt, and varies from 0-180 degrees. The slant is determined from the length of the vector, and varies from 0-90 degrees. Studies of surface perception have dealt exclusively with subjective judgements of slant (e.g., slant-shape invariance and slant aftereffect). The subjective tilt of a surface describes the component of the orientation of the surface in the image plane. While this component has been factored out in most experiments by orienting the stimulus such that that the tilt is vertical (or horizontal), surface tilt is nonetheless a necessary aspect of surface perception.

Figure 2 demonstrates various instances of perceived surface tilt. Note that each figure is ambiguous, being subject to reversals. Significantly, when the figure reverses, both the slant and tilt remain unchanged. The normal vector appears to reverse direction but projects to the same tilt orientation. Although slant and tilt is a natural way of describing surface orientation, other means are conceivable, such as gradient space [Huffman 1971] [Horn 1977]. Several forms of surface orientation descriptor are compared on computational and psychophysical grounds in Stevens [1978], from which it is concluded that slant

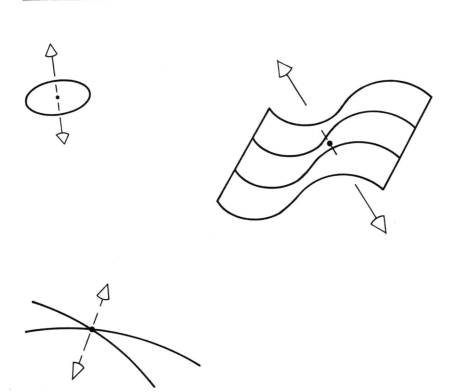

Figure 2. The two degrees of freedom of surface orientation can be described as slant and tilt. Slant is the angle between the line of sight and the surface normal, while tilt is the orientation of the normal in the image plane. Slant and tilt remain unchanged during reversals in surface orientation. Only the projection of the normal reverses direction (obscure one cone at a time when visualizing each surface).

and tilt are probably the components of local surface orientation descriptors incorporated in the human visual system. The question is: How might tilt and slant be inferred from a single image?

Analyzing Contours

The present study involves image contours and excludes sources of information about surface orientation provided by gradients of intensity (for example, shading [Horn 1977]). Contours can be distinguished as *occluding* contours (e.g., silhouette contours) or *surface* contours. Marr [1976] has observed that we derive more three-dimensional understanding of an object from its silhouette than one would expect, but that if the object were assumed to be a generalized cone with convex cross-section, then its shape may be recovered from its occluding contour. Furthermore, since the contour corresponds to surface points that are tangent to the line of sight, the surface orientation is constrained along the contour: the tilt must be perpendicular to the tangent of the contour, and the slant must be 90 degrees.

The visual system does not always assume that a silhouette with an axis of symmetry is a generalized cone. In figure 3a we interpret the silhouette as a cone, however the silhouette in figure 3b appears planar. Observe that both figures are identical above section AA, and have the same axis of symmetry. In terms of surface orientation, the distinction between occluding contours and surface contours may only be important when the underlying surface along the occluding contour is tangent to the line of sight. Otherwise, the visual system appears not to handle occluding contours differently from surface contours in the analysis of surface orientation.

In the following, I will delineate some of the computational problems in deriving surface orientation from surface contours in an orthographic projection. This will be followed with a discussion of deriving surface orientation from perspective projections.

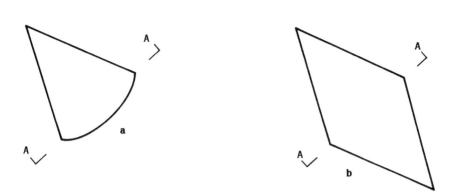

Figure 3. When the silhouette is assumed to be that of a generalized cone, as in Figure 3a, the occluding contours correspond to surface points that are tangent to the line of sight. The occluding contours in Figure 3b, however, are subject to a different analysis, resulting in an interpretation of a slanted planar surface.

Deriving Surface Orientation from an Orthographic Projection

It is particularly difficult to account for the three-dimensionality of an image produced by orthographic projection in terms of depth cues, since an orthographic projection contains no depth information (other than occlusion). Nonetheless, it is common practice to use this projection in pictorially conveying three-dimensional shape. The optics of the eye does produce a perspective projection; however that projection is not significantly different from an orthographic projection when the dimensions of the surface are small relative to the viewing distance.

We will start with the most simplified situation, the planar surface defined by a pair of intersecting lines (see figure 4a). The following discussion pertains to the analysis of surface orientation from local arrangements of linear contours; the more general analysis of curvilinear contours is discussed in [Stevens 1978]. Let us assume that a linear contour in an image is the projection of a linear feature in three dimensions. This allows us to treat a linear contour as the projection of a three-dimensional vector.

A pair of intersecting three-dimensional vectors is sufficient to define a plane. Its orthographic projection would be a pair of intersecting lines. Determining the surface orientation from the projection can then be couched as a problem of deriving the normal.

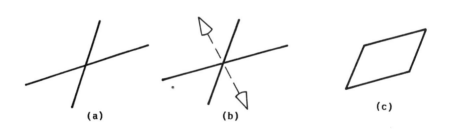

(a)   (b)   (c)

Figure 4. The simple intersection of two contours in **Figure 4a** strongly suggests a spatial orientation. The subjective tilt shown in Figure 4b is a function of the relative line lengths and their angle of intersection. The parallelogram in Figure 4c presents the same geometry and suggests the same surface orientation.

The surface normal cannot be recovered directly from the projection, hence some three-dimensional information is necessary. There are four nontrivial cases in which the normal can be recovered with the addition of knowledge about the three-dimensional configuration. These involve knowing either (1) the three-dimensional (nonforeshortened) lengths of both vectors, (2) that one of the vectors is not foreshortened, (3) the length of one vector and the angle of intersection, or (4) the ratio of lengths and the angle of intersection.

I have found evidence that the visual system uses two of these four cases. In figure 4a the pair of vectors suggests a surface with tilt shown in figure 4b. The conclusion of a series of experiments involving a range of obtuse angles and relative line lengths is that the visual system assumes case 4, that the vectors are equal-length and that their angle of intersection is a right angle. This applies to parallelograms as well (figure 4c), although with parallelograms there is a competing solution that has caused the distributions of tilt judgements to be bimodal. The other solution places the tilt as perpendicular to the longer edges. This is consistent with case 2: the longer vectors are assumed not to be foreshortened. (The surface slant is then simply rotation about the nonforeshortened vector.) Other evidence of case 2 is given by the tilt judgements of scaline triangles (figure 5), where the surface tilt is judged as perpendicular to one of the edges (usually the longest edge).

The surface tilt in figure 6 appears consistent with the nonforeshortened contour assumption as well: The tilt is usually judged as perpendicular to the parallel contours. This raises the question of *triggering criteria*, for why should we see these figures as oriented in space? Is there some simple geometry that triggers a three-dimensional interpretation? One possibility is that the visual system assumes that the obtuse angle is the image of a right angle (this and other triggering criteria can be phrased in terms of symmetry). It is interesting to note that the surface orientation we see may not be consistent with the assumptions that trigger our perceiving the three-dimensionality. For example, in figure 6, if the surface tilt involves the nonforeshortened contour assumption, the angle of intersection

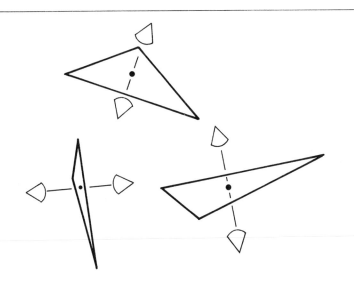

Figure 5. Scalene triangles appear to be spatially oriented such that the tilt is perpendicular to one of the edges. This is equivalent to assuming that the edge is not foreshortened; that the surface is effectively rotated about that axis.

cannot be a right angle in three dimensions.

The Bisector Solution

A third method for orthographic analysis of tilt is demonstrated with figure 7a. The intersection has a three-dimensional interpretation for which surface tilt is shown in figure 7b. The tilt is judged as the bisector of the obtuse angle of intersection. Although the bisector would appear to be an *ad hoc* solution to the tilt, it can be shown to be the tilt solution in which the slant of the surface is minimized. The bisector solution has been

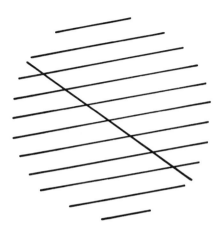

Figure 6. While parallel lines appear in the image plane, if a line is added that cuts obliquely across them, the surface appears slanted. The tilt is usually judged as perpendicular to the parallel lines. Although the obtuse angle of intersection may trigger the three-dimensional interpretation, the tilt is not consistent with the obtuse angle being the image of a right angle.

demonstrated in a rather different figure, the mouse hole (figure 8a). The subjective normal to the wall is shown in figure 8b, which is the bisector of the obtuse angle defined by the axis of symmetry AB and the baseline. An experiment involving a range of configurations suggests that whenever the image is asymmetric, the figure is seen as three-dimensional and the tilt is not significantly different from the bisector. The triggering criterion again appears to be an obtuse angle, an implicit expectation for symmetry.

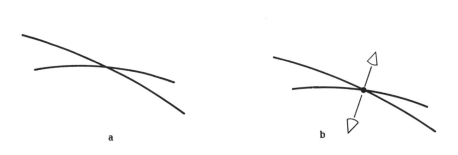

Figure 7. The pair of curvilinear contours in Figure 7a suggests a right-angle intersection on a curved surface. The tilt is judged as the bisector of the angle of intersection in the image, shown in Figure 7b.

Slant from Tilt

Each of the above methods for inferring surface tilt assumes some local geometry of surface contours. How then might surface slant be determined? The slant of the surface can be computed from the configuration in figure 9: the image of three mutually orthogonal axes (one of which is the surface normal given by the tilt). Attneave and Frost [1969] observed that the slant σ of a surface is given by:

$$\sin \sigma = (\cot \alpha \cot \beta)^{1/2}.$$

One can abstract this configuration from figure 4b, figure 7b, and figure 8b. Other work on surface orientation from orthographic analysis in Stevens [1978] suggests that where surface tilt can be determined, this three-axis configuration can

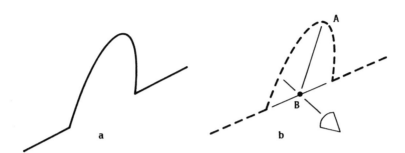

Figure 8. The contour in Figure 8a appears three-dimensional: a mouse hole. the tilt in Figure 8b is judged as the bisector of the angle defined by the axis AB and the baseline.

usually be defined.

Perspective Analysis

Perspective causes the railroad tracks in an image to converge and causes the texture density to increase in the direction of increasing distance. These two effects are often distinguished as "linear perspective" and "texture gradient," respectively. I will discuss texture gradients here.

An image with a texture gradient is almost invariably interpreted as that of a surface receding in depth. While texture gradients have been thought by some to determine surface orientation [Gibson 1950] [Bajcsy 1972], others (for example, Rosinski [1974]) claim that the texture gradient specifies distance up to a scale factor. However, surface orientation and relative distance are mathematically equivalent, hence if the texture gradient provides information in one form, it necessarily provides information in the other form as well. The distinction arises in

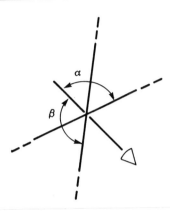

Figure 9. The projection of three mutually orthogonal axes contains sufficient information to allow the slant to be computed. This configuration often arises in orthographic analysis of surface orientation (see Figure 4b, Figure 7b, and Figure 8b).

attempting to actually compute a surface description: despite their equivalence, the computations of distance or surface orientation do not necessarily present equivalent computational problems. In this discussion, we will assume that (1) the surface description consists of local descriptors, and that (2) each descriptor is computed by a local computation that takes input measurements from the immediate vicinity of that image point. This *locality restriction* will be necessary to avoid circuitous arguments about the feasibility of computing one form of descriptor or another.

Let us first consider the feasibility of computing the distance (up to a scale factor) to a surface point from the locally measured texture gradient. We seek an expression relating the texture gradient and the absolute distance to the surface point. The various constants that are introduced would constitute the "scale factor". An expression for absolute distance D in terms of the density gradient $\nabla\rho$ is given below:

$$D = H/[1 - (\nabla\rho\cos^4\sigma/3H^2\rho_s)^2]^{1/2}$$

where

$$\nabla\rho = 3\rho_s H^2 \sin\sigma/\cos^4\sigma$$

and H is the height of the eye above the surface, σ is the surface slant at the point where the gradient is measured, and ρ_s is the actual density of elements on the surface. The expression can be simplified by using the *normalized texture gradient* $\nabla\rho/\rho$ (described later):

$$D = H/[1 - (\nabla\rho\cos\sigma/3\rho)^2]^{1/2}.$$

In this form, the density gradient $\nabla\rho$ is normalized by the measured density ρ, thereby removing the requirement for knowing ρ_s. The factor H can be considered part of the "scale factor", however, for scaled distance to be computed would still require that the local surface slant σ be known or assumed. This problem is usually avoided by assuming a planar, horizontal surface, wherein the slant is given by the angle between the line of sight and the vertical. However if we assume that the surface is planar and horizontal, the distance could as well be inferred from simple trigonometry *without the need for an image*:

$$D = H/\cos\sigma.$$

Furthermore, this assumption would seldom be valid. Since the surface orientation probably cannot be assumed, it would appear that distance to a surface point is not feasibly computed directly from the measured density gradient at the corresponding image point. However, I shall show that surface orientation can be feasibly computed directly from texture gradients.

The Perspective Projection as a Local Transformation

A texture gradient can be described by the partial derivatives of some texture measure in two orthogonal image directions. One approach is to use a fixed image coordinate system, wherein the derivatives in the x and y directions are computed, in a manner analogous to computing intensity gradients. Alternatively, the partial derivatives can be measured in the direction of the gradient and perpendicular to the gradient. This would simplify the description since the partial derivative perpendicular to the gradient is zero. The orientation of the gradient corresponds to the *tilt* of the surface at that point, so this description assumes that the surface tilt is known (a method for inferring the tilt will be shown later).

A surface texture of circles will illustrate this (figure 10). An individual texture element in the image would be an ellipse, with the minor axis parallel to the surface tilt τ. The major axis (or "width") subtends an angle w in the image, and the minor axis (or "height") subtends an angle h. The angle w is inversely proportional to the distance to the surface, while h is further *foreshortened* according to the slant σ between the line of regard and the normal to the surface. That is, "widths" are scaled by distance while "heights" are scaled by distance and foreshortened by slant. Locally, the perspective projection is no more complicated than these two transformations, *given that the direction of the gradient is known*. In general, a length measured on a surface will be subjected to both transformations, however the effects can be decomposed by determining the component h of the projection in the τ orientation and the w component perpendicular to τ.

The image orientation perpendicular to τ corresponds to the orientation *on the surface* of points that are locally equidistant from the viewer. Of course, the image orientation τ corresponds

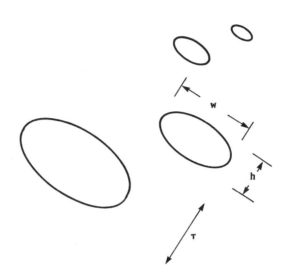

Figure 10. The perspective projection of a patch of surface comprised of circular elements. Define **w** as a length measured perpendicular to the direction of the gradient and **h** as a length measured in the direction of the gradient. From **w** and **h** one can define area, eccentricity, and density.

to the direction on the surface of steepest descent from the viewer.

Normalized Texture Gradients

Five texture measures are naturally defined by this local image coordinate system. Widths (w) and heights (h) are length measurements in the direction of the gradient and perpendicular to the gradient. Eccentricity (e = h/w) and area (a = hw) are then defined, along with the density measure ρ. Corresponding to the projected width and height are surface dimensions L_x and

L_y; the density on the surface is ρ_s. The texture measures can be expressed as:

$$w = (L_x/H)\cos\sigma$$
$$h = (L_y/H)\cos^2\sigma$$
$$e = h/w = (L_y/L_x)\cos\sigma$$
$$a = hw = (L_yL_x/H^2)\cos^3\sigma$$
$$\rho = \rho_s H^2/\cos^3\sigma.$$

The gradients of these measures are:

$$\nabla w = -(L_x/H)\sin\sigma$$
$$\nabla h = -(2L_y/H)\cos\sigma\sin\sigma$$
$$\nabla e = -(L_y/L_x)\sin\sigma$$
$$\nabla a = -(3L_yL_x/H^2)\cos^2\sigma\sin\sigma$$
$$\nabla\rho = 3\rho_s H^2\sin\sigma/\cos^4\sigma.$$

These expressions show the dependence of the magnitude of the gradient on σ, H, and the surface parameters L_x, L_y, and ρ_s. These expressions can be simplified by expressing the variables on the right hand side in terms of the appropriate texture measures, from which we discover some interesting relations between the tangent of the slant and the ratio of a texture gradient to the value of the texture measure at a given point:

$$\nabla w/w = -\tan\sigma$$
$$\nabla h/h = -2\tan\sigma$$
$$\nabla e/e = -\tan\sigma$$
$$\nabla a/a = -3\tan\sigma$$
$$\nabla\rho/\rho = 3\tan\sigma.$$

These expressions demonstrate the feasibility of inferring the local surface slant σ by means of the ratio of two measurements: the first derivative of a texture measure and the measure itself at a given point. The effect is to cancel all dependence on H and the particular surface properties. This ratio will be termed the *normalized texture gradient.*

Normalized texture gradients are potentially important, for they allow the computation of local surface slant for arbitrary surfaces with only *qualitative* assumptions concerning the surfaces. These assumptions are that the texture measure is locally uniform and that the surface is roughly planar in the locality of the measurement.

Although there are several normalized texture gradients from which the visual system could infer surface slant, there is no reason to believe that all are used. It is a matter of current experimentation to determine which gradients are actually used.

Surface Tilt from Texture Gradients

In the above, the surface tilt has been implicit. Tilt corresponds to the orientation of the gradient, the image orientation in which a given texture measure varies most rapidly. A straightforward approach to computing the local gradient for a given measure would be to compute the derivative in various orientations and select the maximum as the magnitude of the gradient and the orientation as the surface tilt. (This orientation would be the same for each measure in a natural scene.) In studying the strategy that the human visual system has adopted, I have found that we can make precise tilt judgements with texture gradient sampling that appear to be so small as to make this approach unreliable. The surface tilt in figure 11a is judged to be perpendicular to the orientation in which successive contours are intersected with equal spacings (figure 11b). In fact, the observer needs only three contours in order to perceive the surface well enough to make the tilt judgements.

Computing the tilt as perpendicular to the orientation of equal spacing is related to the nonforeshortened contour assumption in orthographic analysis of surface tilt. The image orientation perpendicular to the gradient corresponds to the locus of points on the surface that are equidistant from the observer, that is, not foreshortened. Hence in the image, the intersections with successive contours along this locus would be equal-spaced.

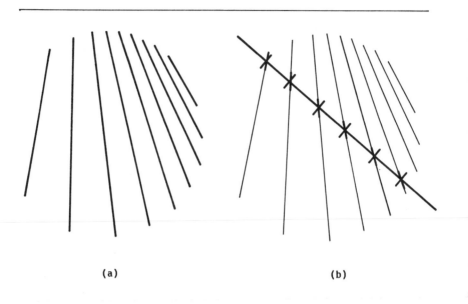

(a)   (b)

Figure 11. The divergent linear contours in Figure 11a suggest a slanted surface. The tilt (shown in Figure 11b) is judged as perpendicular to the orientation in which successive contours are intersected with equal spacing.

References

F. Attneave and R. Frost, "The Determination of Perceived Tridimensional Orientation by Minimum Criteria," *Perception and Psychophysics 6,* 1969.

R. Bajcsy, *Computer Identification of Textured Visual Scenes,* Stanford AI Laboratory Memo 180, 1972.

J. J. Gibson, *The Perception of the Visual World*, Houghton Mifflin, 1950.

B. K. P. Horn, "Image Intensity Understanding," *Artificial Intelligence 8*, also available as MIT AI Laboratory Memo 335, 1977.

D. A. Huffman, "Impossible Objects as Nonsense Sentences," in *Machine Intelligence 6*, R. Meltzer and D. Michie (eds.), The Edinburgh University Press, 1971.

W. H. Ittelson, *Visual Space Perception*, Springer-Verlag, 1960.

K. Koffka, *Principles of Gestalt Psychology*, Harcourt Brace, 1935.

D. Marr, *Analysis of Occluding Contour*, MIT AI Laboratory Memo 372, 1976.

D. Marr, "Representing Visual Information," *AAAS 143rd Annual Meeting, Symposium on Some Mathematical Questions in Biology*, February, (in press), also available as MIT AI Laboratory Memo 415, 1977.

R. R. Rosinski, "On the Ambiguity of Visual Stimulation: A Reply to Eriksson," *Perception and Psychophysics 16*, 1974.

K. A. Stevens, *Analysis and Representation of Visual Surface Orientation*, MIT PhD Dissertation (in preparation), 1978.

REGISTERING REAL IMAGES USING SYNTHETIC IMAGES

BERTHOLD K. P. HORN
BRETT L. BACHMAN

Accurate alignment of images with surface models is an important prerequisite for many image understanding tasks. Berthold Horn and Brett Bachman describe here an automatic method of potentially high accuracy that does not depend on feature extraction or other sophisticated image analysis methods. Instead, all that is required is careful matching of the real image with a synthetic one generated using a digital terrain model and a gradient-space representation of light reflectance. Because this technique, proposed by Horn and developed by Horn and Bachman, is an area-based process, it has the potential for subpixel accuracy -- accuracy not easily attained with techniques dependent on alignment of features such as edges or curves. The method is illustrated by registering LANDSAT images with digital terrain models.

The Registration Problem

Interesting and useful new image analysis methods may be developed if registered image intensity and surface slope information is available. Automatic change detection, for example, seems unattainable without an ability to deal with variations of appearance with changes in the sun's position. In turn, these variations can be understood only in terms of surface topography and reflectance models. Similarly, human cartographers consult both aerial photographs and topographic maps of a region to trace the paths of streams and rivers. Automatic analysis of either of these information sources alone is unlikely to lead to robust methods for performing this task.

An important application of aligned image and surface information lies in the area of automatic terrain classification. To date, no account has been taken of varying surface gradient, sun position or the physics of light reflection in ground cover. Classification ought to be based on measurable properties of the surface, not raw image intensities, which are only indirectly related to these properties. Classification techniques have been limited in their application to flat regions and have had to be retrained for images with different sun angles. Aligning images with surface models will permit removal of the image intensity component due to varyig orientation of the surface element.

Another application may be found in the inspection of industrial parts with complicated surfaces. Aligning images of these parts with models of their surfaces should permit one to determine defects in the surfaces which give rise to differences between real and synthesized images. It may also be possible to determine the position and orientation of a part by such techniques. This would then lead to methods which may guide a computer-controlled manipulator to retrieve one of the top-most parts in a bin full of parts. In this case, further work will be required to ascertain the effects of mutual illumination due to the proximity of parts to one another.

The method depends on matching the real image with a

synthetic image produced from the terrain model. The similarity of the two images depends in part upon how closely the assumed reflectance matches the real one. For mountainous terrain and for images taken with low sun elevations, rather simple assumptions about the reflectance properties of the surface gave very good results. Since all LANDSAT images are taken at about 9:30 local solar time, the sun elevations in this case are fairly small and image registration for all but flat terrain is straightforward.

   This implies that LANDSAT images are actually not optimal for automatic terrain classification, since the intensity fluctuations due to varying surface gradients often swamp the intensity fluctuations due to variations in surface cover. An important application of our technqiue in fact is the removal of the intensity fluctuations due to variations in surface gradient from satellite images in order to facilitate the automatic classification of terrain. To do this, we must model the way the surface reflects light.

The Reflectance Map

Work on image understanding has led to a need to model the image-formation process. One aspect of this concerns the geometry of projection, that is, the relationship between the position of a point and the coordinates of its image. Less well understood is the problem of determining image intensities, which requires modelling of the way surfaces reflect light. For a particular kind of surface and a particular placement of light sources, surface reflectance can be plotted as a function of surface gradient (magnitude and direction of slope). The result is called a reflectance map and is usually presented as a contour map of constant reflectance in gradient space [Moravec 1977].

   The reflectance map may be determined empirically by measuring the reflectance of a small, flat surface sample as it is oriented in many different directions while surrounded by the desired distribution of light sources. Alternatively, a test object such as a sphere or paraboloid, which contains surface elements oriented in all possible directions may be used [Horn 1970] [Horn 1975] [Moravec 1977]. Mathematical models of surfaces have also been developed in order to derive analytical expressions for surface reflectance or at least numerical values obtained by Monte Carlo simulation [Hapke]. In related graphics work, simple phenomenological models have been used [Catmull 1975] [Phong 1975] [Blinn and Newell 1976].

Since the reflectance map gives reflectance as a function of local surface gradient only, it does not take into account effects dependent on the position of the surface element. Two such effects which are not considered are mutual illumination of surface elements and cast shadows. Illumination of portions of a surface by neighboring surface elements when the object concerned has concavities is difficult to model and leads to global computations. Fortunately, this effect is usually small unless the surface reflectance is exceptionally high [Moravec 1977]. The reflectance map correctly accounts for self-shadowed surfaces, but not shadows cast by one surface element on another. Such cast shadows can however be calculated using well-known hidden-surface algorithms to predict which surface elements are not visible from the source [Warnock 1969] [Watkins 1970] [Sutherland *et al.* 1974].

One use of the reflectance map is in the determination of surface shape from intensities [Horn 1970] [Horn 1975] in a single image; here, however, it will be employed only in order to generate synthetic images from digital terrain models.

Reflectance and the Gradient

A gradient has two components, namely the surface slope along two mutually perpendicular directions. If the surface height, z, is expressed as a function of two coordinates x and y, we define the two components, p and q of the gradient as the partial derivatives of z with respect to x and y respectively. In particular, a Cartesian coordinate system is erected with the x-axis pointing east, the y-axis north and the z-axis up. Then, p is the slope of the surface in the west-to-east direction, while q is the slope in the south-to-north direction:

$$p = \partial z/\partial x \qquad q = \partial z/\partial y$$

One can estimate the gradient from the digital terrain model using first differences:

$$p = [z_{(i+1)j} - z_{ij}]/\Delta$$

$$q = [z_{i(j+1)} - z_{ij}]/\Delta$$

where Δ is the grid-spacing. More sophisticated schemes are possible [Horn 1976b] for estimating the surface gradient, but are unnecessary. We assume that the imaging system is on the z-axis at a large distance from the surface, with its optical axis pointing straight down.

In order to be able to calculate the reflectance map, it is necessary to know the location of the light source. Here the primary source is the sun, and its location can be determined easily by using tables intended for celestial navigation or by straightforward computations [Newcomb 1895] [Smart 1931] [Woolard and Clemance 1966] [Horn 1976a]. In either case, given the date and time, the azimuth (θ) and the elevation (ϕ) of the sun can be found. Here, azimuth is measured clockwise from North, while elevation is simply the angle between the sun and the horizon (see figure 1). Now one can erect a unit vector at the origin of the coordinate system pointing at the light source,

$$\mathbf{n_s} = [\sin(\theta)\,\cos(\phi),\ \cos(\theta)\,\cos(\phi),\ \sin(\phi)].$$

Since a surface element with gradient (p, q) has a normal vector $\mathbf{n} = (-p, -q, 1)$, we can identify a particular surface element that happens to be perpendicular to the direction towards the light source. Such a surface element will have a surface normal

$n_s = (-p_s, -q_s, 1)$, where $p_s = \sin(\theta) \cot(\phi)$ and $q_s = \cos(\theta) \cot(\phi)$. We can use the gradient (p_s, q_s) as an alternative means of specifying the position of the source (see figure 1).

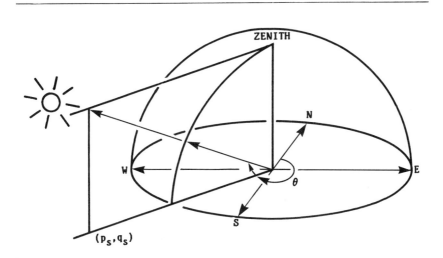

Figure 1. Definition of azimuth and elevation of the sun.

In work on automatic hill-shading, for example, one uses $p_s = -0.707$ and $q_s = 0.707$ to agree with standard cartographic conventions which require that the light source be in the Northwest at 45 degree elevation [$\theta = (7/4)\pi$, $\phi = \pi/4$) [Horn 1976b].

Not all light reflected from the surface comes directly from the sun; some of it is scattered in the atmosphere. One could add a small component to the reflectance map to account for this and rather simple models of how much light a surface element captures from the general sky illumination would do.

This was not done for the examples here since the effect is very small in the near infra-red, as demonstrated by the very dark appearance of shadowed surface elements in bands 6 and 7 of LANDSAT images.

Now reflectance of a surface can be expressed as a function of the incident angle (i), the emittance angle (e), and the phase angle (g) (see figure 2). We use a simple, idealized reflectance model for the surface material:

$$\phi_1(i, e, g) = \rho \cos(i).$$

This reflectance function models a surface which, as a perfect diffuser, appears equally bright from all viewing directions. Here, ρ is an "albedo" factor and the cosine of the incident angle simply accounts for the foreshortening the surface element as seen from the source. It is not necessary for the reflectance to be a function of the incident angle only, in fact more sophisticated models of surface reflectance are possible [Moravec 1977], but are unnecessary for this application.

It is more convenient to express the reflectance as a function of the gradient (p, q). This is straightforward, since the phase angle g is constant [Moravec 1977]. The incident angle is the angle between the local normal $(-p, -q, 1)$ and the direction to the light source $(-p_s, -q_s, 1)$. The cosine of this angle can then be found by taking the dot product of the corresponding unit vectors,

$$\cos(i) = \frac{(1 + p_s p + q_s q)}{(1 + p_s^2 + q_s^2)^{1/2}(1 + p^2 + q^2)^{1/2}}$$

Finally,

$$\phi_1(p, q) = \frac{\rho(1 + p_s p + q_s q)}{(1 + p_s^2 + q_s^2)^{1/2}(1 + p^2 + q^2)^{1/2}}$$

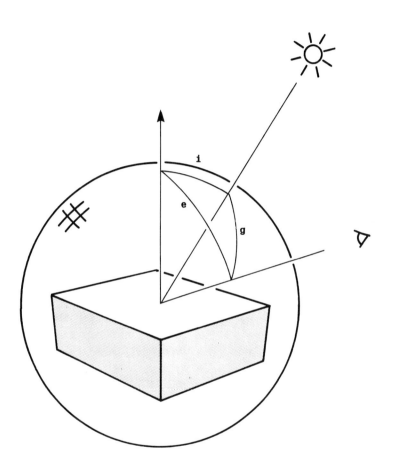

Figure 2. The geometry of light reflection from a surface element is governed by the incident angle, i, the emittance angle, e, and the phase angle, g.

Another reflectance function, similar to that of materials in the maria of the moon and rocky planets [Horn 1975] [Hapke], is a little easier to calculate.

$$\Phi_2(p, q) = \rho \cos(i)/\cos(e) = \rho(1 + p_s p + q_s q)/(1 + p_s^2 + q_s^2)^{1/2}$$

This reflectance function models a surface which reflects equal amounts of light in all directions. For small slopes and low sun elevations, it is very much like the first one, since then $(1 + p^2 + q^2)$ will be near unity. Both functions were tried and both produce good alignment -- in fact, it is difficult to distinguish synthetic images produced using these two reflectance functions.

Synthetic and Real Images

Given the projection equations that relate points on the objects to images of said points, and given a terrain model allowing calculation of surface gradient, it is possible to predict how an image would appear under given illuminating conditions, provided the reflectance map is available. We assume simple orthographic projection here as appropriate for a distant spacecraft looking vertically down with a narrow angle of view. Perspective projection would require several changes in the algorithm. There would no longer be a simple relationship between points in the synthetic image and points in the surface model, for example, and some of the techniques used in computer graphics would be useful [Catmull 1975] [Phong 1975] [Blinn and Newell 1976]. In the case of LANDSAT images, however, the departure from orthographic projection is very small and only in one direction due to the special nature of the scanning device (This distortion along scan lines is easy to deal with if a surface model is available).

The process of producing the synthetic image is simple. An estimate of the gradient is made for each point in the digital

Figure 3. Early morning (9:55 G.M.T.) synthetic image.

Figure 4. Early afternoon (13:48 G.M.T.) synthetic image.

(a)

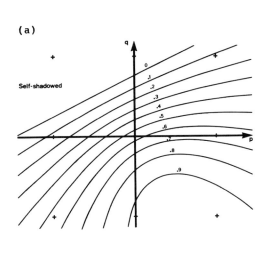

(b)

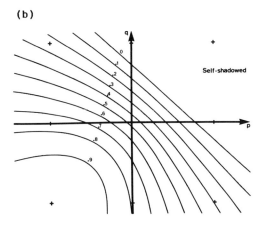

Figure 5a. Reflectance map used in the synthesis of Figure 1. The curves shown are contours of constant $\Phi_1(p, q)$ for $\rho = 1$.

Figure 5b. Reflectance map used in the synthesis of Figure 2.

terrain model by considering neighboring elevations. The gradient's components, p and q, are then used to look up or calculate the expected reflectance. An appropriate intensity is placed in the image at the point determined by the projection equation. All computations are simple and local, and the work grows linearly with the number of picture cells in the synthetic image.

Sample synthetic images are shown in figure 3 and figure 4. The two images are of the same region with differences in assumed location of the light source. In figure 3 the sun is at an elevation of 34 degrees and azimuth of 153 degrees, corresponding to its true position at 9:55 G.M.T., 1972/Oct/9, while for figure 4 it was at an elevation of 28 degrees and an azimuth of 223 degrees, corresponding to its position at 13:48 G.M.T. later on the same day. The corresponding reflectance maps are shown in figure 5.

Reflectance maps for the simpler reflectance function $\Phi_2(p, q)$ under the same circumstances are shown in figure 6. Note that near the origin there is very little difference between $\Phi_1(p, q)$ and $\Phi_2(p, q)$. Since most surface elements in this terrain model have slopes less than $2^{-1/2}$, synthetic images produced using these two reflectance maps are similar.

Since the elevation data is typically rather coarsely quantized as a result of the fixed contour interval on the original topographic map, p and q usually take on only a few discrete values. Models with arbitrarily complex reflectance functions can then be easily accomodated as can reflectance functions determined experimentally and known only for a discrete set of surface orientations.

Since the real image was somewhat smoothed in the process of being reproduced and digitized, we found it advantageous to perform a similar smoothing operation of the synthetic images so that the resolution of the two approximately matched. Alignment of real and synthetic images was, however, not dependent on this refinement.

The image used for this paper's illustrations is a portion

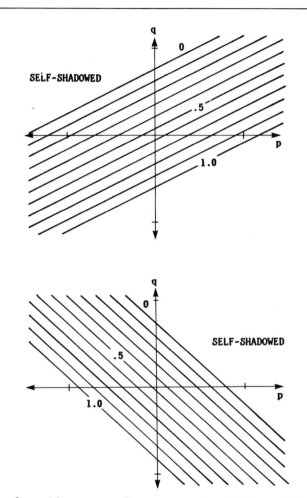

Figure 6a. Alternate reflectance map, which could have been used in place of the one shown in Figure 5a. The curves shown are contours of constant $\phi_2(p, q)$ for $\rho = 1$.

Figure 6b. Alternate reflectance map that could have been used in synthesis of Figure 2.

Figure 7. Enlargement of the transparency containing the real image used in the alignment experiments. The region covered by the digital terrain model is shown outlined.

of a LANDSAT [Bernstein 1976] image acquired about 9:55 G.M.T. 1972/October/9 (ERTS-1 1078-09555). Channel 6 (near infra-red, $.7\mu$ to $.8\mu$) was used, although all four channels appear suitable, with channel 4 (green, $.5\mu$ to $.6\mu$) being most sensitive to moisture in the air column above the surface, and channel 7 (infra-red, $.8\mu$ to 1.1μ) best able to penetrate thin layers of clouds and even snow. An enlargement of a transparency made from the original satellite image is shown in figure 7. This should be compared with the synthetic image, generated from the digital terrain model, shown in figure 3.

Note that the "footprint" of a LANDSAT picture cell (that is, the imaging system's instantaneous field of view) is about 79 x 79 meters [Bernstein 1976], quite compatible with the resolution of the terrain model, 100 x 100 meters. The digitized image used was actually of somewhat lower resolution, however, due to limitations of the optics and elecron-optics of our scanning system. Fortunately, alignment of images with terrain models is possible even with low quality image data. Further application of the aligned image and surface model information in such tasks as terrain classification however will require use of the raw sensor data, which is available on magnetic tape [Bernstein 1976].

Transformation Parameters and Choice of a Similarity Measure

Before we can match the synthetic and the real image, we must determine the nature of the transformation between them. If the real image truly is an orthographic projection obtained by looking straight down, it is possible to describe this transformation as a combination of a translation, a rotation and a scale change. If we use x and y to designate points in the synthetic image and x' and y' for points in the real image, we may write:

$$\begin{bmatrix} x' - x_0' \\ y' - y_0' \end{bmatrix} = s \begin{bmatrix} \cos\theta & \sin\theta \\ -\sin\theta & \cos\theta \end{bmatrix} \begin{bmatrix} x - x_0 \\ y - y_0 \end{bmatrix} + \begin{bmatrix} \Delta x \\ \Delta y \end{bmatrix}$$

where Δx and Δy are the shifts in x' and y' respectively, θ is the angle of rotation and s is the scale factor. Rotation and scaling take place relative to the centers (x_0, y_0) and (x_0', y_0') of the two images in order to better decouple the effects of rotation and scaling from translations. That is, the average shift in x' and y' induced by a change in rotation angle or scale is zero.

In our case, the available terrain model restricts the size of the synthetic image. The area over which matching of the two will be performed is thus always fixed by the border of the synthetic image. The geometry of the coordinate transformation is illustrated in figure 8.

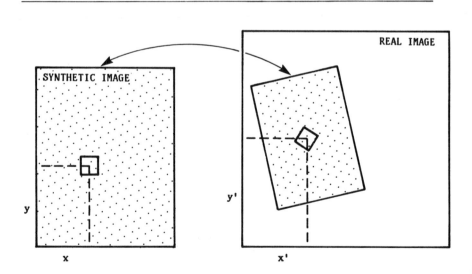

Figure 8. Coordinate transformation from synthetic image to real image.

In order to determine the best set of transformation parameters (Δx, Δy, s, π), one must be able to measure how closely the images match for a particular choice of parameter values. Let S_{ij} be the intensity of the synthetic image at the ith picture cell across in the jth row from the bottom of the image, and define R_{ij} similarly for the real image. Because of the nature of the coordinate transformation, we cannot expect that the point in the real image corresponding to the point (i, j) in the synthetic image will fall precisely on one of the picture cells. Consequently, S_{ij} will have to be compared with $R(x', y')$, which is interpolated from the array of real image intensities. Here (x', y') is obtained from (i, j) by the transformation described in the previous section.

One measure of difference between the two images may be obtained by summing the absolute values of differences over the whole array. Alternately, one might sum the squares of the differences:

$$\sum_{i=1}^{n} \sum_{j=1}^{m} \{S_{ij} - R(x', y')\}^2$$

This measure will be minimal for exact alignment of the images. Expanding the square, one decomposes this result into three terms, the first being the sum of S_{ij}^2, the lst the sum of $R^2(x', y')$. The first is constant, since we always use the full synthetic image; the last varies slowly as different regions of the real image are covered. The sum of $S_{ij}R(x', y')$ is interesting since this term varies most rapidly with changes in the transformation. In fact a very useful measure of the similarity of the two images is the correlation:

$$\sum_{i=1}^{n} \quad \sum_{j=1}^{m} \quad S_{ij}R(x', y')$$

This measure will be maximal when the images are properly aligned. It has the advantage of being relatively insensitive to constant multiplying factors. These may arise in the real image due to changes in the adjustment of the optical or electronic systems.

Note that image intensity is the product of a constant factor which depends on the details of the imaging system (such as the lens opening and the focal length), the intensity of the illumination striking the surface, and the reflectance of the surface. We assume all but the last factor is constant and thus speak interchangeably of changes in surface reflectance and changes in image intensities.

Of course the real image intensity at the point (x', y') has to be estimated from the array of known image intensities. If we let $k = |x'|$, and $l = |y'|$ be the integer parts of x' and y', then $R(x', y')$ can be estimated from R_{kl}, $R_{(k+1)l}$, $R_{k(l+1)}$ and $R_{(k+1)(l+1)}$ by linear interpolation (see figure 9).

$$R_l(x') = (k + 1 - x')R_{kl} + (x' - k)R_{(k+1)l}$$

$$R_{(l+1)}(x') = (k + 1 - x')R_{k(l+1)} + (x' - k)R_{(k+1)(l+1)}$$

$$R(x', y') = (l + 1 - y')R_l(x') + (y' - l)R_{(l+1)}(x')$$

The answer is independent of the order of interpolation and, in fact, corresponds to the result obtained by fitting a polynomical of the form $(a + bx + cy' + dx'y')$ to the values at the four indicated points. Alignment was found not to be impaired, however, when nearest neighbor interpolation was used instead. This may be a result of the smoothing of the real image as previously described.

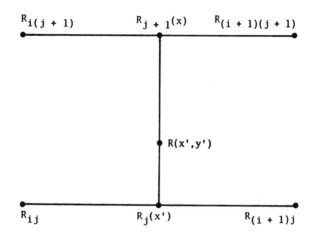

Figure 9. Simple interpolation scheme applied to the real image array.

Locating the Best Match

High output may result as the transformation is changed simply because the region of the real image used happens to have a high average gray-level. Spurious background slopes and false maxima may then result if the raw correlation is used. For this and other reasons, it is convenient to normalize. One approach essentially amounts to dividing each of the two images by its standard deviation; alternately, one can divide the raw correlation by

$$(\sum_{i=j}^{n} \sum_{j=1}^{m} S_{ij}^2)^{1/2} * (\sum_{i=j}^{n} \sum_{j=1}^{m} R^2(x',y'))^{1/2}$$

One additional advantage of this approach is that a perfect match of the two images now corresponds to a normalized correlation of one. An alternate method uses a normalization factor that is slightly easier to compute and which has certain advantages if the standard deviations of the two images are similar. Instead of using the geometric mean, Hans Moravec proposes the arithmetic mean [Moravec 1977]:

$$\left[\sum_{i=1}^{n} \sum_{j=1}^{m} S_{ij}^{2} + \sum_{i=1}^{n} \sum_{j=1}^{m} R^{2}(x',y') \right] / 2$$

The first term need not be recomputed, since the full synthetic image is always used. Since we found the alignment procedure insensitive to the choice of normalization method, we used the second in our illustrations.

Now that we have shown how to calculate a good similarity measure, we must describe an efficient method for finding the best possible transformation parameters. Exhaustive search is clearly out of the question. Fortunately, the similarity measure allows the use of standard hill-climbing techniques. This is because it tends to vary smoothly with changes in parameters and often is monotonic (at least for small ranges of the parameters).

When images are not seriously misaligned, profiles of the similarity measure usually are unimodal with a well-defined peak when plotted against one of the four parameters of the transformation (see figure 10). It is possible to optimize each parameter in turn, using simple search techniques in one dimension. The process can then be iterated. A few passes of this process typically produce convergence. (More sophisticated schemes could reduce the amount of computation, but were not explored).

When the images are initially not reasonably aligned, more care has to be taken to avoid being trapped by local maxima. Solving this problem using a more extensive search

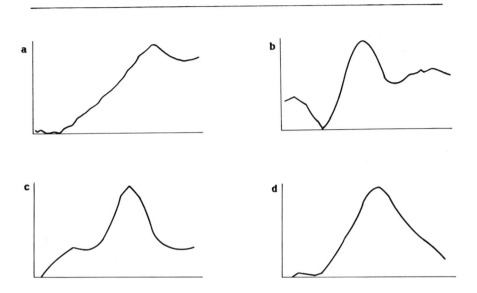

Figure 10a. Variation of similarity measure with translation in x direction.

Figure 10b. Variation of similarity measure with translation in y direction.

Figure 10c. Variation of similarity measure with rotation.

Figure 10d. Variation of similarity measure with scale changes.

leads to prohibitively lengthy computations.

One way to reduce the computation is to use only subimages or "windows" extracted from the original images. This is useful for fine matching, but is not satisfactory here because of the lack of global context.

Alternatively, one might use sampled images obtained by picking one image intensity to represent a small block of image intensities. This is satisfactory as long as the original images are smoothed and do not have any high resolution features. If this is not the case, aliasing due to undersampling will produce images of poor quality unsuitable for comparisons.

One solution to this dilemma is to low-pass filter the images before sampling. A simple approximation to this process uses averages of small blocks of image intensities. The easiest method involves making one image intensity in the reduced image equal to the average of a 2 x 2 block of intensities in the original image. This technique can be applied repeatedly to produce ever smaller images and has been used in a number of other applications [Moravec 1977] [Tanimoto 1976].

The results of the application of this reduction process to real and synthetic images can be seen in figure 11. First, the most highly reduced image is used to get coarse alignment. In this case, extensive search in the parameter space is permissible, since the number of picture cells in the images to be matched is very small. This coarse alignment is then refined using the next larger reduced images (with four times as many picture cells). Finally, the full resolution images are used directly to fine tune the alignment. False local maxima are, fortunately, much rarer with the highly reduced pictures, thus further speeding the search process. It is as if the high resolution features are the ones leading to false local maxima.

Quick convergence was obtained when translation was optimized before rotation, and scale change. In each case the best values found so far for each parameter were used while searching for an optimum value in another parameter.

Results of the Registration Experiments

We matched the real and synthetic images using the similarity measure and search technique just described. We tried several combinations of implementation details, and in all cases achieved alignment which corresponded to a high value of the normalized correlation, and which was very close to that determined

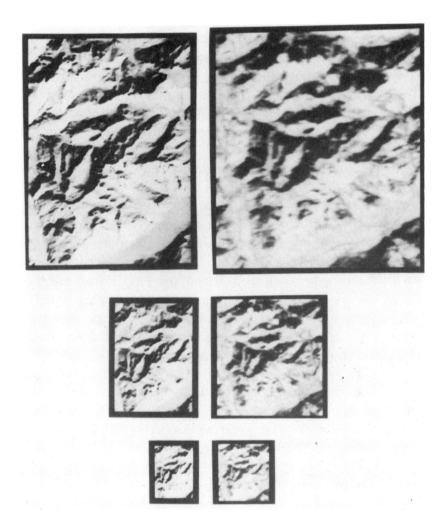

Figure 11. Successive reduction by factors of two applied to both the synthetic (left) and the real (right) image.

manually. For the images shown here, the normalized correlation coefficient reaches .92 for optimum alignment, and the match is such that no features are more than two picture cells from the expected place, with almost all closer than one (The major errors in position appear to be due to perspective distortion, with which the process is not now designed to cope). The accuracy with which translation, rotation and scaling were determined can be estimated from the above statement.

Overall, the process appears quite robust, even with degraded data. Details of interpolation, normalization, search technique, and even the reflectance map did not matter a great deal.

Having stated that alignment can be accurately achieved, we may now ask how similar the real and synthetic images are. There are a number of uninformative numerical ways of answering this question. Graphic illustrations, such as images of the differences between the real and synthetic image, are more easily understood. For example, we plot real image intensity versus synthetic image intensity in figure 12. Although one might expect a straight line of slope one, the scattergram shows clusters of points, some near the expected line, some not.

The clusters of points indicated by the arrow labelled A (figure 12) corresponds chiefly to image points showing cloud or snow cover, with intensity sufficient to saturate the image digitizer. Here the real image intensity exceeds the synthetic image intensity. Arrow B indicates the cluster of points which corresponds to shadowed points. Those near the vertical axis and to its left come from self-shadowed surface elements, while those to the right are regions lying inside shadows cast by other portions of the surface. These cast shadows are not now simulated in the synthetic image. Here the synthetic image is brighter than the real image. Finally, the cluster of points indicated by the arrow C arises from the valley floor, which covers a fairly large area and has essentially zero gradient. As a result, the synthetic image has constant intensity here, while the real image shows both darker features (such as the river) and

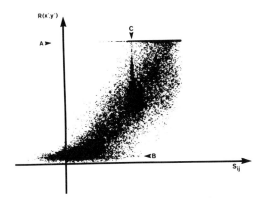

Figure 12a. Scattergram of real image intensities <u>versus</u> synthetic image intensities based on $\Phi_1(p, q)$.

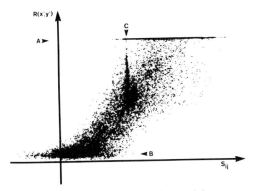

Figure 12b. Scattergram of real image intensities <u>versus</u> synthetic image intensities based on $\Phi_2(p, q)$.

brighter ones (such as those due to the cities and vegetation cover). Most of the ground cover in the valley appears to have higher albedo than the bare rock which is exposed in the higher regions, as suggested by the position of this cluster above the line of slope one.

If we were to remove these three clusters of points, the remainder would form one elongated cluster with major axis at about 45 degrees. This shows that, while there may not be an accurate point-by-point equality of intensities, there is a high correlation between intensities in the real and synthetic images.

Note, by the way, that no quantization of intensity is apparent in these scattergrams. This is a result of the smoothing applied to the synthetic image and the interpolation used on the real image. Without smoothing, the synthetic image has fairly coarse quantization levels because of the coarse quantization of elevations as indicated earlier. Without interpolation, the real image, too, has fairly coarse quantization due to the image digitization procedure.

Finally, note that we achieve our goal of obtaining accurate alignment. Detailed matching of synthetic and real image intensity is a new problem which can be approached now that the problem of image registration has been solved.

When, for example, the surface materials have reflectances covering a range of two-to-one and the sun elevation is 35 degrees, then regions with surface slopes above approximately 0.23 (e about 13 degrees) will have image intensities affected more by surface gradient than by surface cover. Conversely, flatter surfaces will result in images more affected by variations in surface cover than by the area's topography.

One conclusion is that alignment of images with terrain models is feasible without detailed knowledge of the surface materials if the sun elevation is small and the surface slopes are high.

References

R. Bernstein, "Digital Image Processing of Earth Observation Sensor Data," *IBM Journal of Research and Development*, Vol. 20, pp. 40-57, 1976.

J. F. Blinn and M. E. Newwll, "Texture and Reflection in Computer Generated Images," *Comm. A.C.M.*, Vol. 19, pp. 542-547, 1976.

K. Brassel, *Modelle und Versuch zur Automatischen Schraglicht-schatierung*, 7250 Klosters, Switzerland, Buchdruckerei E. Brassel, 1973.

E. A. Catmull, "Computer Display of Curved Surfaces," *Proc. Conf. on Computer Graphics, Pattern Recognition and Data Structure*, (IEEE Cat. No. 75 CH0981-IC), pp. 11-17, 1975.

M. J. Duggin, "Likely Effects of Solar Elevation on the Quantification of Changes in Vegetation with Maturity Using Sequential LANDSAT images," *Applied Optics*, Vol. 16, pp. 521-523, 1977.

B. Hapke, "An Improved Theoretical Lunar Photometric Function," *The Astronomical Journal*, Vol. 71, pp 333-339.

Explanatory Supplement to the Astronomical Ephemeris and the American Ephemeris and Nautical Almanac, Her Majesty's Stationery Office, London, England, 1961.

B. K. P. Horn, "Shape from Shading: A Method for Obtaining the Shape of a Smooth Opaque Object from One View," *MIT Laboratory for Computer Science TR-79*, 1970.

B. K. P. Horn, "Obtaining Shape from Shading Information," *The Psychology of Computer Vision*, P. H. Winston (ed.),

McGraw-Hill, 1975.

B. K. P. Horn, "Celestial Navigation Suite for a Programmable Calculator," unpublished, 1976.

B. K. P. Horn, "Automatic Hill-shading Using the Reflectance Map," unpublished, 1976.

B. K. P. Horn, "Understanding Image Intensity," *Artificial Intelligence*, Vol. 8, pp 201-231., 1977.

H. P. Moravec, "Techniques towards Automatic Visual Obstacle Avoidance," *Proceedings of the Fifth International Conference on Artificial Intelligence*, Cambridge, MA, 1977.

Simon Newcomb, *A Compendium of Spherical Astronomy*, New York, McMillan and Co., 1895, 1906.

D. Nitzan, A. E. Brain and R. O. Duda, "The measurement and use of registered reflectance and range data in scene analysis," *Proc. of the IEEE*, Vol. 65, pp 206-220.

P. Oetking, "Photometric Studies of Diffusely Reflecting Surfaces with Applications to the Brightnes of the Moon," *Journal of Geophysical Research*, Vol. 71, pp. 2502-2514, 1966.

Bui Tuong Phong, "Illumination for Computer Generated Images," *Comm. A.C.M.*, Vol. 18 pp 311-317, 1975.

E. L. Simmons, "Particle Model Theory of Diffuse Reflectance: Effect of Non-uniform Particle Size," *Applied Optics*, Vol. 15, pp 603-604, 1976.

W. M. Smart, *Textbook on Spherical Astronomy*, Cambridge University, 1931, 1965.

I. E. Sutherland, R. F. Sproull and R. A. Schumacker, "A Characterization of Ten Hidden Surface Algorithms," *Computing Surveys*, Vol. 6, pp 1-55, 1974.

S. L. Tanimoto, "Pictorial Feature Distortion in a Pyramid," *Computer Graphics and Image Processing*, Vol. 5, pp 333-352, 1976.

C. J. Tucker, "Asymptotic Nature of Grass Canopy Spectral Reflectance," *Applied Optics*, Vol. 16, pp 1151-1156, 1977.

The American Ephemeris and Nautical Almanac for the Year 1972, U.S. Government Printing Office, 1972

The Nautical Almanac for the Year 1972, U. S. Government Printing Office, 1972.

J. E. Warnock, "A Hidden-line Algorithm for Halftone Picture Representation," *University of Utah, Salt Lake City, Department of Computer Science Report TR-4-15*, 1969.

G. S. Watkins, "A Real-time Visible Surface Algorithm," *University of Utah, Salt Lake City, Department of Computer Science Technical Report UTEC-CSC-70-101*, 1970.

W. W. M. Wendlandt and H. G. Hecht, *Reflectance Spectroscopy*, Interscience Publishers, 1966.

E. W. Woolard and G. M. Clemance, *Spherical Astonomy*, Cambridge University Press, 1966.

The complete version of this paper appears in *Communications of the ACM*, Vol. 21, Nol. 11, November 1978, copyright 1978, Association for Computing Machinery, Inc.

ANALYZING CURVED SURFACES USING REFLECTANCE MAP TECHNIQUES

ROBERT WOODHAM

This section is an overview of Robert Woodham's PhD thesis, in which he develops the reflectance map idea, adding a new perspective by thinking in terms of curvature constraints. Woodham's approach leads to a novel technique called *photometric stereo* in which surface orientation is determined from two or more images taken from the same camera position. The idea of photometric stereo is to vary the direction of the incident illumination between successive views while holding the viewing direction constant. This, in principle, provides enough information to determine surface orientation at each picture element. Since the imaging geometry does not change, the correspondence between picture elements is known *a priori*. This stereo technique is photometric because it uses the intensity values recorded at a single picture element, in successive views, rather than the relative positions of displaced features.

Reflectance Map Techniques for Image Analysis

Understanding the relationship between image intensity and object relief is of fundamental importance to image analysis because knowing the intensity variation across surfaces of smooth objects leads to conclusions about the topography of those surfaces. The problem is difficult because local surface topography cannot, in general, be determined by the intensity value recorded at a single image point. In order to assign a global interpretation to an image, additional assumptions must be invoked. The tools developed here help make these assumptions explicit and thereby deepen our understanding of what can and cannot be computed directly from image intensity.

Image intensity is determined by object relief and by scene illumination, object photometry and imaging geometry. Three local properties of object relief are: *range* (distance from the viewer), *surface orientation* (direction of a surface normal), and *surface curvature* (the principal radii of curvature and associated directions). A *reflectance map* is a convenient way to incorporate a fixed scene illumination, object photometry, and imaging geometry into a single model that allows image intensity to be related directly to surface orientation. Although surface orientation has two degrees of freedom, image intensity provides only one measurement. Still, curvature constraints can be embodied in algorithms for determining surface orientation from the image intensities recorded in a single view.

Developing the Reflectance Map

The fraction of light reflected by a surface in a given direction depends on the optical properties of the object material, the surface microstructure and the spatial and spectral distribution and state of polarization of the incident light. A key photometric observation is that no matter how complex the distribution of incident illumination, for most surfaces, the fraction of the incident light reflected in a particular direction depends only on the surface orientation.

The reflectance characteristics of an object material can be represented as a function $\phi(i,e,g)$ of the three angles i, e and g defined in figure 1. These are called, respectively, the *incident,*

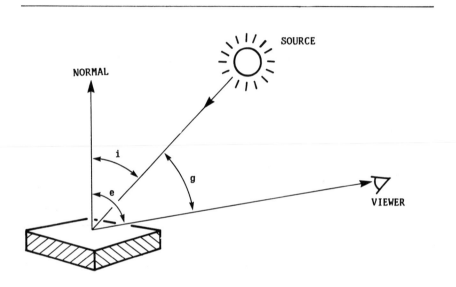

Figure 1. Defining the three angles i, e and g. The incident angle i is the angle between the incident ray and the surface normal. The view angle e is the angle between the emergent ray and the surface normal. The phase angle g is the angle between the incident and emergent rays.

emergent and *phase* angles. The angles i, e and g are defined relative to the object surface. $\phi(i,e,g)$ determines the ratio of radiance to irradiance measured per unit surface area, per unit solid angle, in the direction of the viewer. The reflectance function defined here is related to the bi-directional reflectance-distribution function defined by the National Bureau of Standards [Nicodemus *et al* 1977].

Image-forming systems perform a perspective transformation (figure 2a). If the size of the objects in view is small compared to the viewing distance, then the perspective projection can be approximated as an orthographic projection (figure 2b). Consider an image-forming system that performs an orthographic projection. To standardize the imaging geometry, it is convenient to align the viewing direction with the negative z-axis. Assume appropriate scaling of the image plane so that object point (x,y,z) maps onto image point (u,v) where u = x and v = y. With this imaging geometry, image coordinates (x,y) and object coordinates (x,y) are referred to interchangeably.

If the equation of a surface is given explicitly as z = f(x,y) then a surface normal is given by the vector [∂f(x,y)/∂x,∂f(x,y)/∂y,-1]. If parameters *p* and *q* are defined by:

$$p = \partial f(x,y)/\partial x$$
$$q = \partial f(x,y)/\partial y$$

then the surface normal can be written as [p,q,-1]. The quantity (p,q) is called the *gradient*, and *gradient space* is the two-dimensional space of all such points (p,q). Gradient space has been used in scene analysis [Mackworth 1973]. In image analysis, it is used to relate the geometry of image projection to the radiometry of image formation [Horn 1977]. This relation is established by showing that image intensity is determined by the surface reflectance function φ(i,e,g) and that this function can be represented as a function of the gradient (p,q).

Suppose each surface element receives the same incident illumination. Then, φ(i,e,g) determines the amount of the light reflected, per unit surface area, per unit solid angle, in the direction of the viewer. In an orthographic projection, each

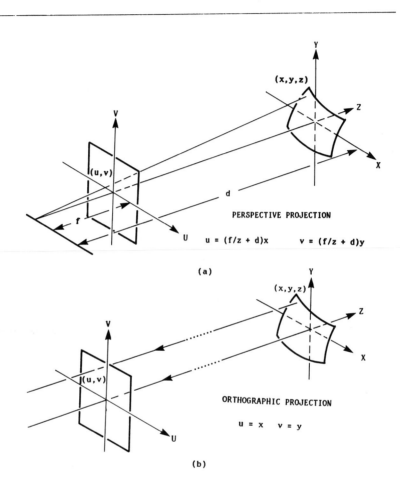

Figure 2. Characterizing image projections. Figure 2a illustrates the well-known perspective projection. (Note: to avoid image inversion, it is convenient to assume that the image plane lies in front of the lens rather than behind it.) For objects that are small relative to the viewing distance, the image projection can be modeled as the orthographic projection illustrated in Figure 2b. In an orthographic projection, the focal length f is infinite so that all rays from object to image are parallel.

picture element subtends the same solid angle. Thus, $\phi(i,e,g)$ determines image intensity. In an orthographic projection, the phase angle g is constant at each object point. The incident angle i and the view angle e depend only on surface orientation. Thus, for the given imaging geometry, for a given distribution of incident illumination and a given object material, the image intensity corresponding to a surface point with gradient (p,q) is unique. The *reflectance map* $R(p,q)$ determines image intensity as a function of p and q.

A reflectance map models the surface photometry of an object material for a particular light source, object surface, and viewer geometry. It corresponds to a viewer-centered representation of the surface reflectance function $\phi(i,e,g)$. If the viewing direction and the direction of incident illumination are known, then expressions for $\cos(i)$, $\cos(e)$, and $\cos(g)$ can be derived in terms of gradient space coordinates p and q. Suppose vector $[p_s, q_s, -1]$ defines the direction of incident illumination. Then:

$$\cos(i) = \frac{1 + pp_s + qq_s}{(1 + p_s^2 + q_s^2)^{1/2}\,(1 + p^2 + q^2)^{1/2}}$$

$$\cos(e) = \frac{1}{(1 + p^2 + q^2)^{1/2}}$$

$$\cos(g) = \frac{1}{(1 + p_s^2 + q_s^2)^{1/2}}$$

These expressions allow one to transform an arbitrary surface photometric function $\phi(i,e,g)$ into a reflectance map $R(p,q)$. Reflectance maps can be determined empirically, derived from phenomenological models of surface reflectance, or derived from analytic models of surface microstructure. Figure 3 illustrates a reflectance map $R(p,q)$ derived from the phenomenological model of a perfect diffuse reflector for which $\phi(i,e,g) = \cos(i)$.

The basic equation describing the image-forming process:

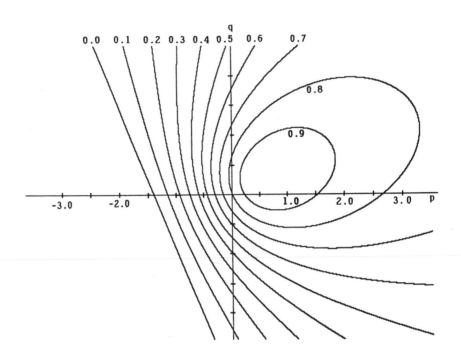

Figure 3. The reflectance map $R(p,q)$ for a Lambertian surface illuminated from gradient point $p_s = 0.7$ and $q_s = 0.3$ plotted as a series of contours (spaced 0.1 units apart). A Lambertian surface appears equally bright from all directions.

$$I(x,y) = R(p,q)$$

It is one equation in the two unknowns p and q. The intensity value recorded at an image point (x,y) is not sufficient to determine the corresponding surface orientation (p,q). Rather, the intensity value determines a contour in gradient space upon which the corresponding gradient must lie.

The Image Hessian Matrix

By taking partial derivatives of the basic equation $I(x,y) = R(p,q)$ with respect to x and y two equations are obtained which can be written as the single matrix equation:

$$\begin{bmatrix} I_x \\ I_y \end{bmatrix} = \begin{bmatrix} p_x & q_x \\ p_y & q_y \end{bmatrix} \begin{bmatrix} R_p \\ R_q \end{bmatrix} \qquad (1)$$

(Subscripts are used to denote partial differentiation.) Similarly, the two first-order equations:

$$dp = p_x dx + p_y dy$$
$$dq = q_x dx + q_y dy$$

can be written as the single matrix equation:

$$\begin{bmatrix} dp \\ dq \end{bmatrix} = \begin{bmatrix} p_x & p_y \\ q_x & q_y \end{bmatrix} \begin{bmatrix} dx \\ dy \end{bmatrix} \qquad (2)$$

Define the matrix H by:

$$H = \begin{bmatrix} \dfrac{\partial^2 f(x,y)}{\partial x^2} & \dfrac{\partial^2 f(x,y)}{\partial x \partial y} \\[2ex] \dfrac{\partial^2 f(x,y)}{\partial y \partial x} & \dfrac{\partial^2 f(x,y)}{\partial y^2} \end{bmatrix}$$

H is called the *image Hessian matrix* of the surface $z = f(x,y)$. A surface $z = f(x,y)$ is called *smooth* if it is twice differentiable with continuous second partial derivatives. For smooth surfaces, the order of differentiation can be interchanged ($p_y = q_x$). For smooth surfaces, the image Hessian matrix is therefore symmetric. Equations (1) and (2) can be rewritten as:

$$[I_x, I_y]' = H [R_p, R_q]' \qquad (3)$$

$$[dp, dq]' = H [dx, dy]' \qquad (4)$$

(where ' denotes vector transpose.)

Equation (4) relates movement in the image to the corresponding movement in gradient space. Suppose image point (x,y) is known to correspond to gradient point (p,q). If two linearly independent directions $[dx_1, dy_1]$ and $[dx_2, dy_2]$ and the corresponding $[dp_1, dq_1]$ and $[dp_2, dq_2]$ are known, then the image Hessian matrix H is determined uniquely at (x,y). Indeed,

$$H = \begin{bmatrix} dp_1 & dp_2 \\ dq_1 & dq_2 \end{bmatrix} \begin{bmatrix} dx_1 & dx_2 \\ dy_1 & dy_2 \end{bmatrix}^{-1} \qquad (5)$$

Equation (3) establishes one correspondence. If $[dx, dy] = [R_p, R_q] ds$ then $[dp, dq] = [I_x, I_y] ds$. (This observation is the basis for methods for determining shape from shading information by characteristic strip expansion [Horn 1975], [Horn 1977].) Image intensity constrains the image Hessian matrix H but does not determine it completely. Now equation (5) can be rewritten as:

$$H = \begin{bmatrix} I_x & dp \\ I_y & dq \end{bmatrix} \begin{bmatrix} R_p & dx \\ R_q & dy \end{bmatrix}^{-1} \qquad (6)$$

The image Hessian matrix H is a viewer-centered representation of surface curvature. Suppose that k_1 and k_2 are the eigenvalues corresponding to eigenvectors ω_1 and ω_2 of the matrix C where:

$$C = (p^2 + q^2 + 1)^{-3/2} \begin{bmatrix} q^2 + 1 & -pq \\ -pq & p^2 + 1 \end{bmatrix} H \qquad (7)$$

Then, $r_1 = 1/k_1$ and $r_2 = 1/k_2$ are the two principal radii of curvature of the surface $z = f(x,y)$, oriented respectively in the image by the directions defined by ω_1 and ω_2. The product term:

$$(p^2+q^2+1)^{-3/2} \begin{bmatrix} q^2+1 & -pq \\ \\ -pq & p^2+1 \end{bmatrix}$$

explicitly compensates the foreshortening due to an oblique viewing direction e.

    Equation (6) represents the information about surface curvature contained locally in image intensity. But since equation (6) admits an infinite number of solutions, additional constraint is required.

Exploiting Curvature Constraint

Situations are now considered in which special properties of surface curvature simplify image analysis. One motivation for this study is practical. There are few industrial fabrication processes capable of producing objects with arbitrary surface curvature. Perhaps more significantly, there are no general drafting techniques available for designing parts with arbitrary surface curvature. In industrial inspection, it is useful to exploit the constraint imposed by a particular fabrication process.

    Another motivation for this study is theoretical. The basic equation $I(x,y) = R(p,q)$ is underdetermined. Yet people seem to provide consistent interpretations of images even without explicit knowledge of the reflectance map. Thus, it is important to explore how assumptions about surface curvature provide constraint and to determine where these assumptions might come from.

    Properties of the image Hessian matrix **H** relate to the curvature of the surface $z = f(x,y)$. The convexity/concavity of the object surface $z = f(x,y)$ is determined by the definiteness of the image Hessian matrix H. The number of finite principal radii of curvature of the object surface $z = f(x,y)$ is determined by the number of nonzero eigenvalues of the image Hessian matrix H. Consider first the convexity/concavity of an object surface.

■   The object surface $z = f(x,y)$ is convex (with respect to the viewer) at image point (x,y) if and only if the corresponding image Hessian matrix H is positive semidefinite at (x,y).

■   The object surface $z = f(x,y)$ is concave (with respect to the viewer) at image point (x,y) if and only if the corresponding image Hessian matrix H is negative semidefinite at (x,y).

Suppose $z = f(x,y)$ is everywhere convex with respect to the viewer. Then, H is everywhere positive semidefinite. Multiplying the two matrix equations (3) and (4) on the left by $[R_p \ R_q]$ and $[dx \ dy]$ respectively, gives rise to the two inequalities:

$$R_p \ I_x + R_q \ I_y \geq 0 \tag{8}$$
$$dx \ dp + dy \ dq \geq 0 \tag{9}$$

Two similar inequalities hold, with the sense of the inequality reversed, if the surface $z = f(x,y)$ is everywhere concave.

Inequality (8) provides additional *a priori* constraint on the set of possible gradient solutions to the basic equation $I(x,y) = R(p,q)$ for a convex surface $z = f(x,y)$. The normal vector $[R_p, R_q]$ to the contour of constant reflectance at any point (p,q) hypothesized to be a solution to the basic equation $I(x,y) = R(p,q)$ must have a nonnegative component in the direction of the normal vector $[I_x, I_y]$ to the contour of constant intensity at (x,y) (figure 4).

Inequality (9) provides additional constraint on the possible change in surface orientation $[dp, dq]$ corresponding to a

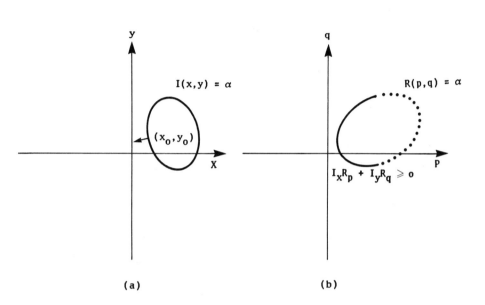

Figure 4. The inequality $R_p I_x + R_q I_y \geq 0$ constrains the reflectance map contour that can correspond to image points on a convex surface. Suppose $I(x_0, y_0) = \alpha$. Then the normal to the reflectance map contour $R(p,q) = \alpha$ at the corresponding (p_0, q_0) must have a nonnegative component in the direction of the normal to the contour of constant intensity at $(x_0, y_0) = \alpha$. Points dotted in (b) can therefore be excluded.

movement [dx,dy] in the image of a convex surface $z = f(x,y)$. The vector [dp,dq] must have a nonnegative component in the direction [dx,dy].

By choosing [dx,dy] appropriately, it is possible to determine either the sign of the change to the view angle e, where $\tan(e) = (p^2 + q^2)^{1/2}$, or the sign of the change to the direction of steepest descent θ, where $\theta = \tan^{-1}(q/p)$. Assumptions about changes in view angle and changes to the direction of steepest descent have been embedded in an algorithm for determining surface orientation from the image intensities recorded in an single view [Woodham 1977]. This algorithm estimates the gradient (p,q) at each image point (x,y) by propagation of the constraint provided by local assumptions about surface curvature.

Consider now the radii of curvature of an object surface. Let $z = f(x,y)$ be the equation of a smooth surface and let λ_1 and λ_2 be the two eigenvalues of the corresponding image Hessian matrix H at image point (x_0,y_0). The surface $z = f(x,y)$ is said to be *planar* at (x_0,y_0) if and only if $\lambda_1 = \lambda_2 = 0$. The surface $z = f(x,y)$ is said to be *singly curved* at (x_0,y_0) if and only if exactly one of λ_1 and λ_2 is equal to zero. The surface $z = f(x,y)$ is said to be *doubly curved* at (x_0,y_0) if and only if both λ_1 and λ_2 are not equal to zero.

The definition of planar, singly curved and doubly curved surfaces given here in terms of the viewer-centered image Hessian matrix H is equivalent to one given in terms of the object-centered principal radii of surface curvature. An eigenvalue λ_i of H is zero if and only if the corresponding principal radius of curvature r_i is infinite.

Reflectance map techniques for analyzing objects whose surfaces are planar are discussed in a paper by Horn [1977]. Consider instead objects that are singly curved. Huffman [1975] refers to singly curved surfaces as "paper" surfaces and proposes that such surfaces possess a complexity that is midway between that of a completely general surface and that of a planar surface. In image analysis, singly curved surfaces do indeed possess a complexity that lies between that of a completely general surface and that of a planar surface as will now be shown.

Let $z = f(x,y)$ be the equation of a surface that is everywhere singly curved. Suppose that a point (x_0, y_0) in the image is known to correspond to a point (p_0, q_0) in gradient space. Then, the image Hessian matrix H at (x_0, y_0) is completely determined. Indeed, H is given as the matrix product:

$$H = \begin{bmatrix} \cos(\alpha) & -\sin(\alpha) \\ \sin(\alpha) & \cos(\alpha) \end{bmatrix} \begin{bmatrix} \lambda & 0 \\ 0 & 0 \end{bmatrix} \begin{bmatrix} \cos(\alpha) & \sin(\alpha) \\ -\sin(\alpha) & \cos(\alpha) \end{bmatrix} \qquad (10)$$

where

$$\lambda = \frac{(I_x^2 + I_y^2)^{1/2}}{R_p \cos(\alpha) + R_q \sin(\alpha)}$$

and

$$\tan(\alpha) = \frac{I_y}{I_x}$$

The constraint that, for a singly curved surface, exactly one eigenvalue of H must be zero provides sufficient additional information to solve for H explicitly. Given any initial image point (x_0, y_0) known to correspond to gradient point (p_0, q_0), the image Hessian matrix H at (x_0, y_0) is determined by (10). The matrix H can then be used to find the new gradient corresponding to an arbitrary movement [dx,dy] in the image using equation (4).

The operations embodied in (10) and (4) above can be iterated to trace out a family of curves on the object surface. This result should not be terribly surprising. The fact that H has one zero eigenvalue means that there is one direction of movement in the image which results in no change to surface orientation. The orthogonal direction α is given by the vector $[I_x, I_y]$. The component of any movement [dx,dy] perpendicular to $[I_x, I_y]$ does not change the gradient (p,q). The component of [dx,dy] in the direction $[I_x, I_y]$ changes the gradient (p,q) in the direction α where the value of λ determines the "scale factor" for that change.

The points in gradient space corresponding to a singly curved surface $z = f(x,y)$ are constrained to lie on a one-parameter curve in gradient space. This is just another manifestation of the observation that singly curved surfaces possess a complexity midway between that of a planar surface, where surface points map into a single point in gradient space, and that of a completely general surface, where surface points map into a two-parameter region in gradient space.

Binford has defined a broader class of surfaces called generalized cones. A *generalized cone* is the surface swept out by moving a simple smooth cross section along some axis, at the same time magnifying or contracting it in a smoothly varying way. Generalized cones are doubly curved. The curvature of a generalized cone, however, conveniently decouples into a term due to the cross section function and a term due to the axial-scaling function. Under appropriate viewing conditions, this decoupling carries over to images of generalized cones. Such images can be analyzed "almost" as if the surface were singly curved. Additional information required to account for the second degree of freedom in surface curvature can be recovered from the object silhouette. Solids of revolution, for example, while doubly curved, do form a simple-to-analyze subclass of generalized cones [Woodham 1978].

Photometric Stereo

The equation $I(x,y) = R(p,q)$ is one equation in the two unknowns p and q. In order to determine the gradient (p,q) corresponding to image point (x,y) more information must be provided. Knowledge of surface curvature provides additional information. Photometric stereo, on the other hand, uses the additional information provided by more equations.

The idea of photometric stereo is to vary the direction of incident illumination between successive views while holding the viewing direction constant. Suppose two images $I_1(x,y)$ and $I_2(x,y)$ are obtained by varying the direction of incident illumination. Since there has been no change in the imaging geometry, each picture element (x,y) in the two images corresponds to the same object point and hence to the same gradient (p,q). The effect of varying the direction of incident illumination is to change the reflectance map $R(p,q)$ that characterizes the imaging situation.

Let the reflectance maps corresponding to $I_1(x,y)$ and $I_2(x,y)$ be $R_1(p,q)$ and $R_2(p,q)$ respectively. There are now two independent equations:

$$I_1(x,y) = R_1(p,q) \tag{11}$$

$$I_2(x,y) = R_2(p,q) \tag{12}$$

These two nonlinear equations will have at most a finite number of solutions. Two reflectance maps $R_1(p,q)$ and $R_2(p,q)$ are required. But, if the phase angle g is the same in both views (i.e. the illumination is rotated about the viewing direction), then the two reflectance maps are rotations of each other.

The images required for photometric stereo can be obtained by explicitly moving a single light source, by using multiple light sources calibrated with respect to each other or by rotating the object surface and imaging hardware together to simulate the effect of moving a single light source. The equivalent of photometric stereo can also be achieved in a single view by using multiple illuminations which can be separated by color.

Photometric stereo is fast. It has been developed as a practical scheme for environments in which the nature and position of the incident illumination can be controlled. Initial computation is required to determine the reflectance map for a particular experimental situation. Once calibrated, however, photometric stereo can be reduced to simple table lookup operations.

In photometric stereo, there is a trade-off to deal with.

Choosing a larger phase angle g leads to more accurate solutions. At the same time, a larger phase angle causes a larger portion of gradient space to lie in the shadow region of one or more of the sources. A practical compromise is achieved by using four light sources and a relatively large phase angle. Solutions are accurate and most of gradient space lies in regions illuminated by at least three of the sources. Three image intensity measurements overdetermine the set of equations and establish a unique solution.

    Photometric stereo can be used in two ways. For a given image point (x,y), equations (11) and (12) can be used to determine the corresponding gradient (p,q). Used in this way, photometric stereo is a general technique for determining surface orientation from image intensity. Figure 5 illustrates the intersection of reflectance map contours obtained using a three-source configuration.

    For a given gradient (p,q), equations (11) and (12) can also be used to determine corresponding image points (x,y). Used in this way, photometric stereo is a general technique for determining points in an image whose corresponding object points have a particular surface orientation. Figure 6 illustrates the intersection of image intensity contours obtained using a three-source configuration.

    This use of photometric stereo is appropriate for the so called industrial bin-of-parts problem. The location in an image of key object points is often sufficient to determine the position and orientation of a known object tossed onto a table or conveyor belt. It is worth noting that object points whose surface normal directly faces the viewer form a unique class of image points whose intensity value is invariant under rotation of the light source about the viewing direction (for a fixed, nonzero phase angle g). Thus, it is possible to locate such object points without explicitly determining the reflectance map $R(p,q)$. Whatever the nature of the function $R(p,q)$, the value of $R(0,0)$ is not changed by rotation about the gradient origin. Figure 7 repeats the example given in figure 6 but for the case $p = 0$, $q = 0$.

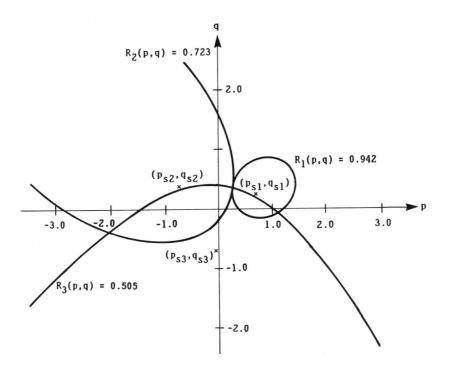

Figure 5. Determining the surface orientation (p,q) at a given image point (x,y). Three (superimposed) reflectance map contours are intersected where each contour corresponds to the intensity value at (x,y) obtained from three separate images (taken under the same imaging geometry but with different light source position). $I_1(x,y) = 0.942$, $I_2(x,y) = 0.723$ and $I_3(x,y) = 0.505$.

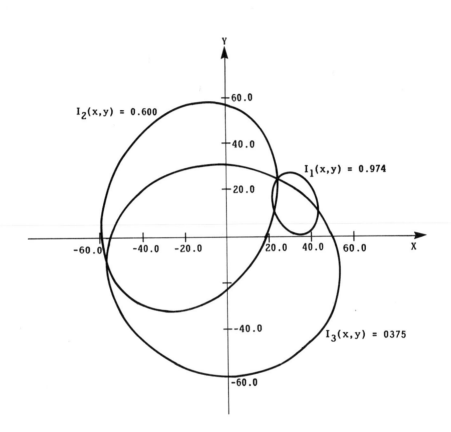

Figure 6. Determining image points (x,y) whose surface orientation is a given gradient (p,q). Three (superimposed) image intensity contours are intersected where each contour corresponds to the value at (p,q) obtained from three separate reflectance maps. (Each reflectance map characterizes the same imaging geometry but corresponds to a different light source position.) $R_1(p,q) = 0.974$, $R_2(p,q) = 0.600$ and $R_3(p,q) = 0.375$.

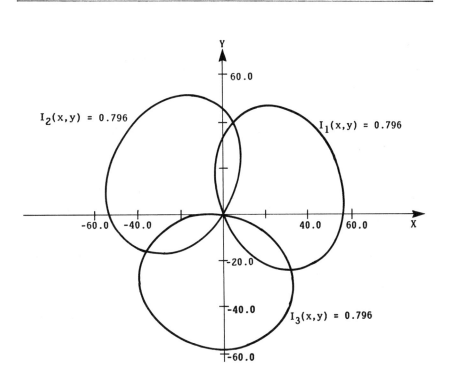

Figure 7. Determining image points whose surface normal directly faces the viewer. Three (superimposed) image intensity contours are intersected where each contour corresponds to the value at (0,0) obtained from three separate reflectance maps. (Each reflectance map characterizes the same imaging geometry but corresponds to a different light source position.) Note that the reflectance map value at (0,0) does not change with light source position (provided the phase angle g is held constant).

References

B. K. P. Horn, "Obtaining Shape from Shading Information," in *The Psychology of Computer Vision*, P. H. Winston (ed.), McGraw-Hill, 1975.

B. K. P. Horn, "Understanding Image Intensities," in *Artificial Intelligence*, Vol. 8, 1977.

D. A. Huffman, "Curvature and Creases: A Primer on Paper," in *Proc. of Conf. on Computer Graphics, Pattern Recognition and Data Structures*, 1975.

A. K. Mackworth, "Interpreting Pictures of Polyhedral Scenes," in *Artificial Intelligence*, Vol 4, 1973.

D. Marr, "Analysis of Occluding Contour," *Proc. R. Soc. Lond. B.*, Vol 7, 1977.

R. J. Woodham, "A Cooperative Algorithm for Determining Surface Orientation from a Single View," in *Proceedings of IJCAI-77*, 1977.

R. J. Woodham, *Reflectance Map Techniques for Analyzing Surface Defects in Metal Castings*, MIT AI Laboratory TR-457, 1978.

ANALYSIS OF SCENES FROM A MOVING VIEWPOINT

MARK A. LAVIN

In this overview of Mark Lavin's PhD thesis, he shows how it is possible to use a series of snapshots of hilly terrain to make a map and to discover position. The work is based on the fact that the two-dimensional structure of the visual field derives in a well-defined, albeit degenerate way from the three-dimensional structure of the environment. Difficult heuristic matching problems arise because features in one snapshot must be matched with those in another. Mathematical problems are also encountered inasmuch as there is a need to deal with the extreme overconstraint inherent in the problem as formulated.

The Motion Stereo Problem

The problem of recovering a three-dimensional description of the environment from a two-dimensional view (or views) is important to all vision systems, biological and artificial. Psychophysics has suggested a number of cues that might be used by a biological vision system to solve the problems involved [Gibson 1950]; many of these cues have been used in machine vision systems. For example, researchers have explored the use of stereopsis [Marr and Poggio 1976], accommodation [Horn 1968], texture gradients [Lieberman 1974], intensity gradients [Horn 1975], and interposition and shape [Waltz 1975]. All these techniques are based on a common observation: The three-dimensional structure of the environment, together with the laws of optics and photometry, determine the structure of the two-dimensional visual field. Given certain assumptions, it is often possible to reverse the mapping, recovering (some of) the three-dimensional information from the two-dimensional image.

The Problem Domain -- an Example

In this work, the following goals were established:

- Devise a problem which requires that three-dimensional motion and structure information be recovered from two-dimensional motion and structure.

- Implement a computer program to solve this problem.

- Evaluate the results with respect to further explorations into the use of motion information in machine vision systems.

Imagine a terrain consisting of smooth hills, rooted in a flat plain, and a camera that can move in three dimensions over the terrain and rotate around a vertical axis. Suppose that the camera moves along a smooth, but unknown path, producing an image of the terrain at regular intervals, i.e., a movie in which the movement arises from the motion of the camera. The problem is this:

■   Given only the two-dimensional information in the movie, construct a three-dimensional model of the terrain (height, latitude, longitude, and shape of the hills) and a description of the movement of the camera through the terrain (the altitude, latitude, longitude, and heading of the camera at the instant each image was taken).

This problem satisfies the first goal of the research in that the only information about the three-dimensional structure of the terrain and motion of the camera is from the two-dimensional motion and structure of the movie. In order to make progress on the problem, it was necessary to simplify it as follows: rather than using an actual gray-scale movie, the input was provided by a simulation program which could produce the equivalent of a line drawing of an arbitrary terrain from a given camera position and heading. The line drawings were represented by graph data structures in which nodes correspond to features (for example, peaks, right and left hill slopes, edge intersections, and bottoms of hills), and the branches indicate adjacency of the features.

Given this scheme for representing visual input, it was possible to construct a computer program, referred to below as DYNAVU, which could address the problem stated in the scenario. A test of DYNAVU consisted of these steps:

■   Creating a tabular description of a terrain in terms of the latitude, longitude, height and radius of hills (hills were simulated as cone- or Gaussian-shaped, and thus completely described by these four parameters).

■   Creating a tabular description of a camera path in terms of latitude, longitude, altitude, and camera heading at the point where each "frame" is produced.

■   Using the input simulation program to produce a series of line-drawing data structures representing the frames of the input movie.

■   Applying DYNAVU to reconstruct a model of the terrain and the camera path.

Figure 1 shows an example of an input movie, consisting of 23 frames taken from a flight over a terrain with seven conical hills. When DYNAVU was applied to this input, it was able to construct a tabular description of the terrain and camera path, which it rendered as a map as shown in figure 2: the circles represent hills in the terrain (with their radii scaled to the computed breadth of the hills), and the short lines represent camera positions and headings from which each frame was taken. For qualitative comparison, figure 3 shows a similar map which was derived directly from the input descriptions of terrain and camera path rather than via a set of movie frames. This true map and the computed map (figure 2) differ in two respects: First, DYNAVU has no initial reference frame, so it introduces an arbitrary scaling, translation and rotation in its model (this could be corrected if a reference standard, such as two known landmarks, were available). Second, the two concentric hills in the computed map show that DYNAVU failed to recognize the identity of a hill which disappeared and then reappeared, owing to a conservative approach to global matching (see below).

The quantitative accuracy of DYNAVU's reconstruction was measured by finding a best-fit mapping between the true terrain/camera path and the computed versions (discounting the effect of the arbitrary scaling, translation, and rotation), and examining the goodness of fit. When this was done for the preceding example, it was found that:

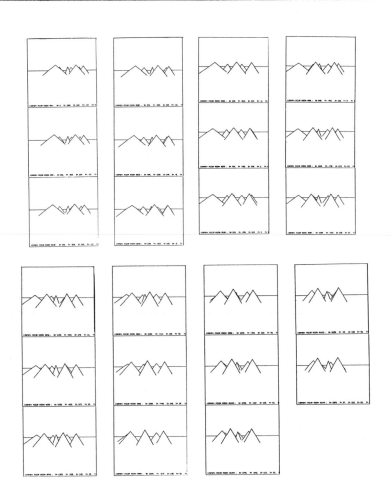

Figure 1. Frames from an input movie.

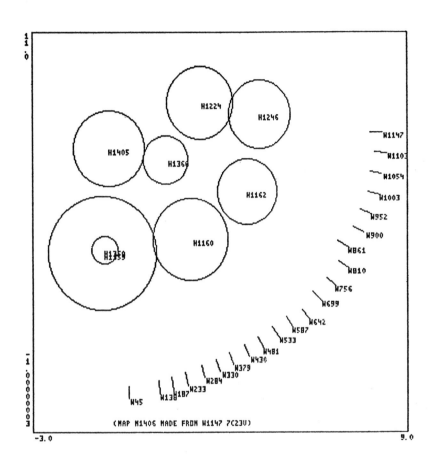

Figure 2. Terrain map computed by DYNAVU.

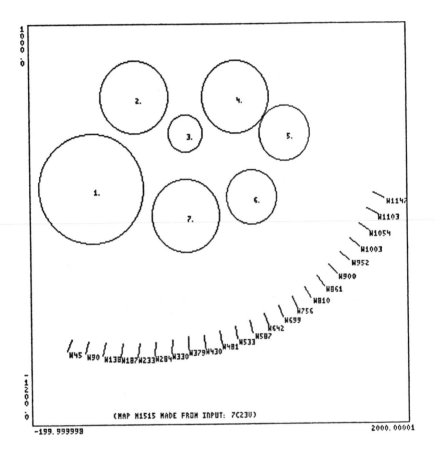

(MAP M1515 MADE FROM INPUT: 7C23U)

Figure 3. True (pre-input) map of terrain.

■   The r.m.s. error of fit in the camera heading over the 23 views was 1.29 degrees; the "true" heading ranged from -20.0 degrees to 66.0 degrees in these views.

■   The r.m.s. error of position for both camera positions and peaks of hills was 42.09 units. This compares favorably with the fact that the original scene as shown in figure 3 is approximately 2000 by 2000 units.

Thus, in this example, DYNAVU was able to reconstruct a fairly accurate model of three-dimensional motion and structure, based only on the movement and structure in its two-dimensional input. The following section sketches the strategies used by DYNAVU to achieve this result.

The Solution Technique

The first step in constructing a program was to divide the problem into three subproblems: extracting information about two-dimensional motion from successive frames of the input movie; using the two-dimensional information to make local inferences about three-dimensional motion and structure; and combining the local pieces of information into a complete global model of the terrain and camera path. Although the third subproblem is domain-specific, the first two subproblems seem inherent in any vision system which attempts to use motion information.

In the context of DYNAVU, the problem of motion detection is a problem of *matching*: the goal is to find a correspondence between features (for example, hill peaks) in successive frames such that two-dimensional features F1 and F2 in successive frames match if and only if they arise from the same three-dimensional object. Since the mapping from three dimensions to two is degenerate, it is necessary to exploit some physical constraints to do the reverse transformations

First, the rule about common derivation can be cast as

follows: two-dimensional features can match only if they could derive from the same type of three-dimensional object; for example, peak vertices can match only peak vertices. This constraint is realized by grouping features (left slopes, right slopes, peaks, etc.) into *contours*, which are subject to the constraint that they must match "at most" one-to-one -- a given contour in one view can match zero or one contours in each of the preceding and succeeding views.

Underlying the remaining three constraints is the assumption of *frame coherence*. That is, in a smoothly moving environment, the appearance of input views does not change radically between frames. This leads to the second matching constraint -- *lateral coherence*, that states that two contours C1 and C2 in successive frames can match only if the difference in their two-dimensional positions does not exceed some bound.

It was found experimentally that lateral coherence alone did not suffice; thus the concept of *depth coherence* (another corollary of frame coherence) was introduced: the depths of two-dimensional features do not change radically between successive images. The *relative* depths of contours (the INFRONTOF relation) is defined (figure 4) when two contours intersect at a T-vertex (the contour forming the crossbar of the T is INFRONTOF the contour forming the stem), or when one contour lies directly above (in two-dimensional Y) another (based on the assumption that the camera has no tilt or roll). Given this depth relation, the remaining two matching constraints can be stated: First (figure 5), for contours C1a and C1b in one image, and C2a and C2b in the successive image, the matches C1a:C2a and C1b:C2b cannot both be valid if (C1a INFRONTOF C1b) AND (C2b INFRONTOF C2a). Second (figure 6), for contour C1 in one image and contours C2a and C2b in the next image, the match C1:C2a is preferred to C1:C2b if and only if (C2a INFRONTOF C2b).

These four constraints (one-to-one, lateral coherence, two forms of depth coherence) define acceptable matches, but do not provide a mechanism for finding the best match. The naive

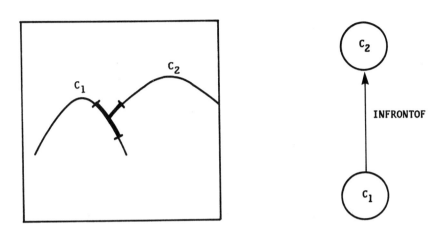

Figure 4a.   T-junction implies **INFRONTOF** relation..

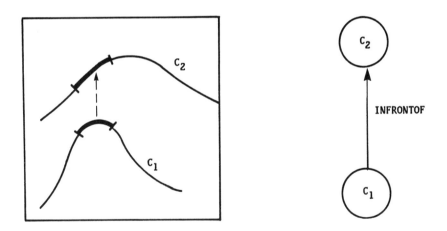

Figure 4b.   ABOVE relation implies **INFRONTOF** relation.

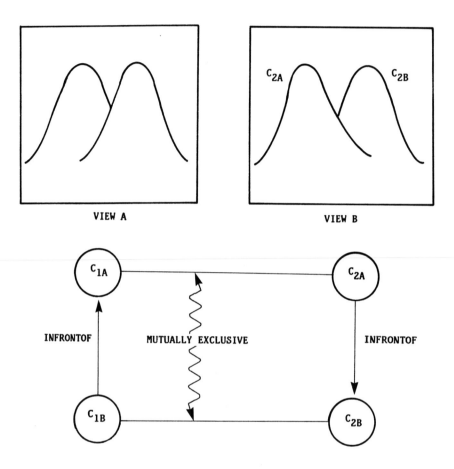

Figure 5. One matching constraint from depth coherence.

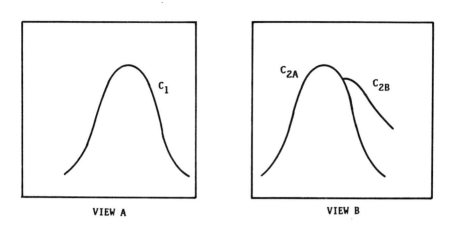

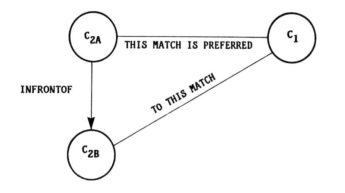

Figure 6. Another matching constraint from depth coherence.

solution of enumerating and testing all combinations grows exponentially with the number of features. Set-reduction matching techniques [Sussengeuth 1965] are not applicable since features can appear and disappear. Thus, it was necessary to develop an *ad hoc* but efficient matching algorithm, which implicitly implements the four constraints.

A binary matrix (see figure 7) is used to represent the correspondence between contours in successive views. The rows represent the contours of the first view, and are ordered by the INFRONTOF relation (front to back), while the columns (similarly ordered) correspond to the contours of the second view. Elements of the matrix are 1 if and only if the corresponding contours are believed to match. Entries are initialized based on lateral coherence. Next, the algorithm scans the array, sequentially eliminating entries precluded by depth coherence (all but the "frontmost" entries in each row and column). Finally all entries which are the sole 1's in their respective rows and columns (corresponding to undisputed one-to-one matches) are retained as the result of the matching operation.

After matching, DYNAVU uses three quantitative techniques for deriving local descriptions of terrain structure and camera motion. All draw those three-dimensional conclusions which best agree with the two-dimensional observations. The definition of agreement between two-dimensional and three-dimensional information depends on a prior model of the image forming process. In the case of DYNAVU, it is assumed that the input views were formed by a perspective projection as illustrated in figure 8. This camera model allows the definition of a measure of error between a two-dimensional datum (a feature with given two-dimensional coordinates, seen from a known viewing point) and a three-dimensional datum (an object with given three-dimensional coordinates). As figure 9 shows, this error measure is the distance from the three-dimensional point to the line-of-sight ray determined by the two-dimensional coordinates and the camera position/heading.

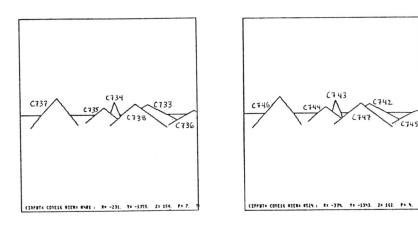

	C747	C746	C745	C744	C743	C742
C738	1	0	0	0	1	1
C737	0	1	0	0	0	0
C736	0	0	1	0	0	0
C735	0	0	0	1	1	0
C733	1	0	0	0	0	1
C734	1	0	0	1	1	0

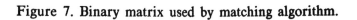

ARROWS INDICATE INFRONTOF RELATIONS

Figure 7. Binary matrix used by matching algorithm.

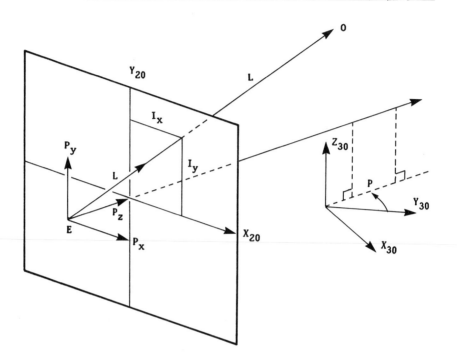

Figure 8. Perspective projection.

The first quantitative technique is used to determine the location of an object point, given two or more views of the point from known camera positions/headings. This is done by finding the three-dimensional location which minimizes the mean squared 3D:2D error according to the error measure stated above. Differentiating the expression for mean squared error with respect to the unknown three-dimensional point yields a set of three simultaneous linear equations which can be solved for the coordinates of the best-fit point.

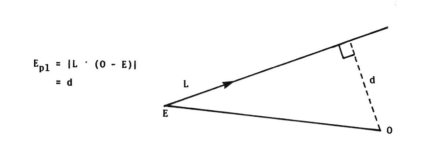

$$E_{pl} = |L \cdot (O - E)|$$
$$= d$$

Figure 9. Definition of 20:30 error measure.

The second quantitative technique is used to determine the position and heading of a camera for a view in which two or more landmarks with known three-dimensional coordinates appear. This problem is solved by finding the position/heading which minimizes the mean squared error measure; however, an analytic solution is not generally possible. Rather, it is necessary to perform a minimizing search over values of the camera heading. For a given value of heading, it is possible to specify the directions (but not the origins) of the rays from the viewing point through the given two-dimensional data. By reversing these rays, and anchoring them to the known three-dimensional landmarks, the problem can be converted to finding a three-dimensional object point from known viewing positions as above. That is, it is possible to solve analytically for a best-fit viewing position (and derive the goodness of fit) for each assumed value of heading. Direct search finds the value(s) of the heading which gives the minimal best-fit error. The computation is simplified when only two known three-dimensional landmarks can be seen; in this case, a closed expression for the best-fit error as a function of heading can be derived. Solving this expression for the heading, and applying the previous technique for locating the viewing position, the entire problem can be solved without direct search.

The two techniques above are used to determine the three-dimensional structure (object locations) and the three-dimensional motion (viewing point positions/headings). The final technique combines both of these functions: Given two views with at least three pairs of corresponding two-dimensional feature points, it is possible to determine (up to arbitrary constants of scaling, rotation, and translation), the three-dimensional positions of all object points, and the two positions/headings of the camera. The technique is again based on the notion of minimizing the mean squared error as defined above. However, it was found that application of a direct search to minimize 3D:2D error was computationally infeasible. Fortuitously, a formula suggested by Ullman [1977] could be extended to serve as a much simpler error measure to be used in a direct search. This search yields zero to four best-fit values of heading change (between views); each leads to a best-fit translation between views, which leads, via the first technique above, to a solution for the locations of the object points.

To summarize what we have discussed so far, the matching algorithm provides a correspondence between two-dimensional features in successive views, and from there, a correspondence between two-dimensional features and descriptions of three-dimensional objects in DYNAVU's internal description of the terrain. The quantitative techniques provide local information about terrain structure and camera movement. DYNAVU's final task is to combine local information into a global description of the terrain and camera path by a "bootstrapping" process. Suppose, at some point in the input, that at least two of the hills currently in view had been previously assigned three-dimensional coordinates. Then, using the second quantitative technique, it would be possible to determine a three-dimensional position/heading for the current viewing point. This information, combined with information from one or more previous views, could be used to determine the three-dimensional location of some previously unlocated hill. That is, known landmarks are used to determine camera positions/headings, which are then used to determine new landmarks. The only problem with this bootstrapping analysis is getting it started; fortunately, the third quantitative technique provides a means of determining an initial set of landmarks and camera positions/headings from which the rest of the model can be built incrementally.

Another task in producing a global description is to find correspondences between newly appearing hills and those which had previously disappeared ("global matching"). This represents an important adjunct to the interframe two-dimensional matching algorithm, since it can introduce information to combat the drift which would naturally develop with the sequential method of combining local evidence. The technique used for global matching is rather conservative (a false positive match would probably lead to severe anomalies); this led to the error indicated by the concentric hills in the map of figure 2. The matching is based on two kinds of constraints: quantitative -- limiting error of fit between two-dimensional and three-dimensional data, assuming the postulated match; and qualitative -- precluding matches that violate the constraint that a hill can not derive from two distinct contours that have some INFRONTOF relation between them.

Evaluation and Further Directions

Testing of DYNAVU revealed several areas where the program ran into difficulty: First, it was found that as the complexity of the two-dimensional views increased, the matching process became increasingly dependent on the choice of a lateral distance threshold and that, ultimately, it was not possible, using the mechanisms outlined above, to prevent some false negative matches and (more seriously) false positive matches. Second, for certain inputs, there was noticeable degradation of the model as the program progressed; that is, the computed description started to deviate more and more from the "true" description as the program built layer upon layer of bootstrapping. Third, it appeared that DYNAVU was sensitive in a rather nonuniform fashion to perturbations of the input information. In particular, correcting the small two-dimensional errors introduced by the input simulation process (generally a few parts in a thousand) dramatically improved the program's performance. These observations led to the following conclusions that apply beyond the limited context of DYNAVU's problem domain:

■   Greater feature density is needed: it became clear that the deficiencies in the matching process stemmed neither from the *ad hoc* matching algorithm, nor even from the choice of matching constraints, but rather from the fact that the input representation (indeed, the problem domain) contained such sparse data that there was not enough information for the matcher to perform efficiently or correctly. This appears to be another instance of the "Waltz effect" [Waltz 1975]: increasing the amount and variety of data available to an analysis program (for example, expanding the set of edge and junction labels) may simplify program structure and greatly improve execution efficiency (compare the simple Waltz label matching scheme with the heuristics and rules of Guzman [1968]).

■   The construction of global conclusions should be limited: it was found that when the two-dimension to three-dimension inference techniques were tested in isolation, they performed satisfactorily. However, when they are combined in DYNAVU, so that the output of one stage became the input of the next, overall errors started to creep into the models of terrain and camera path; local errors of limited scope were exacerbated when combined to draw global conclusions. However, the thrust of this observation is optimistic; drawing global conclusions about three-dimensional motion and structure from two-dimensional data may be not only infeasible, but also unnecessary. In particular, I believe that the local three-dimensional data have immediate use in a vision system -- for segmentation [Aggarwal 1974], object identification [Badler 1975], attitude and motion control [Chien 1975], and so on -- without being combined into one master geometrric of the environment.

These conclusions suggest future directions for research on machine vision systems using motion information. One area of particular interest concerns the construction and analysis of *visual motion fields*. The motion of the observer, coupled with motions in the environment, induce in the visual field of the observer a two-dimensional velocity vector field. This field, like the scalar fields of intensity [Horn 1975], disparity [Marr 1976], and texture density [Gibson 1950], [Lieberman 1974], encodes information about the three-dimensional environment.

Extracting the visual motion field from successive images is problematic. Recently, a number of researchers have devised techniques, based on relaxation processes in discrete networks, which might be adapted to the extraction of the visual motion field in a highly parallel, locally simple way [Horn 1974], [Stevens 1978], [Marr 1976]. In problem domains where there is greater feature density, it is possible to simplify the matching criteria to lateral coherence and *area coherence*: the motion field tends to be piecewise continuous. Further, given sufficient feature density, the interactions among sets of potential matches are greatly simplified, so that the complexity is no longer exponential in the size and feature density of the input [Lavin 1977].

Several operations on the visual motion field have been suggested to derive local inferences about three-dimensional motion and structure. Nakayama and Loomis [1974] suggested an algorithm for region segmentation, based on a gradient and threshold operation applied to the visual velocity field (regions of discontinuity in the field correspond to boundaries of surfaces at different depths, or moving at different velocities). Koenderink and van Doorn [1976] have suggested quantitative extensions to the qualitative observations of Gibson [1955], noting that certain vector field properties of the visual motion field (curl, divergence, deformation) can be related to observer motion and the local orientation of feature-bearing surfaces. As noted by Woodham [1977], the latter is an important step in recovering descriptions of three-dimensional shape.

References

J. K. Aggarwal and R. O. Duda, *Computer Analysis of Moving Images*, Electronics Research Center Information Systems Research Laboratory Technical Report 161, University of Texas at Austin, 1974.

N. I. Badler, *Temporal Scene Analysis: Conceptual Descriptions of Object Movements*, Department of Computer Science Technical Report No. 80 (PhD Thesis), University of Toronto, 1975.

R. T. Chien and V. C. Jones, "Acquisition of Moving Objects and Hand-Eye Coordination," in *Advance Papers of the Fourth International Joint Conference on Artificial Intelligence*, 1975.

J. J. Gibson, *The Perception of the Visual World*, Houghton-Mifflin Co., 1950.

J. J. Gibson, P. Olum, and F. Rosenblatt, "Parallax and Perspective During Aircraft Landings," *The American Journal of Psychology*, Vol. 68, No. 3, 1955.

A. Guzman, *Computer Recognition of Three-Dimensional Objects in a Visual Scene*, MIT Laboratory for Computer Science TR-59 (PhD Thesis), 1968.

B. K. P. Horn, *Focusing*, MIT AI Laboratory Memo 160, 1968.

B. K. P. Horn, "Horn's Lightness Program," in P. Winston (ed.) *Progress in Artificial Intelligence*, MIT AI Laboratory TR-310, 1974.

B. K. P. Horn, *Image Intensity Understanding*, MIT AI Laboratory Memo 335, 1975.

J. J. Koenderink, and A. J. van Doorn, "Local Structure of Movement Parallax of the Plane," *Journal of the Optical Society of America*, Vol. 66, No. 7, 1976.

M. A. Lavin, *Computer Analysis of Scenes from a Moving Viewing Point*, (Ph. D. Thesis), MIT AI Laboratory, 1977.

L. I. Lieberman, *Computer Recognition and Description of Natural Scenes*, PhD Thesis, Department of Computer and Informattion Science, University of Pennsylvania, 1974.

D. Marr and T. Poggio, "Computation of Stero Disparity," *Science*, Vol. 194, No. 4262, 1976.

K. Nakayama and J. M. Loomis, "Optical Velocity Patterns, Velocity-Sensitive Neurons, and Space Perception: a Hypothesis," *Perception*, Vol. 3, 1974.

E. H. Sussenguth, "A Graph-Theoretic Algorithm for Matching Chemical Structures," *Journal of Chemical Documentation*, Vol. 5, 1965.

K. A. Stevens, "Computation of Locally Parallel Structure," *Biol. Cybernetics 29*, 1978, also MIT AI Laboratory Memo 392, 1977.

Shimon Ullman, *The Interpretation of Visual Motion*, PhD Thesis, to be published by MIT Press, 1978.

D. L. Waltz, "Understanding Line Drawings of Scenes with Shadows," in P. Winston (ed.) *The Psychology of Computer Vision,* McGraw-Hill, 1975.

R. J. Woodham, *Reflectance Map Techniques for Analyzing Surface Defects in Metal Castings,* PhD Thesis, MIT AI Laboratory Technical Report 457, 1978.

MANIPULATION
AND
PRODUCTIVITY
TECHNOLOGY

HIROCHIKA INOUE
TOMAS LOZANO-PEREZ
BERTHOLD HORN
JOHN HOLLERBACH

Section Contents

Productivity technology to us means intelligent robots in the boring and dangerous jobs where humans should not be. Creating such robots requires an understanding of vision, manipulation, and problem solving. In this chapter we concentrate on manipulation since the other two essential ingredients are discussed elsewhere.

■   *Inoue* opens the chapter with a discussion of a program that assembles a radial bearing using a manipulator with a force-sensing wrist designed by Minsky. He shows that force-sensing enables assembly operations that cannot be done by dead reckoning.

■   *Lozano* investigates the problem of making a high-level language for mechanical manipulation using Inoue's demonstration as a focal point. He concentrates on the problem of grasping.

■   *Horn* gives a sample mathematical analysis of a simple multijoint manipulator. Although such an analysis increases our understanding of the behavior of *simple* systems, the complexity of the resulting equations precludes their exclusive use for controlling realistic manipulators.

■   *Hollerbach* addresses control from another perspective, asking and answering questions about how people control their own limbs, particularly in the act of writing. He uses a human-like mechanical arm for theory-testing simulations.

Artificial Intelligence Applied to Productivity Technology

The Artificial Intelligence literature is full of papers that illustrate what can be done with intelligent computers connected to the world with flexible, well-instrumented manipulators and with some sort of eye. Programs have assembled bearings with 20 micrometer tolerances; they have identified and reoriented scattered parts lying on a light table; and they have inspected metal castings for grain-size defects.

The roots of this technology extend back to the work on computer vision and manipulation that was very prominent in Artificial Intelligence during the middle and late 1960s. MIT and Stanford, for example, were experimenting with programs that demonstrated the ability to understand a visual scene, and the Stanford Research Institute was working with motion, problem solving, and obstacle avoidance using Shakey, a wheeled robot.

During this phase, there was a great deal of effort aimed at transforming blocks world images into line drawings. Programs of many kinds were written to analyze intensity profiles, to extract feature points from them, to group the feature points into line segments, and to convert the line segments into clean, complete drawings.

Originally, researchers were optimistic that this blocks world would soon turn to the industrial world and the robot projects would become productivity technology projects. But as it became clear that the problems were much harder than anticipated, the hope for continuous maturing faded, and the robot projects became productivity technology projects more by metamorphosis than by smooth, continuous change.

Still, the early work did produce the repertoire of basic vision, manipulation, and problem–solving techniques that are, in more contemporary forms, making for progress against three kinds of industrial problems:

■   In the area of vision, one problem is inspection for defects. A second is helping in guiding parts into place. A third is reorienting parts that are randomly jumbled together in a bin.

■   In the area of manipulation, one problem is that of using sensors to determine forces to be applied, as when inserting a peg into a tight-fitting hole. Another is that of smoothly controlling multijointed manipulators during rapid motion.

■   In the area of programming-language design, the main problem is to create problem-solving systems that accept rough assembly instructions, preferably in English, and produce the detailed streams of low-level instructions that interpret sensor signals and control manipulator motors.

Already much has been accomplished. The following representative sample is from the progress reports of MIT, Stanford, and SRI, the largest US Artificial Intelligence centers doing productivity technology.

■   A total system has been illustrated that used force and touch, tools, and some simple vision to assemble a ten-part water pump.

■   Coordinated manipulator action has been illustrated through the assembly of a hinge using two cooperating manipulators.

■   Close-tolerance manipulation has been illustrated through the assembly of a bearing with 20-micrometer tolerances. This work is the subject of the section by Inoue.

■   Accurate part location using vision has been illustrated through the precise determination of the position of semiconductors in preparation for lead attachment.

■   An ability to perceive, describe, and identify three-dimensional shapes was illustrated by a complicated system that combined laser rangefinding with new theory of representation based on generalized-cylinders.

■   The reorienting of scattered parts has been illustrated through the identification and correct adjustment of steel castings spread on a light table. This demonstration makes heavy use of binary image processing techniques.

■   The use of visual feedback has been illustrated through the location of bolt holes using a solid-state camera mounted on a bolt-bearing arm.

■   The use of vision for inspection has been illustrated through a program that examines jet engine turbine blades for grain-size defects.

To be sure, these are illustrations, not total solutions. There is a gap between a mature technology and these first crude harbingers of coordinated motion, force sensing, visual inspection, and bin-picking.

The Future

Looking to the future, several things seem to be on the critical path. For example, there certainly is a need for better vision processing. *Better* means both faster and more sophisticated. Vision, however, is not discussed in any of the sections here since another chapter is devoted entirely to the general subject.

Next there is a need for a language for programming assembly. This may seem odd, but the need is certainly not for another minor variation on the traditional programming languages. Instead, the need is for a language that is strong on problem solving, sufficiently strong for the programmer to specify what he wants in high-level, comfortable, human terms. Eventually, a really talented system would be fed directly from manuals used to instruct people. There has been progress on the critical modules of such a system, and with enough work, there need be little of the current danger that expensive assembly will merely be replaced by expensive programming. The section by Lozano-Perez illuminates the issues involved.

There is a need for better control ideas. Dynamic control of the trajectory of a many-jointed manipulator seems to require large calculations, if the motion is to be done smoothly, yet at speed. As Horn's section shows, mathematical analysis is possible (and even straightforward), but the resulting equations are far too complex for real-time control with a low-capacity computer. The problem can be simplified by placing constraints on manipulator design, for example by designing the axes of rotation of the last three joints to intersect, but even the simplified problem is not yet solved.

Finally there is a need for better equipment. Better solid-state cameras, better force sensors, and better mechanical designs are usually at the top of every list. Industry is doing a good job with cameras, but there is no corollary hope for rapid progress with manipulators, either for autonomous robots or for teleoperator applications.

In the manipulator area, one idea of promise is that of copying human arms. Lack of redundancy is one reason today's manipulators are so limited. In the past, absence of redundancy made sense -- it renders solution of the state equations easier because of the invertibility of the matrices resulting from a one-to-one correspondence between task requirements and control inputs. With redundancy the inversion of matrices is no longer possible, and solution of the state equations becomes more difficult.

But while simplifying the control strategy, lack of

redundancy renders certain actions impossible in a constrained environment. For reasons of obstacle avoidance or working space constraints, the disposition of some of the joints may become fixed. It then becomes impossible to achieve a general positioning and orienting ability at the manipulator end. A redundant manipulator would provide extra degrees of freedom to achieve required movements at the manipulator end while fulfilling working space constraints. Moreover, the most favorable joint disposition could be chosen from the multiple configurations that satisfy the constraints.

Consequently, a manipulator design closer to that of a human arm with multiple redundancy may be called for. The adequacy of human arms for manipulation tasks provides an existence proof that there is a redundant manipulator design that works. Past manipulator designs have stressed design and control simplicity over similarity to human arms.

To cope with multiple degrees of freedom, animal control may involve certain stereotyped patterns of muscle contraction combining different muscles and joints that limit the degrees of freedom. The solution to a motor task then involves the selection of the best stereotyped pattern for the situation and the fine tuning of this pattern according to the precise task requirements. The need for a general solution to the noninvertible state equations is obviated. Hollerbach goes into detail in his section on understanding human handwriting.

FORCE
FEEDBACK IN
PRECISE
ASSEMBLY
TASKS

HIROCHIKA INOUE

In order to assemble automatically physical objects with small clearances, great positional accuracy is required, both in the initial positioning of the parts to be assembled and in the subsequent motions of the robot arm. However, robot arms, being large mechanical devices, typically have rather poor positional accuracy. Hirochika Inoue describes the use of force feedback to correct inaccurate initial positioning of the parts to be mated and to overcome the inaccuracy of an arm. In the experiment described, the tolerances were an order of magnitude smaller than the inherent positional accuracy obtainable with the particular arm used.

The Little Robot System

The Little Robot System developed by D. Silver is shown in figure 1. This medium size, five degree of freedom, seven axis robot arm is controlled by the MIT AI Laboratory's PDP-6 computer through the programming language LISP. The arm is controlled by means of force and position feedback. By using force feedback, one can write very simple programs which achieve tolerances exceeding the positional accuracy of the arm.

The robot arm's force sensor complex is located in its wrist. Consisting of six linear variable differential transformers (LVDT's), the force sensor complex measures the forces and torques acting on the wrist. Figure 2 shows the geometry of these six LVDT's. The equations below describe the relationship between force and torque components in the wrist centered rectangular coordinate system and the force component acting at the position of each LVDT. The angle "a" is a rotational displacement between the robot wrist axis and the force sensor complex axis.

Fx,Fy,Fz forces in the x, y, and z axis,
Tx,Ty,Tz torques about x, y, and z axis,
f1,f2 ... forces at each of the six LVDT's.

```
Fx = -f2*cos(45+a) - f4*cos(45-a) + f5*cos(45+a)
Fy = -f2*sin(45+a) + f4*sin(45-a) + f5*sin(45+a)
Fz = f1 + f3 + f6
Tx = f1*d*cos(a) - f3*d*sin(a) + f6*d*sin(a)
Ty = f1*d*sin(a) + f3*d*cos(a) - f6*d*cos(a)
Tz = f2*d - f4*d + f5*d
```

Force and torque components in the hand coordinate may be obtained from those in the wrist coordinate system by the following equations.

Figure 1. Whole view of the Little Robot System

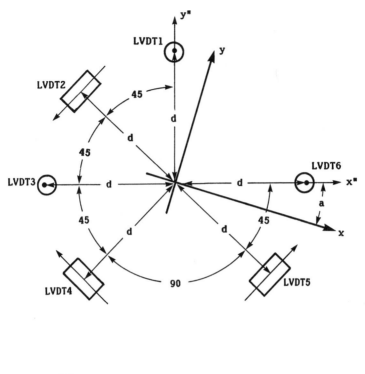

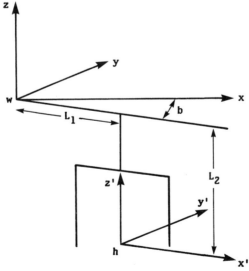

Figure 2. Force sensor complex and the coordinate systems.

```
Fx' = Fx*cos(b) - Fy*sin(b)
Fy' = Fx*sin(b) + Fy*cos(b)
Fz' = Fz
Tx' = (Tx - L2*Fy)*cos(b) - (Ty + L2*Fx)*sin(b)
Ty' = (Tx - L2*Fy)*sin(b) + (Ty + L2*Fx)*cos(b) + L1*Fz
Tz' = Tz - L1*(Fy*cos(b) + Fx*sin(b))
```

The stress-strain matrix of the sensor complex has not been analyzed in detail. Therefore an approximation technique is used. First, the displacements (both linear and angular) in the rectangular sensor coordinate system must be related to the displacements measured by the LVDT's. Suppose dx", dy", and dz" are small linear displacements in the sensor coordinate system, and that da", db", and dc" are small rotations around the sensor's x, y, and z axis (respectively). These displacements and rotations in the sensor's coordinate system are related to the displacements detected by the six LVDT's (t1, t1, ... t6) by the following equations.

```
dx" = -(t2 + t4)/sqrt(2)
dy" = (t4 + t5)/sqrt(2)
dz" = (t3 + t6)/2
da" = (t3 + t6 - 2*t1)/2
db" = (t3 - t6)/2
dc" = (t2 + t5)/2
```

The displacements and rotations in the sensor's coordinate system can be transformed into displacements and rotations in the wrist coordinate system. Finally, the overall stiffness coefficients (k1, k2, ... k6) must be determined experimentally for the wrist so that the following equations hold.

```
Fx = k1*dx, Fy = k2*dy,  Fz = k3*dz
Tx = k4*da,  Ty = k5*db,  Tz = k6*dc
```

The equations developed above enable the PDP-6 to

determine torques and forces acting on the hand by observing displacements of the LVDT's. The PDP-6 servos the robot arm every 1/60 of a second. The PDP-6 is in turn controlled by LISP programs in the PDP-10 via primitives which set and examine PDP-6 variables. These variables are divided into two classes: those which are inputs to the PDP-6, and those which are outputs from the PDP-6. The variable names make use of prefixes according to the table below.

Prefix meanings

X X-axis	Y Y-axis	Z Z-axis	R rotation about Z-axis
G grip	V vice	T tilting-part-holder	

suffix	prefix	meaning	unit	type
		PDP-6 output variables		
POS	X,Y,Z,R,G,V,T	position	inch/rad	floating
DLT	X,Y,Z,R,G,V,T	position error	pot. unit	fixed
FRS	X,Y,Z,G,V	calib. force	LVDT unit	fixed
TRC	X,Y,Z	calib. torque	LVDT unit	fixed
		PDP-6 input variables		
DES	X,Y,Z,R,G,V,T	destination	inch/rad	floating
FDS	X,Y,Z,R,G,V	force dest.	LVDT unit	fixed
FRE	X,Y,A,R,G,V	mode switch		0 or -1
GAN	X,Y,A,R,G,V,T	position servo gain		fixed
FGN	X,Y,Z,R,G,V	force servo gain		fixed

The mode switch (suffix FRE) is used to indicate whether the motion along the particular axis is to be position control servoed (mode = 0) or is to be force control servoed (mode = -1).

In writing LISP control programs for the robot arm, five primitives are frequently used. These are:

(SETM % value) sets the PDP-6 variable to the value

(GETM %) gets the value of the PDP-6 variable as a fixed point number

(GETMF %) gets the value of the PDP-6 variable as a floating point number

(WAIT exp) evaluates "exp" every 1/30 of a second until "exp" evaluates to T

(SEQ v1 v2 v3) returns T when v1 is equal to v2 within the tolerance v3

Using these primitives, one can write many useful LISP functions.

```
(DEFUN X= (X) (SETM XDES X) (SETM XFRE 0))
                ;position control
(DEFUN DX= (DX) (X= (PLUS (GETMF XPOS) DX)))
                ;relative position control
(DEFUN FX= (FX) (SETM XFDS FX) (SETM XFRE -1))
                ;force control
(DEFUN ?X () (SEQ (GETM XDLT) 0 THRESHOLD-P))
                ;check position control
(DEFUN ?FX ()(SEQ (GETM XFRS)(GETM XFDS))(THRESHOLD-F))
                ;check force
```

The programs above can be combined to perform more interesting actions.

```
(DEFUN FOO () (FZ= .01) (WAIT '(?FZ)) (DR= 3.14) (WAIT '(?R)))
```

The program above moves the hand down until either the hand or something held in the hand touches the table. When this happens the hand rotates once. An important property of this program is that contact with the table is maintained while the hand is rotating because the instruction

$$(FZ= .01)$$

is still in effect.

Applications of Force Feedback in Machine Assembly

Precise machine assembly often involves the following basic actions:

■   putting a peg into a hole with close tolerance

■   screwing a nut onto a bolt (to a particular torque)

■   picking up a thin piece from a flat table

While the positional accuracy of the little robot system is only 01 inches, force feedback can be used to perform these basic actions to with .001 inches.

Figure 3 illustrates a specially designed bearing complex consisting of two radial ball bearings, two spacers, a cylinder, a washer, a nut, and a shaft with a threaded end. The dimensions of the parts are given in figure 4. The tolerances are 0.001 inch for the shaft-bearing pair and the bearing-cylinder pair, 0.002 inches for the shaft-spacer1 pair, 0.01 inch for the shaft-spacer2 pair, and 0.06 inch for the shaft-washer.

Peg-into-Hole assembly

Placing a peg into a hole involves three consecutive phases. The first phase, "drop-into," partially drops the shaft into the mouth of the cylindrical hole. The next phase, "mate," adjusts the relative position and orientation between the shaft and the hole. Finally, the third phase, "push-into," pushes the shaft into the hole to complete the assembly task.

The clearances and the shoulder shape of the shaft determine the difficulty of this task. In the field of machine design, the standards of fit are well defined, depending on the machining accuracy. However, no such standards have been established for automatic assembly. Presumably these standards should be defined by considering positioning error, clearances

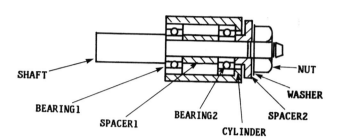

Figure 3. The object to be assembled.

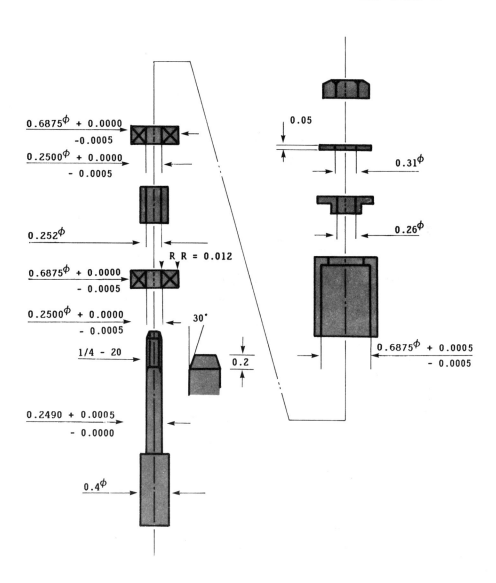

Figure 4. Size and clearances of the parts.

5-1. INITIAL ENVIRONMENT

5-2. BEARING1

5-3. SPACER1

5-4. BEARING2

5-5. CYLINDER

5-6. TILT SHAFT VERTICALLY

5-7. SPACER2

5-8. PICK UP WASHER

5-9. WASHER

5-10. NUT

Figure 5. Assembly of the bearing complex.

between parts, shoulder shape, and the particular assembly algorithm.

Qualitatively, a fit is either "loose" or "close." An example of a loose fit is the shaft-spacer2 pair. On the other hand, the bearing-cylinder pair is a good example of a "close" fit. Since a close fit is more difficult to achieve than a loose fit, both a close fit and a loose fit peg-into-hole algorithm will be developed.

Suppose the errors in the X and Y position repeatability are e/2. Then the hand must be located within the e*e error square centered at the reference point. Similarly, if the hand is holding something with a hole in it, the center of the hole is within the same error square. The tolerance defines a circle whose diameter is equal to "c." If the tolerance circle completely covers the error square, the fit is so loose that the peg will go into the hole without any change in their initial orientation. The fit is loose if

$$c > sqrt(2)*e.$$

Conversely, if the tolerance circle does not cover the error square, some re-orientation will be necessary because the fit is so close. In actual experiments another source of error, grasp-point error, must be anticipated in addition to the position servo error. The grasp error, which results from the grasping action, is sometimes much larger than the positioning error of the servo-mechanism. If a hand has parallel jaws, like the one in the little robot system, then the grasp-point error occurs only in the direction perpendicular to the squeezing axis.

A Loose fit Peg-into-Hole algorithm

For purposes of illustration, assume that the problem is to put spacer2 into the shaft. Let's assume that the hand has already managed to grasp spacer2 such that the cylindrical hole's axis is aligned with the arm's Z-axis. See figure 7. The drop-into

algorithm must move spacer2 down until it lands on the shaft
(which is pointing straight up). There are three possibile contact
situations, illustrated in figure 6. The spacer may offset to the

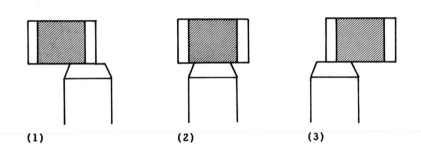

(1)   (2)   (3)

Figure 6. Landing situations.

left, nearly centered, or offset to the right. Depending on which
situation actually occurs, a different search tactic must be used to
complete the drop-into phase. To avoid the necessity of
discovering which contact situation occured, one can deliberately
miss. Then the spacer is always offset to the right, and only a
simple search in the negative X direction is needed.

```
(DEFUN DROP-INTO-L ()      ;assume the hand is holding the spacer
       (DX= shift) (WAIT '(?X));approximately centered above the shaft
       (FZ= small-contact-force) (WAIT '(FZ?))
       (FX= small-sliding-force)
       (WAIT '(OR (?FX) (SEQ (GETM ZFRS) 0 threshold)))
       (DZ= 0.0))
```

The program above loosely drops the spacer onto the
shaft by first shifting the x-position, then moving spacer2 down
until it lands on the shaft and maintaining a small force against

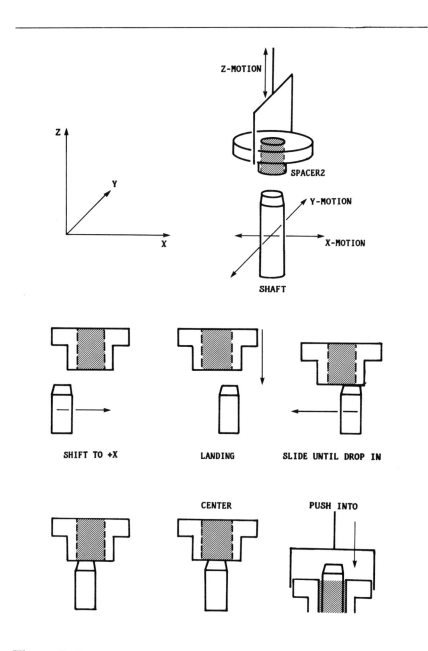

Figure 7. Peg-into-Hole assembly with "loose fit."

it, and then sliding the shaft towards "-X" until the spacer drops onto it. The drop is detected by either the force in the X direction being achieved because the shaft came into contact with the wall of the hole, or by the force along the Z-axis becoming nearly zero.

When the DROP-INTO-L program has completed, the shaft should be at least partially into the hole in spacer2. The next step is to MATE the shaft with the center of spacer2. This is done by moving the shaft in the plus and minus Y direction to find the two edges of the spacer in that dimension, then repeating with the X dimension. The center is of course midway between the two extremes.

```
(DEFUN MATE-V ()
    (PROG (X1 Y1)
          (FY= small-edge-finding-force-to-+Y) (WAIT '(?FY))
          (SETQ Y1 (GETMF YPOS))
          (FY= small-edge-finding-force-to--Y) (WAIT '(?FY))
          (Y= (//$ (+$ Y1 (GETMF YPOS)) 2.0)) WAIT '(?Y))
                            ;the Y coordinate is the average of the two extrema
          (FX= small-edge-finding-force-to-+X) (WAIT '(?FX))
          (SETQ X1 (GETMF XPOS))
          (FX= small-edge-finding-force-to--X) (WAIT '(?FX))
          (X= (//$ (+$ X1 (GETMF XPOS)) 2.0)) (WAIT '(?X)))
```

Once the hole in spacer2 is centered on the shaft, it must be pushed down the shaft until it arives at the end. Since the shaft may be tilted, simply adjusting the Z coordinate of the hand would not be sufficient. What might be a difficult problem if one only used position control has a simple solution if one uses force control, as in the PUSH-INTO-V program below.

```
(DEFUN PUSH-INTO-V ()
    (FX= 0) (FY= 0) (FZ= inserting-force) (WAIT '(?FZ)) )
```

The sequence of DROP-INTO-L, MATE-V, and

PUSH-INTO-V gives a simple stereotyped action for the peg-into-hole assembly problem with loose fit. Actually, the MATE-V function can be omitted because DROP-INTO-L partially centers the shaft, and the PUSH-INTO-V program adapts the position of the shaft to the center of the hole in spacer2. This action is performed by PEG-IN-HOLE-L.

```
(DEFUN PEG-IN-HOLE-L () (DROP-INTO-L) (PUSH-INTO-V))
```

Close fit Peg-into-Hole algorithm

The bearing-cylinder pair is a good example of a close fit because the tolerence circle diameter "c" satisfies the equation

$$c < sqrt(2)*e.$$

The function DROP-INTO-L will not work reliably because the tolerance circle does not cover all of the error square. A simple technique for solving this difficulty is to tilt the peg or the hole. By tilting, the area of the peg tip is reduced, so the tolerance circle diameter is increased. For example, the diameter of the tolerance circle of the bearing-cylinder pair is 0.001 inches without tilting, but is 0.688 with tilting. Note that

$$sqrt(2)*e = 0.009 \text{ inches}.$$

Assume that the cylinder and the shaft with bearings on it are both held horizontally. See figure 8. If the gripper is on the cylinder, then the program DROP-INTO-C performs the drop-into action for a pair with close fit.

```
(DEFUN DROP-INTO-C ()
        (DR= 0.1) (DY= shift) (WAIT '(AND (?R) (?Y))
        (FX= landing-force) (WAIT '(?FX))
        (DX= 0.0))
```

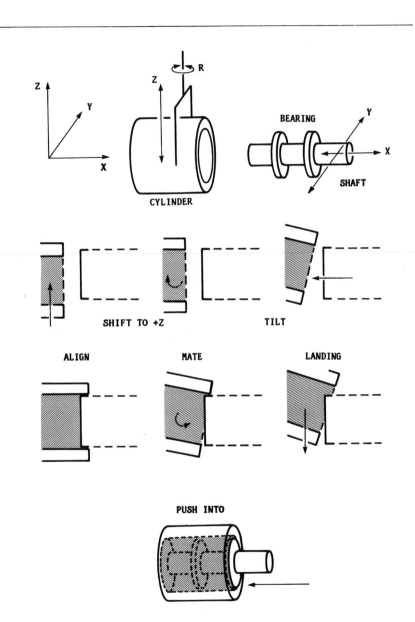

Figure 8. Peg-into-Hole assembly with "close fit."

After DROP-INTO-C has completed, the cylinder must be aligned to the orientation of the shaft, and the Y, Z position of the bearing must be adapted to the cylinder. MATE-H, the program which does this, first moves the bearings up and down to find the center (axis) of the cylinder. Then the bearing is moved in the Y direction to make contact with the side of the cylinder. Keeping this contact, the cylinder is rotated back.

```
(DEFUN MATE-H ( )
 (PROG (Z1)
        (FZ= small-edge-finding-force+z) (WAIT '(?FZ))
        (SETQ Z1 (GETMF ZPOS))
        (FZ= small-edge-finding-force-z) (WAIT '(?FZ))
        (Z= (//$ (+$ Z1 (GETMF ZPOS)) 2.0))
        (FY= small-contact-force-in-Y-axis) (WAIT '(?FY))
        (FZ= 0) (R= 0.0) (WAIT '(?R))
```

The program PUSH-INTO-H applies the horizontal force to push the bearing assembly into the cylinder. It is the same as PUSH-INTO-V except for the direction.

```
(DEFUN PUSH-INTO-H ( )
        (FY= 0) (FZ= 0)
        (FZ= inserting-force) (WAIT '(?FZ)))
```

The entire close fit peg-in-hole assembly operation is accomplished by the PEG-HOLE-C program.

```
(DEFUN PEG-HOLE-C ( )
        (DROP-INTO-C) (MATE-H) (PUSH-INTO-H)).
```

Screwing a Nut onto a Bolt

The action for screwing a nut onto a bolt is also broken into the three consecutive phases "drop-into," "mate," and "screw-into." Since the programs DROP-INTO-L and MATE-V can be used for the first two phases, only a program SCREW-INTO needs to be written.

To screw a nut onto a bolt, the nut must be turned in a clockwise direction while exerting a small downward pressure. The X, Y position of the nut is made to accommodate the screw by setting the X, Y forces to zero. The robot stops when it feels the specified fastening torque.

```
(DEFUN SCREW-INTO ()
         (FZ= small-down-force) (FX= 0) (FY= 0)
         (FR= fastening-torque) (WAIT '(?FR)))
```

Just as with the loose peg-in-hole program, the MATE-V activity is not needed because SCREW-INTO does the mating. The program SCREW-NUT combines all the phases.

```
(DEFUN SCREW-NUT () (DROP-INTO-L) (SCREW-INTO))
```

Picking up a Thin Piece

Automatic assembly requires that the robot be able to handle many small, thin pieces such as washers. It is hard to pick up such thin objects from a flat table. If the position of the hand is slightly higher than the table the robot will miss the washer, while one dare not position the hand lower than the table. Force feedback is used by the PICKUP program to maintain contact with the table while centering the thin piece. Centering is used to correct for small errors in the positioning of the part.

```
(DEFUN PICKUP ()
        (G= (+$ diameter-of-washer) 0.2))
        (Z= small-height-off-table) (WAIT '(AND (?Z) (?G)))
        (FZ= small-landing-force) (WAIT '(?FZ))
        (FG= small-grasping-force) (WAIT '(?FG))
        (DG= 0.2) (WAIT '(?G))     ;open hand a little
        (DR= 1.57) (WAIT '(?R))    ;turn the hand 1.57 radians
        (FG= grasping-force) (WAIT '(?FG)))
```

A LANGUAGE FOR AUTOMATIC MECHANICAL ASSEMBLY

TOMAS LOZANO-PEREZ

In many laboratories, robots use sophisticated manipulators and force feedback to assemble devices like the bearing described by Inoue in the last section. The programs driving such impressive demonstrations have been straightforward, but painful to write because high-level languages are only now under development for automatic assembly. These languages will enable people to instruct robots in terms of high-level goals, possibly given in English, rather than through low-level, tedious programming. This section describes the work of Lozano-Perez on such a high-level language. It is an overview of his MS thesis.

The Mechanical Assembly Problem

Assembly programming is still in the assembly-language era, so to speak. The programmer is forced to think in terms of instructions like these:

Move in the direction d *at speed* s *until you reach position* p.
Exert a force f *by moving in the direction* d.

It would be better, and certainly cheaper, if the programmer could think instead in terms of suggestions like these for assembling part of an engine:

Insert the piston pin partway into the piston.
Place the rod's pin end on the piston pin inside the piston.
Push the pin through the rod and the piston.

That is, we would like to tell our robots what to do in terms that are comfortable to us, leaving them to fill in the details. Rough English descriptions, or something close to English but less ambiguous, is what we have in mind. A mechanical assembly language that works with such descriptions is on the critical path toward economically viable robot systems.

Our short-range goal, then, is to do something about creating such a language. Indeed, this paper is about **LAMA**, an acronym for Language for Automatic Mechanical Assembly.

The translation between what the human foreman-programmer describes and what the manipulator controller wants, in our design, is to take place in two steps:

■   First, the human's *Assembly Description*, with many missing details, is converted into an *Assembly Plan*, which has the gaps filled in, but remains very high level. A very verbose and careful human's assembly decription would differ only slightly or not at all from the assembly plan.

■   Second, the *Assembly Plan* is converted into a *Manipulator Program*, with things worked out to the level of coordinates, trajectories, forces, and torques. This conversion requires, in part, a *pick and place* phase and a *feedback strategy* phase.

The pick and place phase converts the assembly plan into a program that assumes ideal position information and positioning accuracy. It must specify the manipulator motions that achieve the desired relationships between the parts. Both of these assumptions are untenable. The role of feedback planning is to expand skeleton programs embodying feedback strategies to carry out the assembly operations taking into account the imperfection of the data and the positioning errors in the manipulator. The resulting program is the desired *manipulator program.*

The *pick and place* and *feedback strategy* phases have been examined in detail and prototype programs have been implemented that do these jobs [Lozano-Perez 1976]. Here, we will focus on the phase dealing with feedback strategy.

First, however, we survey of some of the decisions that must be made when specifying an automatic mechanical assembly in general. We also give a more complete overview of the design of an overall system. Three basic themes underlie the design:

■   High level assembly operations can be represented by program plans (called *skeletons*) which can be expanded as required by using facts about the specific task at hand.

■   The desired effect of the basic manipulator motions can be described in terms of a few geometrical and spatial relations. We believe that the assembly problem can be seen as the problem of achieving a certain set of geometrical relations between objects while avoiding unwanted collisions.

■   Choices for location and motion parameters should be
      made by identifying all the constraints on the solution,
      finding a range of values in which the solution may lie
      and picking an element from that range.

Now let us highlight the difficulties of programming
assembly operations by examining a particular assembly task in
some detail.

Figure 1 shows the piston subassembly from a model
aircraft engine. We will use it to emphasize the number and
complexity of the decisions to be made in planning an assembly.
The assembly has been carried out using the Silver robot
manipulator at the MIT Artificial Intelligence Laboratory [Silver
1973]. This manipulator is not a fully general position and
orientation generator because it has only five degrees of freedom,
not six. They are divided in the following manner: (1) an xy
table, (2) a wrist which can displace and rotate along the z axis
and (3) a vise which rotates about the x axis (see figure 2). The
manipulator is equipped with a force sensing wrist capable of
resolving the xyz components of the forces and torques acting on
the wrist. This allows the manipulator to generate and detect
forces. The use of force feedback enables the Silver Robot
System to perform precise assembly tasks whose critical
clearances are below its positional accuracy [Inoue 1974].

The hard part of this engine subassembly is inserting the
piston-pin through the piston pin-hole *and* through the
piston-rod. The obvious way to do this (for a human) is to line
up the holes in the piston-rod and the piston and then push the
piston-pin through both holes. This operation is impossible
using the manipulator configuration we have described. Recall
we only have two sets of parallel fingers available; one set is the
hand, the other the vise. This restriction forces us to break the
problem up into three parts.

First the pin is inserted partway into the piston. Then
the piston-rod's pin-end can be placed onto the pin inside the

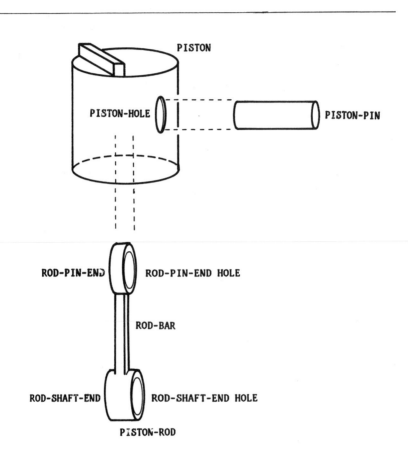

Figure 1. The piston sub-assembly.

piston. And finally, the pin pushed through the rod and the piston-hole.

This *description* of the piston assembly simply specifies three snapshots of the system state. Each state is specified in terms of the spatial relations between the parts involved. The verbs used in the description (insert, place and push) give some

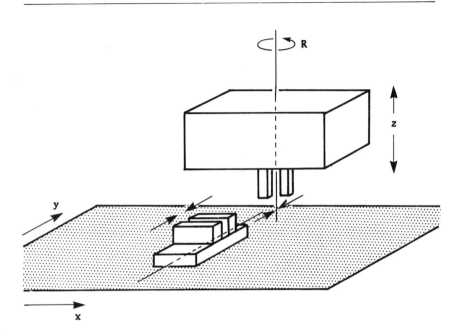

Figure 2. Diagram of Little Robot System, see [Silver 1973].

information as to the nature of the operation necessary to achieve each state. Note that no mention was made of the manipulator. The constraint that only one hand and a vise are available dictates the nature of the solution, but the manipulator motions necessary to carry out the solution are not specified, nor are they obvious.

The assembly can be carried out by first placing the pin in the vise such that its main axis is horizontal (figure 3a). Then the piston can be placed on the pin so that the cavity is facing upward. The rod can then be placed on the portion of pin that is projecting into the piston's cavity (figure 3b). The

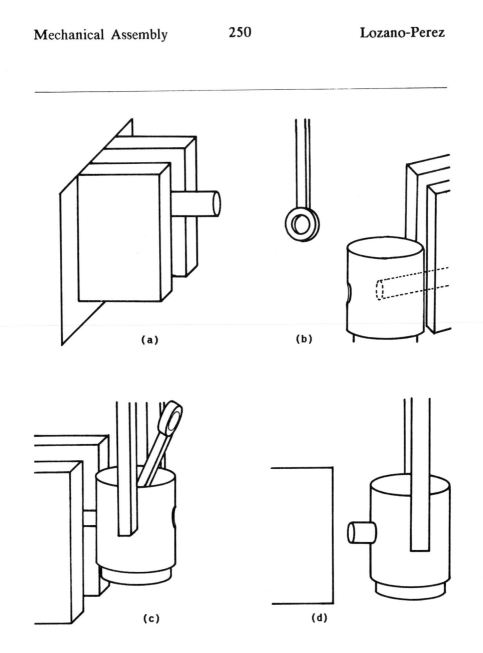

(a)   (b)

(c)   (d)

Figure 3. Steps in the assembly of the piston.

manipulator can then grasp the piston, remove the piston from the vise, and after closing the vise, push the part of the pin protruding from the piston against the vise. We call this the *assembly plan*.

For each operation in the assembly plan, the *manipulator program* must specify the position and orientation of the fingers such that they can securely grasp some part of the object to be moved. The program must also specify a trajectory for the manipulator that is not likely to damage the manipulator or disturb any of the other parts.

The assembly description and the assembly plan mention only the spatial relationships that must hold between the parts in the goal state. These relationships involve much greater positional accuracy than is directly achievable by the manipulator to be used. These relationships can be achieved by employing force feedback techniques such as those described in Inoue [1974].

Inoue has developed a program which, driven by force feedback, does peg-in-hole insertion. Unfortunately, his program cannot be used directly in the task at hand. Inoue's program assumes that the motions of the hand correspond directly to motions of the hole. The assembly plan described above specifies that the piston-rod be held at the opposite end from the point of insertion. This is because the insertion is happening *inside* the piston. Inoue's program must be changed to account for this.

Like most programs, Inoue's has parameters. The length of certain motions and the magnitude of some forces are not specified. These parameters must be specified for the task at hand.

Inoue's program also lacks error detection capabilities. When the manipulator is told to move in a given direction until a force above some threshold is felt, no position bounds are specified. This can give rise to severe errors.

These considerations point to one, very important, conclusion: Inoue's program is not so much a general utility program as a specification of an assembly strategy to be adapted to many different geometric environments. This is true of most manipulator programs because of their dependence on assumptions about the geometry of the task.

Let us summarize the problems to be faced in specifying an assembly operation.

■   Describe the objects to be assembled.

■   Specify a plan for the assembly. The details of the plan will depend on the manipulator configuration available and on the capabilities of the assembly system.

■   Determine the grasping position and orientation for the objects involved in each operation.

■   Determine a collision-free path between the origin and destination of all motions.

■   Tailor the assembly strategies to fit the particular geometric environment. This involves providing parameters to the strategies.

■   Examine the strategies for likely errors and determine the actions to be taken in case of failure.

The current implementation of **LAMA** has focused on a subset of these problems. The most important are grasping, tailoring assembly strategies, and error prediction.

Computing a grasp point on an object from a description of the object and its surrounding environment is a very difficult computational problem. The basic mechanism needed to solve the problem is the ability to detect that attempting to grasp some part of the object will cause a collision. This involves computing the geometric intersection of the solids making up the manipulator description with the object to be grasped and with any nearby object. A non-null intersection indicates a collision. A simple approach to solving this problem would be to guess a grasp point and then test whether it is safe. Typically there is an infinite number of possibilities and the challenge is to choose a grasp point with some confidence that it is a *good* choice. Trial and error methods are unsatisfactory in this context because not only do they have very poor worst-case behavior but once a result is found, it is very difficult to evaluate it without knowing the alternatives. Our approach to grasping relies on describing the range of possible grasp points as a few sets of parameterized grasp positions which can be evaluated and compared as units.

We pointed out the dependence of manipulator programs on the particular geometry they were designed for. A useful mechanical assembly system must have some means of representing assembly strategies that does not make too many assumptions about the environment where they are to be used. Our approach to making the strategies as general as possible is to have each of the steps in the strategy be essentially a goal statement. Each operation is decribed in terms of the geometric relations it is meant to achieve in a coordinate system specified by the strategy. The assembly strategies can then be adapted to a particular situation by computing the parameters needed to achieve the goal of the individual steps of the strategy.

Once we have available a description of the goal of each step, then some errors can be predicted by simulating the operations, taking into account some of the uncertainty in the positions of objects. These error predictions can be used to solicit corrective actions from the user.

Next we describe in more detail how the assembly strategies are used.

The LAMA System

In particular, we now describe how we believe the piston assembly will be processed by **LAMA** when it is completely implemented. Prototype programs currently exist to do parts description, the pick and place phase and a simple feedback strategy phase. No program exists to do the assembly planning.

The parts to be assembled must first be described to the system. The user uses the system interactively to define models of the parts. Complex objects are described as unions of a few kinds of primitive object types. The primitive objects currently available in implemented parts of **LAMA** are a cuboid and a cylinder (both as solids and holes).

Figure 4 shows a schematic description of the models for

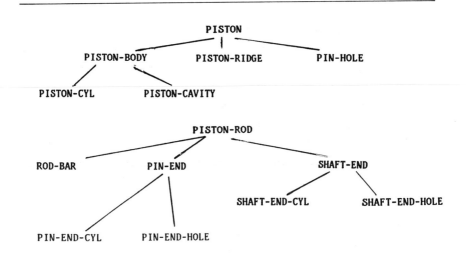

Figure 4. Parts descriptions for piston sub-assembly.

the parts in the piston assembly. Note that the parts are arranged hierarchically. This allows a convenient treatment of subparts of objects. Any desired subpart can be represented as a node in the part model tree. Each node has information regarding the size, type and relative position of the subpart. All the subparts, including the holes, are approximated as rectangular or octagonal right prisms. This provides a uniform internal representation for all the object types. This representation simplifies the definitions of the spatial modelling operations. By generalizing to polyhedra the desired volumes can be approximated to any required accuracy.

The next step is that of describing the assembly. Ideally, we would like to specify the assembly process by simply describing the completed assembly. A more realistic goal is that of accepting assembly instructions similar to those given to people, as discussed.

The assembly description for the piston assembly is shown in figure 5. The assembly description specifies only that

---

```
(INSERT OBJ1: [PISTON-PIN]
        OBJ2: [PISTON PIN-HOLE]
        SUCH-THAT: (PARTLY (FITS-IN OBJ1 OBJ2)))
(INSERT OBJ1: [PISTON-PIN]
        OBJ2: [ROD SMALL-END-HOLE])
(PUSH-INTO OBJ1: [PISTON-PIN]
        OBJ2: (AND [PISTON PIN-HOLE]
                   [PISTON-ROD SMALL-END]))
```

Figure 5. Initial assembly description for the piston assembly.

---

operations, such as insertion, are to be performed on the parts. The individual operations are often underspecified. Parameters are missing or only weakly constrained, for example, insert the pin *partway* into the piston. No mention is made of the manipulator or of the strategies to be used to carry out the operations. Merely saying *insert* is not enough to specify an assembly operation. The actual motions carried out are sensitive to the shape and relative sizes of the parts.

The first step in the transformation from user input to manipulator program is to completely specify the assembly description. This is the task of the Assembly Planner. It must first introduce into the description those operations that will achieve the prerequisites of the operations in the initial description. This requires specification of some high level manipulator commands such as GRASP, UNGRASP and PLACE. Then the operations must be completely specified and strategy choices made for them. The end result of this process is an assembly plan. In this plan each operation is fully specified and the positions and orientations of the parts involved are well constrained. An important point to note is that the plan still does not *determine* the manipulator motions necessary to carry out the assembly. The assembly plan corresponding to the assembly description in figure 5 is shown in figure 6.

```
(GRASP OBJ: [PISTON-PIN])
(PLACE-IN-VISE OBJ: [PISTON-PIN]
                SUCH-THAT:
                    (PARALLEL [PISTON-PIN] [TABLE]))
(UNGRASP OBJ: [PISTON-PIN])
(GRASP OBJ: [PISTON]
         SUCH-THAT: (FACING+ ([PISTON] TOP) DOWN))
(INSERT OBJ1: [PISTON-PIN]
         OBJ2: [PISTON PIN-HOLE]
         SUCH-THAT: (PARTLY (FITS-IN OBJ1 OBJ2) 0.25))
(UNGRASP OBJ: [PISTON])
(GRASP OBJ: [PISTON-ROD]
         SUCH-THAT: (FACING+ ([ROD-BAR] TOP) UP))
(INSERT OBJ1: [PISTON-PIN]
         OBJ2: [PISTON-ROD SMALL-END-HOLE])
(UNGRASP OBJ: [PISTON-ROD])
(GRASP OBJ: [PISTON])
(REMOVE-FROM-VISE OBJ: [PISTON])
(PUSH-INTO OBJ: [PISTON-PIN]
            SUCH-THAT:
               (AND (FITS-IN [PISTON-PIN]
                            [PISTON PIN-HOLE])
                    (FITS-IN [PISTON-PIN]
                            [PISTON-ROD SMALL-END]))))

(UNGRASP OBJ: [PISTON])
```

Figure 6. Assembly plan for the piston assembly.

The current implementation assumes that the Assembly Plan is directly available as an input to the system. We can then focus on the process of transforming an assembly plan into a manipulator program.

Once the assembly plan has been fully specified, a detailed pick and place computation can be carried out. This will determine precisely where the objects are to be grasped and what paths they must follow to avoid collisions. Unfortunately, the Pick and Place computation is not independent of the nature of the assembly strategies. Where the object is grasped and where it is placed prior to an operation depends on the details of the operation. The solution is to do the grasp computation at the initial position of the object to be moved, before the operation is instantiated. This determines the range of possible grasp points. After this, the assembly step is expanded. The instantiation process places additional constraints on both the initial position of the part and its grasp point. Then, an exact grasp point is chosen and the path computed *after* the operation has been expanded.

The pick and place computation exercises most of the spatial expertise of the system. The basic operation in both grasping and collision avoidance is detecting the possibility of a collision by intersecting volumes. In finding a collision-free trajectory we are interested in whether the volume swept out, by the manipulator and the object it carries, collides with other objects in the workspace. Similarly, in grasping we are interested in the locations on the object where the hand can be placed such that no collisions will result. Since there is a whole range of grasping positions for a given object, this amounts to intersecting the volume of the hand, swept out over the possible grasping positions, with the workspace.

We have characterized the types of grasping positions for the primitive objects as a series of *grasp sets*. Grasp sets are parameterized ranges of hand positions over a surface of the object. Figure 7 shows a graphical representation of the grasp sets for cuboids and cylinders. Complex objects are analyzed by considering how to grasp each of their component objects while taking into account the interactions with other parts of the object as well as with the rest of the environment.

Figure 8 shows the system's representation for the *peg-in-hole insertion* strategy. It is very similar to the program presented in Inoue [1974]. The Feedback Strategy phase simulates this *skeleton program*, predicts contacts and estimates the direction and magnitude of the forces that will be produced.

Note that each step in the skeleton program is annotated by the geometric relations it generates between the manipulated parts. This information can be used in two ways:

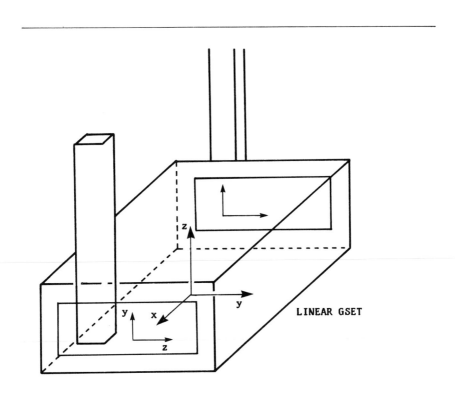

Figure 7. The grasp sets.

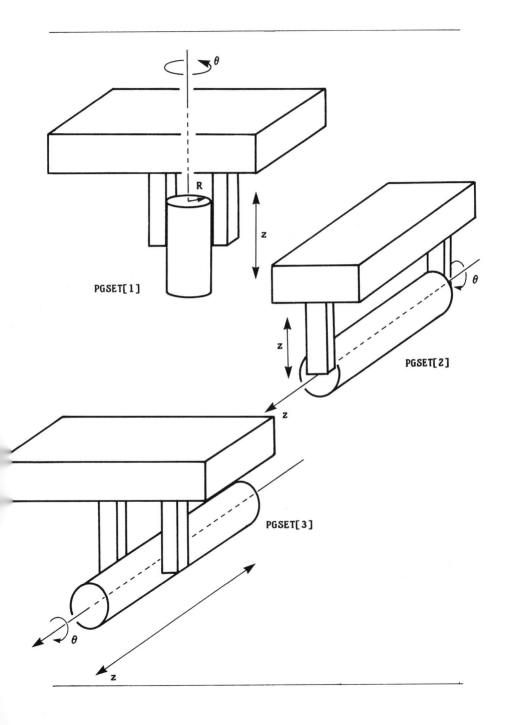

PGSET[1]

PGSET[2]

PGSET[3]

■   To generate numerical values for parameters in the programs. For example, the size of the shift in the y direction in the DROP-INTO operation can be determined by examining the geometrical relations it is meant to achieve.

■   To generate tests for likely failure situations given the particular execution environment. A good example of this is the operation of moving the piston-rod near the piston-pin for the insertion of the rod's pin-end onto the pin inside the piston. By examining the clearance between the tip of the pin and the piston wall given the errors in grasping and positioning, we can predict that sometimes the rod will contact either the pin or the piston. A test for this situation can be generated and instructions as to corrective action could be solicited from the user.

The Feedback Strategy Phase

The result of the operation of the Feedback Strategy phase is a manipulator program. Let us consider the operation of the Feedback Strategy phase during the expansion of the PEG-IN-HOLE operation in which the piston-rod is to be inserted onto the piston-pin, while the pin is inside the piston. A preliminary implementation currently exists of the program that does the simple code generation shown here.

The assembly plan (figure 6) has the following entries for the operation of inserting the piston-rod on the piston-pin:

```
(GRASP OBJ : [PISTON-ROD]
      SUCH-THAT : (FACING+ ([ROD-BAR] TOP) UP))

(INSERT OBJ1 : [PISTON-PIN]
       OBJ2 : [PISTON-ROD PIN-END-HOLE])

(UNGRASP OBJ : [PISTON-ROD])
```

We must first find a grasp point on the piston-rod. There are two possible grasp positions on the rod; one along the sides of the piston-rod's pin-end, the other on the flat ends. The choice will depend on two factors: (1) flat surfaces are preferred to curved surfaces and (2) possible collisions. Collisions are predicted by simulating the assembly operations while assuming the hand can be at both of the legal grasp positions. The Feedback Strategy phase can then consider the effects on each of the grasp ranges simultaneously.

The first task in expanding an assembly strategy is to select the local reference system. The REFERENCE statement in PEG-IN-HOLE indicates that the reference frame's x axis is ALIGNED&CENTERED with the HOLE's front face. This leaves one rotational degree of freedom unspecified. The current system always tries to line up unspecified degrees of freedom in the reference with global axes. In this case, the reference's z is aligned to the global z.

The INITIAL statement specifies the constraints on the initial position of the parts. In PEG-IN-HOLE it specifies that the HOLE and the PEG be ALIGNED&CENTERED and IN-FRONT-OF each other. Figure 9a shows a top view of the interaction volume of the piston-rod's pin end and indicates the intersection of that volume with that of the piston. The intersection divides the range of legal positions into two ranges on either side of the piston wall. The current system chooses to use the range where the objects are closer to each other as the range of legal positions of the piston-rod.

The first step in the DROP-INTO strategy calls for the object

```
(STRATEGY
 PEG-IN-HOLE (PEG HOLE)
 (TYPE (PEG CYL) (HOLE CYL-HOLE))
 (REFERENCE (ALIGNED&CENTERED (REFERENCE X)
                              (HOLE FRONT)))
 (PRE-REQS (CLEARANCE < 0.01))
 (INITIAL (AND (ALIGNED&CENTERED (PEG FRONT)
                                 (HOLE FRONT))
               (IN-FRONT-OF PEG HOLE)))
 (DROP : (DROP-INTO PEG HOLE)
  SUCH-THAT (PARTLY (FITS-IN PEG HOLE)))
 (MATE : (MATE PEG HOLE)
  SUCH-THAT (ALIGNED- PEG HOLE))
 (INSERT : (PUSH-INTO PEG HOLE)
  SUCH-THAT (FITS-IN PEG HOLE)))

(STRATEGY
 DROP-INTO (PEG HOLE)
 (ROTATE : (CHANGE R BY 0.1)
  SUCH-THAT (ALMOST (ALIGNED- PEG HOLE) 0.1))
 (SHIFT : (CHANGE Y)
  SUCH-THAT (LEFT-OF (PEG CENTER) (HOLE CENTER)))
 (LANDING : (CHANGE X)
  SUCH-THAT (CONTACT (PEG FRONT) (HOLE FRONT))))

(STRATEGY
 MATE (PEG HOLE)
 (EDGE+ : (CHANGE Z)
  SUCH-THAT (AND (ABOVE (PEG CENTER) (HOLE CENTER))
                 (CONTACT PEG (HOLE SIDE))))
 (SAVE1 : (SETQ Z1 ZPOS))
 (EDGE- : (CHANGE Z)
  SUCH-THAT (AND (BELOW (PEG CENTER) (HOLE CENTER))
                 (CONTACT PEG (HOLE SIDE))))
 (SAVE2 : (SETQ Z2 ZPOS))
 (CENTER : (MOVE Z)
  SUCH-THAT (BETWEEN (PEG CENTER) Z1 Z2))
 (CONTACT : (CHANGE Y)
  SUCH-THAT (CONTACT PEG (HOLE SIDE)))
 (MATE : (CHANGE R WITH
               (AND (ZFORCE = 0.)
                    (YFORCE = "MAINTAIN-CONTACT")))
  SUCH-THAT (ALIGNED- PEG HOLE)))

(STRATEGY
 PUSH-INTO (PEG HOLE)
 (PUSH : (CHANGE X WITH (AND (YFORCE = 0.)
                            (ZFORCE = 0.)))
  SUCH-THAT (FITS-IN PEG HOLE)))
```

Figure 8. Peg-in-hole strategy. The representation of Inoue's peg-in-hole insertion strategy in LAMA.

in the hand to be rotated 0.1 radians. The Feedback Strategy phase must establish that this rotation will not have any bad effects. This is done by simulating the motion. In this case, contacts with the pin and/or the piston are possible. These accidental contacts determine that the force parameter be *"detect-contact"* and that an error should be generated if the termination condition indicates a contact. The code that does this is shown here:

```
(CHANGE R BY 0.1 WHILE (RFORCE < "detect-contact"))
(COND ((CONTACT? R 0.0 0.1) (ERROR)))
```

At this point the user is asked about the likelihood and seriousness of the predicted error. The user can choose to ignore the error condition.

The next step involves a shift in the y position of the rod so as to place the hole to the left of the pin. The motion is constrained as follows:

- Hole's center LEFT-OF Peg's center: This restriction is placed on the displacement operation itself. Figure 9b shows (in dashed lines) the volume taken up by the piston-rod over the range of positions consistent with this relation.

- Hole CONTACT Peg: This restriction is imposed by the next operation in which the rod is moved along x until contact is achieved. Thus the rod's position for the shift in y is also constrained so as to allow the contact to happen. This is equivalent to constraining the position of the rod's pin-end-hole to OVERLAP in y that of the piston-pin's front face. Figure 9b shows (in solid lines) the volume of the rod over the range of positions consistent with this relation.

A position consistent with both of these relations is obtained by computing the range of values of the position parameters that satisfy each relation and then intersecting the ranges. Figure 9b shows a graphical representation of the ranges and their intersection.

A simulation of the motions shows that the rod can come in contact with the pin and with the inside of the piston (figure 9c). These contacts cannot always be avoided by adjusting the starting position of the piston-rod and so they must be expected to happen. This dictates that the force threshold be *"detect-contact"*. The distance parameter of the motion is chosen as the midpoint of the range of legal displacements (indicated by *'y'*). This choice is quite arbitrary. The conditional statement after the motion merely tests whether the contact occurred. The

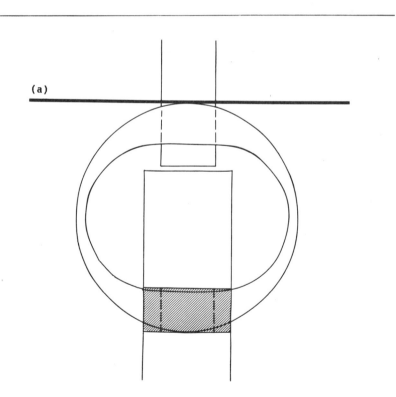

(a)

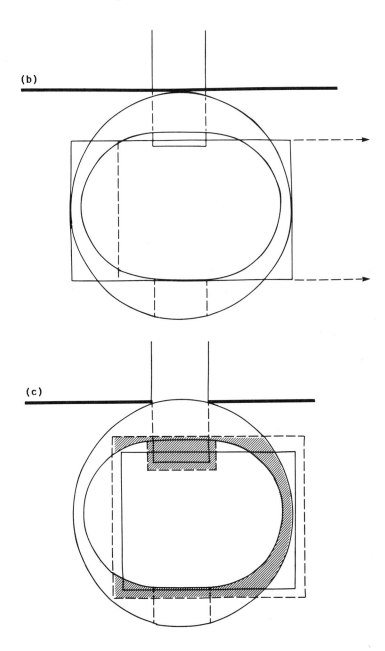

Figure 9. The position ranges for the piston-rod insertion

user is again given the option to ignore the contact if it happens. In this case that is the best course. The code generated is:

```
(CHANGE Y BY "y" WHILE (YFORCE < "detect-contact"))
(COND ((CONTACT? Y 0.0 "y") (ERROR)))
```

After the shift operation, the landing step is simulated. A contact can always be achieved, but there is a region of uncertainty where contact with the inside of the piston is possible before contact with the pin. The contact is ambiguous, so the error cannot be detected by using the location of the contact. The code generated simply makes sure that the contact is in fact detected. The displacement used in the motion is the displacement necessary to go past the last possible contact with the piston-pin and collide unambiguously with the piston wall.

```
(CHANGE X BY "x" WHILE (XFORCE < "detect-contact"))
(COND ((CONTACT? X 0.0 "x")) (T (ERROR)))
```

This completes the DROP-INTO operation. The complete program can be seen in figure 10.

The next step is to compute a path from the position where the piston-rod is first grasped to that where the INSERT is to happen. A straight line path to this position is not possible since it implies going through the piston. The collision avoidance routine generates a path that goes above the piston and moves down to the desired position.

Relation to other Work

The problem of construction planning has been very important in the study of problem solving. During the last three or four years several programs have been developed to do construction planning in the Blocks World domain. Fahlman's [1973] BUILD is expert in planning Blocks World assemblies. The programs of Sussman and Sacerdoti have explored general issues of planning

```
(STRATEGY
  DROP-INTO (PEG HOLE)
  (ROTATE : (CHANGE R BY 0.1)
   SUCH-THAT (ALMOST (ALIGNED- PEG HOLE) 0.1))
  (SHIFT : (CHANGE Y)
   SUCH-THAT (LEFT-OF (PEG CENTER) (HOLE CENTER)))
  (LANDING : (CHANGE X)
   SUCH-THAT (CONTACT (PEG FRONT) (HOLE FRONT))))

(DEFUN
  DROP-INTO (PEG HOLE)
  (CHANGE R BY 0.1 while (rforce < "detect-contact"))
  (cond ((contact?) (error?)))
  (CHANGE Y by "y" while (yforce < "detect-contact"))
  (cond ((contact?) (error?)))
  (CHANGE X by "x" while (xforce < "detect-contact"))
  (cond ((contact?)) (t (error?))))
```

Figure 10. DROP-INTO strategy and its expansion into LAMA. The text in italics indicates the parts generated by the Feedback Strategy phase.

and debugging in the context of assembly problems. Sussman [1973] treated assemblies of blocks exclusively while Sacerdoti [1975] has also considered the assembly (and disassembly) of a water pump.

Of these programs, only BUILD considered the issues of stability, contact, etc., which are vital to the process of mechanical assembly. But even BUILD, being limited to block structures could ignore most of the problems of spatial interactions. BUILD also ignored the manipulation aspect of the construction. Sacerdoti's planning system NOAH in SRI's Computer Based Consultant project avoids all these problems because it assumes a human as the manipulator. The work on LAMA has focussed on the problems introduced by more realistic objects and the errors of a real manipulator.

The approach taken in LAMA to assembly strategies was influenced principally by the work of Sussman [1973] and

Goldstein [1974] in debugging programs. They both stressed the usefulness of having a statement of purpose for each operation in a program. The elegant method of Ambler and Popplestone [1971] for computing the position and orientation of objects given relations such as AGAINST and FITS-IN provided some of the key ideas on how to describe the goals of strategy steps.

There are, at least, five other projects that have direct relevance to the task of building an automatic mechanical system. These projects are being conducted by the IBM Thomas J. Watson Research Center, the Stanford AI Laboratory, the Stanford Research Institute, the University of Edinburgh, and the C. S. Draper Laboratory.

The IBM system design, AUTOPASS [Lieberman and Wesley 1975], is closest to LAMA. It is to be imbedded in PL/I and will provide the user with a selection of high level assembly operations, the most general being a PLACE command in which the destination is specified as geometric relations between objects.

The Stanford system, AL [Finkel et al. 1974], is a complex ALGOL-like language with many new data-structure and control primitives. The design includes a Very High Level Language capability. Both AL and AUTOPASS, as well as LAMA, rely to a large extent on modeling the effect on the world of the assembly operations.

Russell Taylor in his dissertation [1976] develops mechanisms to predict errors in location values from the AL planning model and uses this information to generate AL code automatically. He also introduces skeleton programs or strategies which describe and summarize the coding decisions that have to be made. The semantics for the strategies are fixed at system creation time.

The goal of all these systems is to expand a task-level description into an program for a specific manipulator. LAMA shares many of the ideas and the approaches of both AL and AUTOPASS. LAMA differs mainly in that it allows user-defined assembly strategies to be manipulated by the system. The key idea is to allow the specification of strategies to be independent of the operations performed by the system.

The Edinburgh group [Ambler *et al*. 1974] has worked on the problem of assembling an object whose parts must be visually located and pulled out of a heap. An early speculative paper from their group [Popplestone 1971] anticipated many of the ideas and approaches adopted in this research, even to the choice of a model aircraft engine as the example.

The Draper Lab [Nevins *et al*. 1975] group has investigated direct applicability of a mechanical assembly system in the short range. This has led to emphasis on the type of capabilities that can be made available on a minicomputer. They have also carried out extensive theoretical analysis of the requirements of assemblies in terms of manipulator design and control as well as assembly strategies.

Work being pursued at the Stanford Research Institute on Advanced Automation [Rosen *et al*. 1976] has taken a direction similar to that taken by the Draper Lab. SRI has focussed on mechanical assembly techniques with industrial potential in the short range.

References

A. P. Ambler and R. J. Popplestone, *Inferring the Positions of Bodies from Specified Spatial Relationships*, AISB Summer Conference, University of Sussex, 1974.

A. P. Ambler *et al*., "A Versatile System for Computer Controlled Assembly," *Artificial Intelligence*, Vol. 6, No. 2, 1975.

S. E. Fahlman, "A Planning System for Robot Construction Tasks," *Artificial Intelligence*, Vol. 6, No. 2, 1975, also MIT AI Laboratory TR-283, 1973.

R. Finkel, R. Taylor, R. Bolles, R. Paul, and J. Feldman, *AL, A Programming System for Automation*, Stanford AI Laboratory Memo 177, 1974.

I. P. Goldstein, "Understanding Simple Picture Programs," *Artificial Intelligence*, Vol. 6, No. 3, 1975, also MIT AI Laboratory TR-294, 1974.

H. Inoue, *Force Feedback in Precise Assembly Tasks*, MIT AI Laboratory Memo 308, 1974.

L. I. Lieberman and M. A. Wesley, *AUTOPASS, A Very High Level Programming Language for Mechanical Assembler System*, IBM Research Report RC-5599, 1975.

T. Lozano-Perez, *The Design of a Mechanical Assembly System*, MIT AI Laboratory TR-397, 1976.

J. L. Nevins *et al.*, *Exploratory Research in Industrial Modular Assembly*, Charles Stark Draper Laboratory, NSF Report covering December 1974 to August 1975.

R. J. Popplestone, *How Could FREDDY Put Things Together*, Dept. of Machine Intelligence and Perception, University of Edinburgh, Memo MIP-R-88, 1971.

C. Rosen *et al.*, *Exploratory Research in Advanced Automation*, Stanford Research Institute, NSF Report, 1976.

E. D. Sacerdoti, *A Structure for Plans and Behavior*, Stanford Research Institute Artificial Intelligence Center Technical Note 109, 1975.

D. Silver, *The Little Robot System*, MIT AI Laboratory Memo 273, 1973.

G. J. Sussman, *A Computer Model of Skill Acquisition*, MIT AI Laboratory TR-297, 1973.

R. H. Taylor, *A Synthesis of Manipulator Control Programs From*

Task-Level Specifications, Stanford AI Laboratory Memo 282, 1976.

The complete version of this paper is in *Proceedings of the Fifth International Joint Conference on Artificial Intelligence*, Cambridge, Massachusetts, 1977.

KINEMATICS, STATICS, AND DYNAMICS OF TWO-DIMENSIONAL MANIPULATORS

BERTHOLD K. P. HORN

In order to get some feeling for the kinematics, statics, and dynamics of manipulators, it is useful to separate visualization of linkages in three-space from basic mechanics. The general-purpose two-dimensional manipulator is analyzed in this paper in order to gain a basic understanding of the mechanics issues without encumbrance from the complications of three-dimensional geometry.

Introduction

Kinematics deals with the basic geometry of the linkages. If we consider an articulated manipulator as a device for generating position and orientation, we need to know the relationships between these quantities and the joint variables, since it is the latter that we can easily measure and control. Position here refers to the position in space of the tip of the device, while orientation refers to the direction of approach of the last link. While position is fairly easy to understand in spaces of higher dimensionality, rotation or orientation rapidly becomes more complex. This is the main impetus for our study of two-dimensional devices. In two dimensions, two degrees of freedom are required to generate arbitrary positions in a given work space and one more is needed to control the orientation of the last link.

The device studied in detail has only two joints and so can be used as a position generator. A three-link device is a general-purpose two-dimensional device that can generate orientation as well.

It will become apparent that the calculation of position and orientation of the last link given the joint variables is straightforward, while the inverse calculation is hard and may be intractable for devices with many links that have not been designed properly. The calculation of joint angles given desired position and orientation is vital if around or follow a given trajectory.

If a manipulator has just enough degrees of freedom to cover its work space, there will in general be a finite number of ways of reaching a given position and orientation. This is because the inverse problem essentially corresponds to solving a number of equations in an equal number of unknowns. If the equations were linear we would expect exactly one solution. Since they are trigonometric polynomials in the joint variables -- and hence nonlinear -- we expect a finite number of solutions. Similarly, if we have too few joints, there will in general be no solution, while with too many joints we expect an infinite number of ways of reaching a given position and orientation. Usually there are some arm configurations that present special problems because the equations become singular. These often occur on the boundary of the work space, where some of the links become parallel.

Statics deals with the balance of forces and torques required when the device does not move. If we consider an articulated manipulator as a device for applying forces and torques to objects being manipulated, we need to know the relationship between these quantities and the joint torques, since it is the latter that we either directly control or can at least measure. In two dimensions, two degrees of freedom will be required to apply an arbitrary force at the tip of the device and one more if we want to control torque applied to the object as well.

Clearly then the two-link device to be discussed can be thought of as a force generator, while the three-link device can apply controlled torques as well. The gravity loading of the links has to be compensated for as well and fortunately it can be considered separately from the torques required to produce tip forces and torques.

Dynamics deals with the manipulator in motion. It will be seen that the joint torques control the angular accelerations. The relationships are not direct however. First of all, the sensitivity of a given joint to torque varies with the arm configuration; secondly, forces appear that are functions of the products of the angular velocities; and thirdly there is considerable coupling between the motions of the links. The velocity product terms can be thought of as generalized centrifugal forces.

The equations relating joint accelerations to joint torques are nonlinear, but given the arm state -- that is both joint variables and their rate of change with time -- it is straightforward to calculate what joint torques are required to achieve given angular accelerations. We can, in other words, calculate the time-history of motor torques for each joint required to cause the arm to follow a given trajectory.

Notice that this is an open-loop dead-reckoning approach which in practice has to be modified to take into account friction and small errors in estimating the numerical constant in the sensitivity matrix. The modification can take the form of a small amount of compensating feedback.

This, however, should not be confused with the more traditional, analog servo methods which position-controls each joint independently. Since the dynamic state of the manipulator is a global property, one cannot expect general success using local, joint independent position-control.

To summarize: we will deal with unconstrained motion of the manipulator as it follows some trajectory as well as its interaction with parts that mechanically constrain its motion. Both aspects of manipulator operation are of importance if it is to be used to assemble or disassemble artifacts.

Two-link Manipulator Kinematics

In two dimensions one clearly needs two degrees of freedom to reach an arbitrary point within a given work space. Let us first study a simple two-link manipulator with rotational joints. Note that the geometry of the two-link device occurs as a subproblem in many of the more complicated manipulators. Given the two joint angles, let us calculate the position of the tip of the device. Define vectors corresponding to the two links:

$$\underline{r}_1 = l_1 \; [\cos(\theta_1), \sin(\theta_1)]$$
$$\underline{r}_2 = l_2 \; [\cos(\theta_1 + \theta_2), \sin(\theta_1 + \theta_2)]$$

The the position of the tip $\underline{r}$ can be found simply by vector addition.

$$x = l_1 \; \cos(\theta_1) + l_2 \; \cos(\theta_1 + \theta_2)$$
$$y = l_1 \; \sin(\theta_1) + l_2 \; \cos(\theta_1 + \theta_2)$$

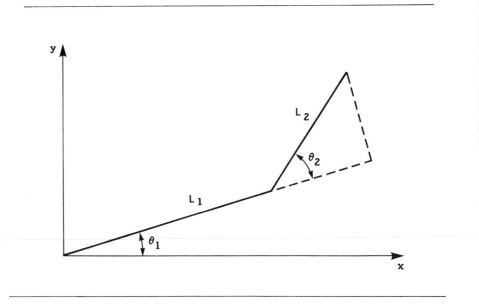

This can be expanded into a slightly more useful form:

$$x = [l_1 + l_2 \cos(\theta_2)] \cos(\theta_1) - l_2 \sin(\theta_2) \sin(\theta_1)$$
$$y = [l_1 + l_2 \cos(\theta_2)] \sin(\theta_1) - l_2 \sin(\theta_2) \cos(\theta_1)$$

The Inverse Problem

While the forward calculation of tip position from joint angles is always relatively straightforward, the inversion is intractable for manipulators with more than a few links unless the device has been specially designed with this problem in mind. For our simple device we easily get:

$$\cos(\theta_2) = \frac{(x^2 + y^2) - (l_1^2 + l_2^2)}{2 \, l_1 \, l_2}$$

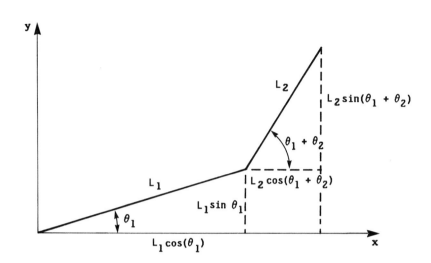

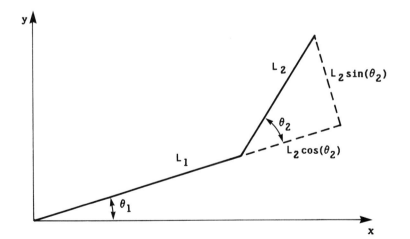

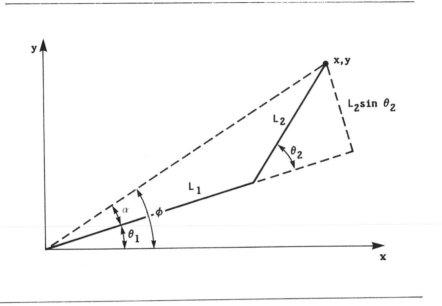

There will be two solutions for θ_2 of equal magnitude and opposite sign. Expanding $\tan(\theta_1) = \tan(\theta - \alpha)$ and using $\tan(\theta) = y/x$ we also arrive at:

$$\tan(\theta_1) = \frac{-l_2 \sin(\theta_2)\, x + [l_1 + l_2 \cos(\theta_2)]y}{l_2 \sin(\theta_2)\, y + [l_1 + l_2 \cos(\theta_2)]x}$$

The reason this was so easy is that we happened to have already derived all the most useful formula using geometric and trigonometric reasoning. A method of more general utility depends on algebraic manipulation of the expressions for the coordinates of the tip. Notice that these expressions are polynomials in the sines and cosines of the joint angles. Such systems of polynomials can be solved systematically -- unfortunately the degree of the intermediate terms grows explosively as more and more variables are eliminated. So this method, while quite general, is in practice limited to solving only simple linkages.

The Work Space

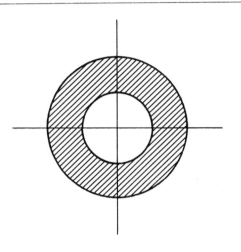

$$(l_1 - l_2)^2 \le l_1^2 + 2\, l_1\, l_2\, \cos(\theta_2) + l_2^2 \le (l_1 + l_2)^2$$

So:

$$|l_1 - l_2| \le \sqrt{x^2 + y^2} \le |l_1 + l_2|$$

The set of points reachable by the tip of the device is an annulus centered on the origin. Notice that points on the boundary of this region can be reached in one way, while points inside can be reached in two. The width of the annulus is twice the length of the shorter link and its average radius equals the length of the longer one.

When $l_1 = l_2 = l$ say, the work space becomes simpler, just a circle. The origin is a singular point in that it can be reached in an infinite number of ways since θ_1 can be chosen

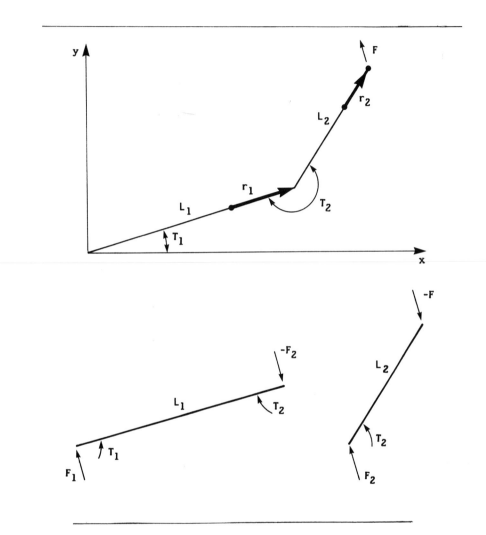

freely.

Statics

So far we have thought of the manipulator as a device for
placing the tip in any desired position within the work space --
that is, a position generator. Equally important is the device's

ability to exert forces on objects. Let us assume that the manipulator does not move appreciably when used in this way so that we can ignore torques and forces used to accelerate the links. Initially we will also ignore gravity; we will later calculate the additional torques required to balance gravity components.

We have direct control over the torques T_1 and T_2 generated by the motors driving the joints. What forces are produced by these torques at the tip? Since we do not want the device to move, imagine its tip pinned in place. Let the force exerted by the tip on the pin be $\underline{F} = (u,v)$. To find the relationships between the forces at the tip and the motor torques, we will write down one equation for balance of forces and one equation for balance of torques for each of the links. Writing down the equations for balance of forces in each of the two links we get:

$$\underline{F}_1 = \underline{F}_2 \quad \text{and} \quad \underline{F}_2 = \underline{F}, \quad \text{that is} \quad \underline{F} = \underline{F}_1 = \underline{F}_2$$

Next picking an arbitrary axis for each of the links we get the equations for balance of torques:

$$T_1 - T_2 = \underline{r}_1 \times \underline{F}$$
$$T_2 = \underline{r}_2 \times \underline{F}$$

Where $[a,b] \times [c,d] = ad - bc$ is the vector cross-product.

$$T_1 = \underline{r}_1 \times \underline{F} + T_2$$
$$= \underline{r}_1 \times \underline{F} + \underline{r}_2 \times \underline{F}$$
$$= (\underline{r}_1 + \underline{r}_2) \times \underline{F}$$

If $T_2 = 0$, then $\underline{r}_2 \times \underline{F} = 0$ and so $\underline{r}_2$ and $\underline{F}$ must be parallel, while $T_1 = 0$, gives $(\underline{r}_1 + \underline{r}_2) \times \underline{F} = 0$ and $(\underline{r}_1 + \underline{r}_2)$ is parallel to $\underline{F}$. These directions for $\underline{F}$ are counter-intuitive if anything! Expanding the cross-products we get:

$$T_1 = [l_1 \cos(\theta_1) + l_2 \cos(\theta_1 + \theta_2)] v$$
$$- [l_1 \sin(\theta_1) + l_2 \sin(\theta_1 + \theta_2)]u$$
$$T_2 = [l_2 \cos(\theta_1 + \theta_2)]v$$
$$- [l_2 \sin(\theta_1 + \theta_2)]u$$

Using these results we can easily calculate what torques the motors should apply at the joints to produce a desired force at the tip.

The Inverse Statics Problem

Now suppose we want to invert this process to calculate the force at the tip given measured joint torques. Fortunately this inversion is straightforward; we simply solve the pair of equations for u and v:

$$u = \frac{\{l_2 \cos(\theta_1 + \theta_2) T_1 - [l_1 \cos(\theta_1) + l_2 \cos(\theta_1 + \theta_2)] T_2\}}{[l_1 l_2 \sin(\theta_2)]}$$

$$v = \frac{\{l_2 \sin(\theta_1 + \theta_2) T_1 - [l_1 \sin(\theta_1) + l_2 \sin(\theta_1 + \theta_2)] T_2\}}{[l_1 l_2 \sin(\theta_2)]}$$

Now we can see in quantitative terms the force components produced by each joint torque acting on its own: There are singularities in the transformation when $\sin(\theta_2) = 0$, that is when $\theta_2 = 0$ or π. Obviously when the links are parallel, the joint torques have no control over the force component along the length of the links. Again we see the special nature of the boundary of the work space.

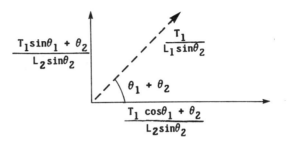

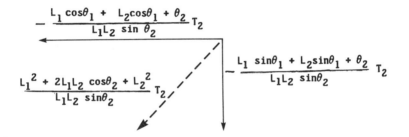

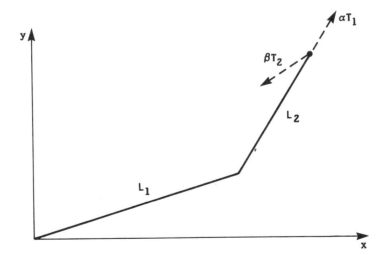

Balancing Gravity

Let us assume for concreteness that the center of mass of each link is at its geometric center and let us define a gravity vector $g = [0,-g]$ acting in the negative y direction. We could now repeat the above calculation with two additional components in the force-balance equations due to the gravity loading. Inspection of the equations shows that the resultant torques are linear in the applied forces, so we can use the principle of superposition, and calculate the gravity induced torques separately. Where there is no applied force at the tip we find

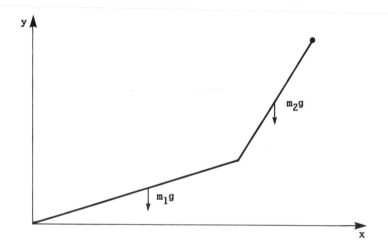

that $\underline{F}_2 = m_2 g$ and

$$\underline{F}_1 = \underline{F}_2 + m_1 \underline{g} = (m_1 + m_2)\underline{g}$$

Considering the torques we find:

$$T_{2g} = -m_2(1/2)\underline{r}_2 \times \underline{g} = g[(1/2)m_2 \, l_2 \, \cos(\theta_1 + \theta_2)]$$
$$T_{1g} = T_{2g} - m_1 \, 1/2 \, \underline{r}_1 \times \underline{g} - m_2 \, \underline{r}_1 \times \underline{g}$$
$$= g[(1/2)m_1 + m_2) \, l_1 \, \cos(\theta_1) + (1/2)m_2 l_2 \, \cos(\theta_1 + \theta_2)]$$

These terms can now be added to the torque terms derived earlier for balancing the force applied at the tip.

Dynamics

Now let us determine what happens if we remove the pin holding the manipulator tip in place and then apply torques to the joints. What angular accelerations of the links will be produced? Knowing the relation between these two quantities will allow us to control the motions of the device as it follows some desired trajectory. We could proceed along lines similar to the ones followed when we studied statics, simply adding Newton's law.

$$\underline{F} = m\underline{a} \qquad or \qquad T = I\alpha$$

where $\underline{F}$ is a force, m mass and $\underline{a}$ linear acceleration. Similarly T is a torque, I moment of inertia and α angular acceleration. The quantities involved would have to be expressed relative to some Cartesian coordinate system. We would be faced with large sets of nonlinear equations, since the mechanical constraints introduced by the linkage would have to be explicitly included and the coordinates of each joint expressed. In general, this method becomes quite unwieldly for manipulators with more than a few links. The more general form of Newton's law indicates a better approach:

$$F_i = d/dt \, (mv_i)$$

where F_i is a component of the force and mv_i is a component of the linear momentum. It is possible to develop a similar equation in a generalized coordinate system that does not have to be Cartesian. It is natural to chose the joint angles as the generalized coordinates. These provide a compact description of the arm configuration and the mechanical constraints are implicitly taken care of. It can be shown that:

$$Q_i = d/dt\ p_i - \partial L/\partial q_i$$

where Q_i is a generalized force, p_i generalized momentum and q_i one of the generalized coordinates. There is one such equation for each degree of freedom. Q_i will be a force for an extensional joint, and a torque for a rotational joint. In both cases, $Q_i q_i$ has the dimensions of work.

Dynamics using Lagranges Equation

In this relation, L is the Lagrangian or "kinetic potential," equal to the difference between kinetic and potential energy, K - P. The generalized momentum p_i can be expressed in terms of L:

$$p_i = \partial L/\partial \dot{q}_i$$

This is analogous to

$$mv = d/dv\ (1/2\ mv^2).$$

The dot represents differentiation with respect to time. Finally:

$$d/dt\ (\partial L/\partial \dot{q}_i) - \partial L/\partial q_i = Q_i$$

Once again there is one such equation for each degree of freedom of the device.

It will be convenient to ignore gravity on the first round -- so there will be no potential energy term. Next we will take the simple case of equal links and let the links be sticks of equal mass m and uniform mass distribution. The moment of inertia for rotation about the center of mass of such a stick is $(1/12)ml^2$. These assumptions allow a great deal of simplification of intermediate terms without losing much of importance. In fact the final result would be the same, except for some numerical constants if we had considered the more general case.

Kinetic energy of a rigid body can be decomposed into a component due to the instantaneous linear translation of its center of mass $(1/2 \ mv^2)$ and a component due to the instantaneous angular velocity $(1/2 \ I_\omega{}^2)$. The angular velocities obviously are just $\dot{\theta}_1$ and $(\dot{\theta}_1 + \dot{\theta}_2)$. The magnitudes of the instantaneous linear velocities of the center of mass are:

$$|1/2 \ \underline{r}_1 \ \dot{\theta}_1|$$
$$|\underline{r}_1\dot{\theta}_1 + 1/2 \ \underline{r}_2(\dot{\theta}_1 + \dot{\theta}_2)|$$

The squares of these quantities are:

$$(1/4)1^2 \ \dot{\theta}_1{}^2 \qquad \text{and}$$
$$1^2[\dot{\theta}_1{}^2 + \cos(\theta_2)\dot{\theta}_1(\dot{\theta}_1 + \dot{\theta}_2) + 1/4(\dot{\theta}_1 + \dot{\theta}_2)^2]$$

The total kinetic energy of link 1 is then:

$$1/2(1/12) \ ml^2\dot{\theta}_1{}^2 + (1/2)m(1/4)1^2 \ \dot{\theta}_1{}^2 = 1/2((1/3)ml^2) \ \dot{\theta}_1{}^2$$

The same result could have been obtained more directly by noting that the moment of inertia of a stick about one of its ends is $(1/3)ml^2$.

The total kinetic energy of link 2 is:

$$1/2((1/12)ml^2)(\dot{\theta}_1 + \dot{\theta}_2)^2$$
$$+ (1/2)ml^2[(5/4 + \cos(\theta_2))\dot{\theta}_1{}^2$$
$$+ (1/2 + \cos(\theta_2))\dot{\theta}_1\dot{\theta}_2 + (1/4)\dot{\theta}_2{}^2]$$
$$= (1/2)ml^2 \ [(4/3 + \cos(\theta_2)) \ \dot{\theta}_1{}^2 + (2/3 + \cos(\theta_2)) \ \dot{\theta}_1\dot{\theta}_2$$
$$+ 1/3 \ \dot{\theta}_2{}^2]$$

Finally, adding all components of the kinetic energy and noting the P = 0, we determine the Lagrangian:

$$L = (1/2)ml^2 \left[(5/3 + \cos(\theta_2))\ \dot\theta_1^{\ 2} \right.$$
$$\left. + (2/3 + \cos(\theta_2))\ \dot\theta_1\dot\theta_2 + 1/3\ \dot\theta_2^{\ 2} \right]$$

Next we will need the partial derivative of L with respect to θ_1, θ_2, $\dot\theta_1$, $\dot\theta_2$. For convenience let $L' = L/(1/2)ml^2$.

$$\partial L'/\partial\theta_1 = 0$$
$$\partial L'/\partial\theta_2 = -\sin(\theta_2)\ \dot\theta_1(\dot\theta_1 + \dot\theta_2)$$
$$\partial L'/\partial\dot\theta_1 = 2(5/3 + \cos(\theta_2))\dot\theta_1 + (2/3 + \cos(\theta_2))\dot\theta_2$$
$$\partial L'/\partial\dot\theta_2 = (2/3 + \cos(\theta_2))\ \dot\theta_1 + 2\ (1/3)\ \dot\theta_2$$

We will also require the time derivatives of these last two expressions:

$$d/dt\ (\partial L'/\partial\dot\theta_1)$$
$$= \ddot\theta_1\ 2\ (5/3 + \cos(\theta_2)) + \ddot\theta_2(2/3 + \cos(\theta_2))$$
$$- \sin(\theta_2)\dot\theta_2(2\dot\theta_1 + \dot\theta_2)$$
$$d/dt\ (\partial L'/\partial\dot\theta_2)$$
$$= \ddot\theta_1\ (2/3 + \cos(\theta_2)) + \ddot\theta_2\ 2(1/3)$$
$$- \sin(\theta_2)\ \dot\theta_1\dot\theta_2$$

When we plug all this into Lagrange's equation

$$d/dt\ (\partial L/\partial\dot\theta_i) - \partial L/\partial\theta_i = T$$

we get:

$$\ddot\theta_1\ 2(5/3 + \cos(\theta_2)) + \ddot\theta_2\ (2/3 + \cos(\theta_2))$$
$$= T_1/(1/2)ml^2 + \sin(\theta_2\ )\ \dot\theta_2(2\dot\theta_1 + \dot\theta_2)$$
$$\ddot\theta_1\ (2/3 + \cos(\theta_2)) + \ddot\theta_2\ 2(1/3)$$
$$= T_2/(1/2)ml^2 - \sin(\theta_2)\ \dot\theta_1^{\ 2}$$

And if you think that was painful, try it the other way! So finally we have a set of equations that allow us to calculate joint torques given desired joint accelerations. Notice that we need to know the arm state, θ_1, θ_2, $\dot\theta_1$, and $\dot\theta_2$ in order to do this. In part this is because of the appearance of velocity-product terms, representing centrifugal forces and the like, and in part it is because the coefficients of the accelerations vary with the arm configuration. It is useful to separate out these latter terms which constitute the sensitivity matrix.

$$\begin{bmatrix} 2(5/3 + \cos(\theta_2)) & (2/3 + \cos(\theta_2)) \\ (2/3 + \cos(\theta_2)) & 2(1/3) \end{bmatrix}$$

If we ignore the velocity-product terms, this matrix tells us the sensitivity of the angular accelerations with respect to the applied torques. It can be shown that the terms in this matrix will depend only on the generalized coordinates (and not the velocities), that the matrix must be symmetrical and that the diagonal terms must be positive.

This, by the way, implies that if one makes the torques large enough to overcome the velocity-product terms, the links will move in the expected direction. The analog, positional approach to arm control depends critically on this property. Notice the couplings between links -- that is torque applied to one joint will cause angular accelerations of both links in general.

The Inverse Matrix

If we wish to know exactly what accelerations will be produced by given torques we have to solve for $\ddot{\theta}_1$ and $\ddot{\theta}_2$ in the above equations.

$$\ddot{\theta}_1 = [2(1/3)\ T_1' - (2/3 + \cos(\theta_2))\ T_2']\ /\ (16/9 - \cos^2(\theta_2))$$

$$\ddot{\theta}_2 = \frac{[-(2/3 + \cos(\theta_2))\ T_1' + 2(5/3 + \cos(\theta_2))T_2']}{(16/9 - \cos^2(\theta_2))}$$

where

$$T_1' = T_1/(1/2 \; ml^2) + \sin(\theta_2)\dot{\theta}_2(2\dot{\theta}_1 + \dot{\theta}_2)$$
$$T_2' = T_2/(1/2 \; ml^2) - \sin(\theta_2) \; \dot{\theta}_1^2$$

Taking Gravity into Acount

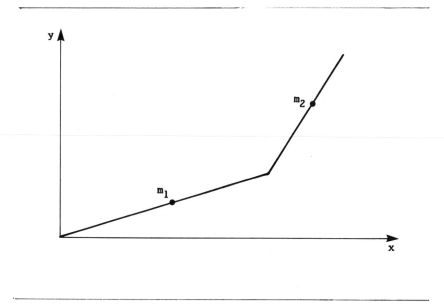

We can define the potential energy P as the sum of the products of the link masses and the elevation of their center of mass relative to some arbitrary place.

$$P = \{gm_1 \; (1/2)l_1 \; \sin(\theta_1)\}$$
$$+ \; \{gm_2[l_1 \; \sin(\theta_1) + (1/2)l_2 \; \sin(\theta_1 + \theta_2)]\}$$

We could now repeat the above calculation, subtracting this term from the kinetic energy. Because of the linearity of the equations, we can again make use of superposition and calculate the torques required to balance gravity separately. Now the partial derivative of P with respect to the angular velocities are 0 so we only need the following:

$$T_{1g} = \partial P / \partial \theta_1 = g[(1/2\ m_1 + m_2)l_1\ \cos(\theta_1)$$
$$+\ 1/2\ m_2 l_2\ \cos(\theta_1 + \theta_2)]$$
$$T_{2g} = \partial P / \partial \theta_2 = g[1/2\ m_2\ l_2\ \cos(\theta_1 + \theta_2)]$$

Adding a Third Link

A manipulator not only has to be able to reach points within a given work space, it also has to be able to approach the object to be manipulated with various orientations of the terminal device. That is, we need a position and orientation generator. Similarly it can be argued that it should not only be able to apply forces to the object, but torques as well. Additional degrees of freedom are required to accomplish this. If we are confined to operation in a two-dimensional space only one extra degree of freedom will be needed, since rotation can take place only about one axis, the axis normal to the plane of operation. It turns out that the same can be said about torque, since applying a torque can be thought of as an attempt to cause a rotation. So in two dimensions, a three link manipulator is sufficient for our purposes. We will now repeat our analysis of kinematics, statics, and dynamics for this device, but with fewer details than before.

Kinematics with Three Links

$$x = l_1\ \cos(\theta_1) + l_2\ \cos(\theta_1 + \theta_2) + l_3\ \cos\ (\theta_1 + _2 + \theta_3)$$
$$y = l_1\ \sin(\theta_1) + l_2\ \sin(\theta_1 + \theta_2) + l_3\ \sin(\theta_1 + \theta_2 + \theta_3)$$
$$\phi = \theta_1 + \theta_2 + \theta_3$$

While we could proceed to solve the inverse problem of finding joint angles from tip position and orientation by geometric, trigonometric or algebraic methods, it is simpler to make use of the results for the two-link manipulator. One can easily calculate

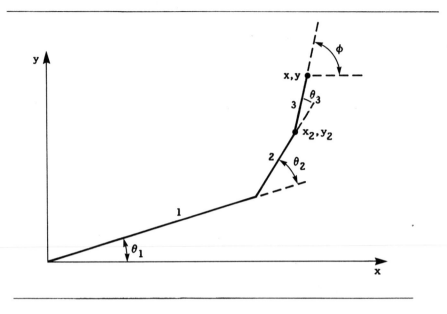

the position of joint 2, knowing

$$x_2 = x - l_3 \cos(\phi)$$
$$y_2 = y - l_3 \sin(\phi)$$

Now one can simply solve the remaining two-link device precisely as before:

$$\cos(\theta_2) = [(x_2{}^2 + y_2{}^2) - (l_1{}^2 + l_2{}^2)] / 2\, l_1\, l_2$$
$$\tan(\theta) = y_2/x_2$$
$$\tan(\alpha) = l_2 \sin(\theta_2) / [l_1 + l_2 \cos(\theta_2)]$$
$$\qquad = 2\, l_1\, l_2 \sin(\theta_2) / [(x_2{}^2 + y_2{}^2) + (l_1{}^2) + (l_1{}^2 - l_2{}^2)]$$
$$\theta_1 = \theta - \alpha$$
$$\theta_3 = \phi - \theta_2 - \theta_1$$

To determine how much of the work space that can be reached by the manipulator is usable with arbitrary orientation of the last link, we could, as before, proceed with an algebraic approach.

For example we might start from $|\cos(\theta_2)| \leq 1$ and the realization that the worst case situations occur when the last link is parallel to the direction from the origin to the tip. The situation is easy enough to visualize, so we will use geometric reasoning instead.

Not all points in the annular work space previously determined can be reached with arbitrary orientation of the last link. A method for constructing the usable work space is simply to construct a circle of radius l_3 about each point. A point is in the usable work space if the circle so constructed lies inside the annulus previously determined.

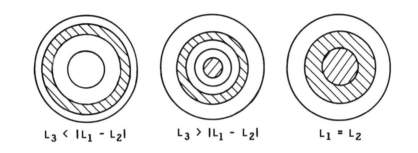

$L_3 < |L_1 - L_2|$ $L_3 > |L_1 - L_2|$ $L_1 = L_2$

Statics with Three Links

We have control of over the three torques T_1, T_2, and T_3. We would like to use these to apply force $\underline{F} = (u,v)$ and torque T to the object held by the tip of the device. We do not want to consider motion of the manipulator now, so again imagine its tip solidly fixed in place. We proceed by writing down one equation for force balance for each link and one equation for torque balance for each link.

$$\underline{F}_1 = \underline{F}_2, \ \underline{F}_2 = \underline{F}_3 \text{ and } \underline{F}_3 = \underline{F} \text{ so } \underline{F} = \underline{F}_1 = \underline{F}_2 = \underline{F}_3$$
$$T_3 = T + \underline{r}_3 \times \underline{F}$$
$$T_2 = T_3 + \underline{r}_2 \times \underline{F}_3$$
$$T_1 = T_2 + \underline{r}_1 \times \underline{F}_2$$
$$T_1 = T + (\underline{r}_1 + \underline{r}_2 + \underline{r}_3) \times \underline{F}$$
$$T_2 = T + (\underline{r}_2 + \underline{r}_3) \times \underline{F}$$
$$T_3 = T + (\underline{r}_3) \times \underline{F}$$

Let's abbreviate the trigonometric terms by subscripts on the letters "s" and "c", so for example
$$s_{23} = \sin(\theta_2 + \theta_3).$$

$$\underline{r}_1 = l_1[c_1, s_1]$$
$$\underline{r}_2 = l_2[c_{12}, s_{12}]$$
$$\underline{r}_3 = l_3[c_{123}, s_{123}]$$

and so

$$(\underline{r}_3) \times \underline{F} = (l_3 c_{123})v - (l_3 s_{123})u$$
$$(\underline{r}_2 + \underline{r}_3) \times \underline{F} = (l_2 c_{12} + l_3 c_{123})v - (l_2 s_{12} + l_3 s_{123})u$$
$$(\underline{r}_1 + \underline{r}_2 + \underline{r}_3) \times \underline{F}$$
$$= (l_1 c_1 + l_2 c_{12} + l_3 c_{123})v - (l_1 s_1 + l_2 s_{12} + l_3 s_{123})u$$

This can be written in matrix form.

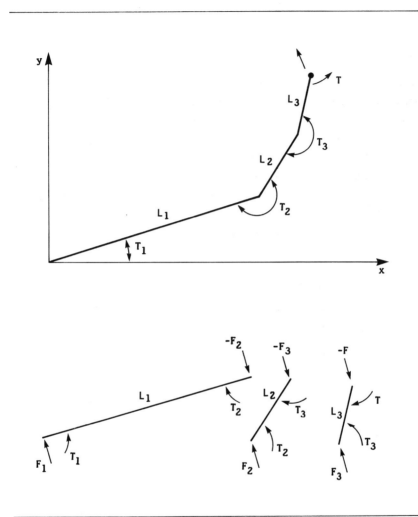

$$
\begin{bmatrix} T_1 \\ T_2 \\ T_3 \end{bmatrix} = \begin{bmatrix} -(l_1 s_1 + l_2 s_{12} + l_3 s_{123}) & (l_1 c_1 + l_2 c_{12} + l_3 c_{123}) & 1 \\ -(l_2 s_{12} + l_3 s_{123}) & (l_2 c_{12} + l_3 c_{123}) & 1 \\ -(l_3 s_{123}) & (l_3 c_{123}) & 1 \end{bmatrix} \begin{bmatrix} u \\ v \\ T \end{bmatrix}
$$

This tells us how to calculate what motor torques are needed to apply a given force and torque to the object held by the manipulator. Notice that we could have arrived at this result by first considering the tip pinned in place only (that is, T=0) and then separately reason out that to apply torque T, each joint torque would have to be increased by T.

The determinant of the above matrix is $l_1 l_2 \sin(\theta_2)$. If θ_2 is neither 0 nor π, we can invert the matrix and solve for u, v, and T given the three joint torques.

$$
\begin{bmatrix} u \\ v \\ T \end{bmatrix} = \frac{1}{l_1 l_2 s_2} \begin{bmatrix} l_2 c_{12} & -(l_1 c_1 + l_2 c_{12}) & l_1 c_1 \\ l_2 s_{12} & -(l_1 s_1 + l_2 s_{12}) & l_1 s_1 \\ l_2 l_3 s_3 - (l_1 l_3 s_{23} + l_2 l_3 s_3) & l_1 l_2 s_2 + l_1 l_3 s_{23} \end{bmatrix} \begin{bmatrix} T_1 \\ T_2 \\ T_3 \end{bmatrix}
$$

Gravity

Gravity is again very simple to take into account. If we assume that the center of mass of each link is in its geometric center we find that:

$$
\underline{F}_3 = m_3 \underline{g}
$$
$$
\underline{F}_2 = (m_2 + m_3) \underline{g}
$$
$$
\underline{F}_1 = (m_1 + m_2 + m_3) \underline{g}
$$

From these, we can derive the torques induced by gravity:

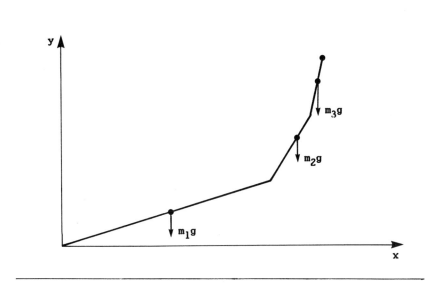

$$T_{3g} = -m_3 \ (1/2)\underline{r}_3 \ \times \ \underline{g} = g[(1/2)m_3l_3c_{123}]$$

$$T_{2g} = T_{3g} - m_3 \ (1/2)\underline{r}_2 \ \times \ \underline{g} - m_3\underline{r}_2 \ \times \ \underline{g}$$

$$= g[(1/2)m_2 + m_3)l_2c_{12} + (1/2)m_3l_3c_{123}]$$

$$T_{1g} = T_{2g} - m_1 \ (1/2)\underline{r}_1 \ \times \ \underline{g} - (m_2 + m_3)\underline{r}_1 \ \times \ \underline{g}$$

$$= g[((1/2)m_1 + m_2 + m_3)l_1c_1$$

$$+ ((1/2)m_2 + m_3)l_2c_{12} + (1/2)m_3l_3c_{123}]$$

Dynamics with Three Equal Links

For definiteness we will again consider a simple case where l_1, l_2, and l_3 are all equal to a length l. The more general case involves a lot more arithmetic and the form of the final result is the same, only numerical constants will be changed. Further, we will ignore gravity for now, and assume the links to be uniform sticks of mass m and inertia $(1/12)ml^2$ about their center of mass. Once again we start by finding the rotational and

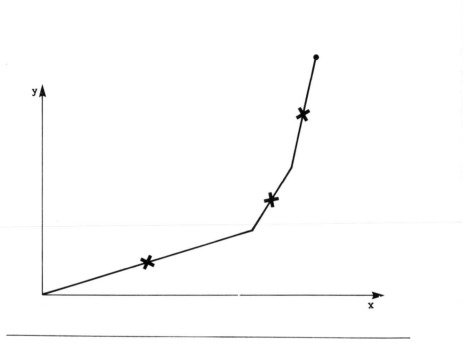

translational velocities of each of the links. Evidently the angular velocities of the three links are $\dot{\theta}_1$, $(\dot{\theta}_1 + \dot{\theta}_2)$, and $(\dot{\theta}_1 + \dot{\theta}_2 + \dot{\theta}_3)$.

The square of the magnitude of the instantaneous linear velocity of the center of mass of link 1 is simply

$$|(1/2)\underline{r}_1\dot{\theta}_1|^2 = 1^2((1/4)\dot{\theta}_1^2)$$

For the square of the magnitude of the velocity of the center of link 2 we have

$$|\underline{r}_1\dot{\theta}_1 + (1/2)\underline{r}_2(\dot{\theta}_1 + \dot{\theta}_2)|^2$$
$$= 1^2[\dot{\theta}_1^2 + \cos(\theta_2)\dot{\theta}_1(\dot{\theta}_1 + \dot{\theta}_2) + 1/4\,(\dot{\theta}_1 + \dot{\theta}_2)^2]$$
$$= 1^2[\dot{\theta}_1^2(5/4 + \cos(\theta_2)) + \dot{\theta}_1\dot{\theta}_2((1/2) + \cos(\theta_2)) + \dot{\theta}_2^2\,(1/4)]$$

For the square of the magnitude of the velocity of the center of link 3 we have

$$|\underline{r}_1\dot{\theta}_1 + \underline{r}_2(\dot{\theta}_1 + \dot{\theta}_2) + (1/2)\underline{r}_3(\dot{\theta}_1 + \dot{\theta}_2 + \dot{\theta}_3)|^2$$
$$= 1^2[\dot{\theta}_1^2 + 2\cos(\theta_2)\dot{\theta}_1(\dot{\theta}_1 + \dot{\theta}_2)$$
$$+ (\dot{\theta}_1 + \dot{\theta}_2)^2$$
$$+ \cos(\theta_3)(\dot{\theta}_1 + \dot{\theta}_2)(\dot{\theta}_1 + \dot{\theta}_2 + \dot{\theta}_3)$$
$$+ 1/4(\dot{\theta}_1 + \dot{\theta}_2 + \dot{\theta}_3)^2$$
$$+ \cos(\theta_2 + \theta_3)\dot{\theta}_1(\dot{\theta}_1 + \dot{\theta}_2 + \dot{\theta}_3)]$$
$$= 1^2[\dot{\theta}_1^2 (9/4 + 2\cos(\theta_2) + \cos(\theta_3) + \cos(\theta_2 + \theta_3))$$
$$+ \dot{\theta}_1\dot{\theta}_2(11/2 + 2\cos(\theta_2)$$
$$+ 2\cos(\theta_3) + \cos(\theta_2 + \theta_3))$$
$$+ \dot{\theta}_2^2(5/4 + \cos(\theta_3))$$
$$+ \dot{\theta}_2\dot{\theta}_3(1/2 + \cos(\theta_3))$$
$$+ \dot{\theta}_3^2(1/4)$$
$$+ \dot{\theta}_3\dot{\theta}_1(1/2 + \cos(\theta_3) + \cos(\theta_2 + \theta_3))]$$

Isn't that lovely. We are now ready to add up the kinetic energy due to rotation and that due to linear translation of the center of mass for all three links to obtain the Lagrangian.

$$L = 1/2\ m1^2\ [\dot{\theta}_1^2(4 + 3\cos(\theta_2) + \cos(\theta_2 + \theta_3) + \cos(\theta_3))$$
$$+ \dot{\theta}_1\dot{\theta}_2(19/3 + 3\cos(\theta_2) + \cos(\theta_2 + \theta_3) + 2\cos(\theta_3))$$
$$+ \dot{\theta}_2^2(5/3 + \cos(\theta_3))$$
$$+ \dot{\theta}_2\dot{\theta}_3(2/3 + \cos(\theta_3))$$
$$+ \dot{\theta}_3^2\ (1/3)$$
$$+ \dot{\theta}_3\dot{\theta}_1(2/3 + \cos(\theta_2 + \theta_3) + \cos(\theta_3))]$$

So this is the Lagrangian for this system and from it we will be able to calculate the relation between joint torques and joint accelerations. Let us use the shorthand notation for trigonometric terms introduced in the discussion of the statics of this device, e.g., $s_{23} = \sin(\theta_2 + \theta_3)$.

We will next derive the partial derivates of the Lagrangian with respect to θ_1, θ_2, θ_3, $\dot{\theta}_1$, $\dot{\theta}_2$, $\dot{\theta}_3$. Let

$L = 1/2\ ml^2 L'$ as before.

$$-\partial L'/\partial\theta_1 = 0$$
$$-\partial L'/\partial\theta_2 = \dot{\theta}_1^{\,2}(3\ s_2 + s_{23}) + \dot{\theta}_1\dot{\theta}_2(3\ s_2 + s_{23}) + \dot{\theta}_3\dot{\theta}_1(s_{23})$$
$$-\partial L'/\partial\theta_3 = \dot{\theta}_1^{\,2}(s_{23} + s_3) + \dot{\theta}_1\dot{\theta}_2(s_{23} + 2\ s_3)$$
$$+ \dot{\theta}_2^{\,2}(s_3) + \dot{\theta}_2\dot{\theta}_3(s_3) + \dot{\theta}_3\dot{\theta}_1(s_{23} + s_3)$$

The partial derivates of the Lagrangian with respect to angular velocity are:

$$\partial L'/\partial\dot{\theta}_1 = 2\dot{\theta}_1(4 + 3c_2 + c_{23} + c_3)$$
$$+ \dot{\theta}_2(19/3 + 3c_2 + c_{23} + 2c_3) + \dot{\theta}_3(2/3 + c_{23} + c_3)$$
$$\partial L'/\partial\dot{\theta}_2 = \dot{\theta}_1(19/3 + 3c_2 + c_{23} + 2c_3)$$
$$+ 2\dot{\theta}_2(5/3 + c_3) + \dot{\theta}_3(2/3 + c_3)$$
$$\partial L'/\partial\dot{\theta}_3 = \dot{\theta}_1(2/3 + c_{23} + c_3)$$
$$+ \dot{\theta}_2(2/3 + c_3) + 2\dot{\theta}_3(1/3)$$

Next we will need the time rate-of-change of the last three quantities above:

$$d/dt\ (\partial L'/\partial\dot{\theta}_1) = 2\ddot{\theta}_1(4 + 3c_2 + c_{23} + c_3)$$
$$+ \ddot{\theta}_2(19/3 + 3c_2 + c_{23} + 2c_3) + \ddot{\theta}(2/3 + c_{23} + c_3)$$
$$- 2\dot{\theta}_1(3s_2\dot{\theta}_2 - s_{23}(\dot{\theta}_2 + \dot{\theta}_3) - s_3\dot{\theta}_3)$$
$$- \dot{\theta}_2(3s_2\dot{\theta}_2 + s_{23}(\dot{\theta}_2 + \dot{\theta}_3) - 2s_3\dot{\theta}_3)$$
$$- \dot{\theta}_3(s_{23}(\dot{\theta}_2 + \dot{\theta}_3) - s_3\ \dot{\theta}_3)$$
$$d/dt(\partial L'/\partial\dot{\theta}_2) = \ddot{\theta}_1(19/3 + 3c_2 + c_{23} + 2c_3)$$
$$+ 2\ddot{\theta}_2(5/3 + c_3) + \ddot{\theta}_3(2/3 + c_3)$$
$$- \dot{\theta}_1(3s_2\dot{\theta}_2 - s_{23}(\dot{\theta}_2 + \dot{\theta}_3) - s_3\dot{\theta}_3) - 2\dot{\theta}_2(s_3\dot{\theta}_3) - \dot{\theta}(s_3\dot{\theta}_3)$$
$$d/dt\ (\partial L'/\partial\dot{\theta}_3) = \ddot{\theta}_1(2/3 + c_{23} + c_3) + \ddot{\theta}_2(2/3 + c_3) + 2\ddot{\theta}_3(1/3)$$
$$- \dot{\theta}_1(s_{23}(\dot{\theta}_2 + \dot{\theta}_3) - s_3\dot{\theta}_3) - \dot{\theta}_2(s_3\dot{\theta}_3)$$

Finally, inserting these terms into Lagrange's equation gives:

$$T_1' = d/dt(\partial L'/\partial \dot\theta_1) - \partial L'/\partial \theta_1$$

$$= 2\ddot\theta_1 (4 + 3c_2 + c_{23} + c_3)$$

$$+ \ddot\theta_2(19/3 + 3c_2 + c_{23} + 2c_3)$$

$$+ \ddot\theta_3(2/3 + c_{23} + c_3)$$

$$- \dot\theta_1\dot\theta_2(6s_2 + 2s_{23}) - \dot\theta_2{}^2(3s_2 + s_{23})$$

$$- \dot\theta_2\dot\theta_3(2s_{23})$$

$$- \dot\theta_3{}^2(s_{23} + s_3) - \dot\theta_3\dot\theta_1(2s_{23} + s_3)$$

$$T_2' = d/dt(\partial L'/\partial \dot\theta_2) - \partial L'/\partial \theta_2$$

$$= \ddot\theta_1(19/3 + 3c_2 + c_{23} + 2c_3) + 2\ddot\theta_2(5/3 + c_3) + \ddot\theta_3(2/3 + c_3)$$

$$+ \dot\theta_1{}^2(3s_2 + s_{23}) - \dot\theta_2\dot\theta_3(2s_3) - \dot\theta_3{}^2(s_3) - \dot\theta_3\dot\theta_1(2s_3)$$

$$T_3' = d/dt(\partial L'/\partial \dot\theta_3) - \partial L'/\partial \theta_3$$

$$= \ddot\theta_1(2/3 + c_{23} + c_3) + \ddot\theta_2(2/3 + c_3) + \ddot\theta_3(2/3)$$

$$+ \dot\theta_1{}^2(s_{23} + s_3) + \dot\theta_1\dot\theta_2(2\,s_3) + \dot\theta_2{}^2(s_3)$$

As in the two-link case, the equations above can be expressed in matrix terms. The torque vector is equal to a sensitivity matrix times the angular acceleration vector, plus a vector of torques due to velocity products. The sensitivity matrix is symmetric, and its diagonal elements are always positive. The terms in this matrix depend only on the joint angles because all the velocity-product terms are segregated out.

Given the arm state (joint angles and joint angular velocities), we can calculate what torques need to be applied to each of the joints in order to achieve a given angular acceleration for each of the joints. We only need to invert the sensitivity matrix.

Extensions to Three Dimensions

Once the basic principles are understood, we can proceed to introduce the extensions necessary to deal with manipulators in three dimensions. There is little difficulty as regards position and force since in an n-dimensional space these quantities can be conveniently represented by n-dimensional vectors. A general position or force generator will need n degrees of freedom.

Unfortunately we are not so lucky with orientation and torque. These can not be usefully thought of as vectors. For example, in three dimensions we know that rotations don't commute, while vector addition does. It is a misleading coincidence that it takes three variables to specify a rotation in three dimensions.

It takes $n(n-1)/2$ variables to specify a rotation in n-dimensional space. Why? A general rotation can be made up of components each of which carries one axis part way towards a second axis. There are n axes, and so "n choose 2" distinct pairs of axes. There are therefore that number of "elementary" rotations. It is not correct to think of rotations "about an axis"; in our two-dimensional example such rotations would carry one out of the plane of the paper, and in four dimensions, not all possible rotations would be generated by considering only combinations of the four rotations about the coordinate axes.

Another way of approaching this problem is to look at matrices that represent coordinate transformations that correspond to rotations. Such matrices are ortho-normal and of size n*n. How many of the n^2 entries can be freely chosen? The condition of normality generates n constraints, and the condition of orthogonality another $n(n-1)/2$. So we have

$$n^2 - n - n(n-1)/2 = n(n-1)/2$$

degrees of freedom left.

To specify position and orientation, or force and torque in n dimensions requires $n(n-1)/2+n$ variables. A general purpose n-dimensional manipulator thus needs to have $n(n+1)/2$ degrees of freedom. For n=3, this is 6. The coincidence that it takes 3 variables to specify a rotation in three dimensions allows some simplifications. A torque, for example, can be calculated by taking cross-products. In higher dimensions, one needs to look at exterior tensor products. A useful way of specifying rotations in three dimensions is by means of Euler angles: roll, pitch, and yaw, for example. It is straightforward to convert between this representation and the ortho-normal matrix notation.

Kinematics

It is no longer sufficient to represent each link as a vector, since the joints at its two ends may have axes that are not parallel. The way to deal with this problem is simply to erect a coordinate system fixed to each link. Corresponding to each joint there will be a coordinate transformation from one system to the next. This transformation can be represented by a 3x3 rotation matrix plus an offset vector. It is convenient to combine these into one 4x4 transformation matrix that has (0 0 0 1) as its last row. This allows one easily to invert the transformation, so as to allow conversion of coordinates in the other direction as well.

The entries in this matrix will be trigonometric polynomials in the joint angles. In order to determine the relation between links separated by more than one joint, one can simply multiply the transformation matrices corresponding to the intervening joints. Doing this for the complete manipulator, one obtains a single matrix that allows one to relate coordinates relative to the tip or terminal device to coordinates relative to the base of the device. In fact the 3x3 rotation submatrix gives us the rotation of the last link relative to the base and and hence its orientation, while the offset 3x1 submatrix is the position of the tip of the last link with respect to the base.

Given the joint variables, it is then a relatively straightforward matter to arrive at the position and orientation of the terminal device or tip. These values are of course unique for a particular set of joint variables.

The Inverse Problem in Three Dimensions is Intractable

Unfortunately the inversion is much harder. One way to approach this problem would be to consider the 3x3 rotation submatrix made up entirely of polynomials in sines and cosines of joint angles and the 3x1 offset submatrix which contains link-lengths as well and try to solve for the sines and cosines of

the six joint angles. There are twelve equations in twelve
unknowns, so we expect there to be a finite number of solutions.
When solving polynomial equations by eliminating variables the
degree of the resulting polynomials grows as the product of the
polynomials combined. We could easily end up with one
polynomial in one unknown with a degree of several thousand.
So in general this problem is intractable.

There are a number of conditions on the link geometry
that make this problem solvable by noniterative techniques.
Several such configurations are known, but one of the easiest to
explain involves decoupling the orientation from the position.
One then has to solve two problems that are much smaller, each
having only three degrees of freedom. Suppose for example that
the last three rotational joints intersect in one point, call it the
wrist. Then these last three can take care of the orientation,
while the remaining three position the wrist. Given the
orientation of the last link it is easy to calculate where the wrist
should be relative to the tip position. Given the position of the
wrist one can solve the inversion problem for the first three
links. This can usually be done by careful inspection rather than
blind solution of trigonometric polynomials. Often also the first
three links are simply a combination of the two-link geometry we
have already solved and an offset polar-coordinate problem.

Now that we know the first three joint angles we can
calculate the orientation of the third to which the wrist attaches.
Comparing this with the last link, it is simple to calculate the
three wrist angles by matrix multiplication and solving for the
Euler angles appropriate to the design of the wrist.

Statics

By controlling the six joint torques we can produce a given force
and torque at the terminal device. The same coordinate
transformation matrices used for solving the kinematics prove
useful here. Cross-products give us the required torques, with
joint motors supporting the components around the joint axes,

while the pin joints transmit the other components. The calculations are straightforward.

Gravity compensation calculations also follow the familiar pattern. In many cases manipulators intended for positional control have been used to generate forces and torques in a different manner. The idea is to use the inherent compliance of the device as a kind of spring and to drive the joints to angles slightly away from the equilibrium position. Since the stress-strain matrix of such a device is very complex and it has different spring constants in different directions, as well as coupling between forces and torques, this technique on its own is not very useful. One solution relies on a force and torque sensor in the wrist. From the output of such a device one can calculate the forces and torques at the tip and servo the joint angles accordingly. The advantage of this technique is that friction in the first three joints does not corrupt the result and that the measurement is made beyond the point where the heaviest and stickiest components of the manipulator are.

Dynamics

The main additional difficulty of manipulators in higher dimensions is that inertia too now has several components instead of just one. The dynamic behavior of a rigid body as regards rotation can be conveniently expressed as a symmetrical, square inertia matrix. This relates the applied torque components to the resulting angular accelerations. The same general idea carries through, with the distinction that the calculations get very messy and have to be approached in a systematic fashion. A practical difficulty is the measurement of the components of the inertia matrices for each of the links of the manipulator.

Of course the problem is somewhat complicated should the manipulator actually manipulate something.

References

B. K. P. Horn and H. Inoue, *Kinematics of the MIT-AI-Vicarm Manipulator*, MIT AI Laboratory Working Paper 69, 1974.

M. E. Kahn, *The Near-minimum-time Control of Open-loop Articulated Kinematic Chains*, Stanford Artificial Intelligence Memo 106, 1969.

R. Paul, *Modelling, Trajectory Calculation and Servoing of a Computer Controlled Arm*, Stanford Artificial Intelligence Memo 177, 1972.

D. L. Pieper, *The Kinematics of Manipulators Under Computer Control*, Stanford Artificial Intelligence Memo 72, 1968.

J. J. Uicker, *On the Dynamic Analysis of Spatial Linkages using 4*4 Matrices*, PhD Dissertation, Northwestern University, 1965.

J. J. Uicker,"Dynamic Force Analysis of Spatial Linkages", *Transactions ASME*, 1967.

UNDERSTANDING MANIPULATOR CONTROL BY SYNTHESIZING HUMAN HANDWRITING

JOHN HOLLERBACH

One goal of research in Artificial Intelligence is that of understanding natural systems from a computation-centered point of view. This can and does lead to cycles of research that shuttle between experiments with human subjects and experiments with implemented computer models. This section by John Hollerbach, a preview of his PhD thesis, illustrates this style of research in the context of understanding human motor control, with particular emphasis on handwriting. Hollerbach begins by enumerating some assumptions, then builds them into a program for a human-like manipulator, next compares his robot's writing with measurements made using human subjects, and finally comes full circle back to new conjectures to be tested by traversing the research cycle again.

Synthetic Handwriting with a Mechanical Arm

The mechanical arm employed in this study was the MIT VICARM, a 6-joint manipulator. The backdrivable torque motors powering each joint allow the production of ballistic movements. Potentiometers and tachometers on each joint yield position and velocity records for each movement, although this was not used to modify the preprogrammed motor currents.

Handwriting for the majority of people involves essentially two orthogonal joints, a finger joint for up-down movement and the wrist for back-forth movement. This allows for separate programming of the two joints and a conceptual simplification of the control strategy. Often mentioned in the literature, joint orthogonality was confirmed by a series of experiments on human subjects. The best choice of orthogonal joints in the VICARM was the wrist hinge joint for up-down movement and the largest shoulder joint for the back-forth movement. Fortunately the disparate size of these joints did not factor significantly in the simulation of handwriting.

The problem of keeping the penpoint on the surface is solved differently by different people, commonly involving the thumb, forefinger, or wrist. This effect was mimicked on the VICARM with a constant force spring attachment to a pen mounted in a linear bearing, automatically keeping the pen on the surface with near-constant pressure.

A number of ideas and strategies for handwriting were attempted on the VICARM. Many of them produce equally smooth and humanlike handwriting, making it impossible purely on performance grounds to select one strategy over another. The eventual strategies I selected represent the simplest set, in some sense, that captures the complexity of handwriting.

- A fixed time quantum. The most basic assumption in the simulation was that there is a fixed time quantum during which force is held constant. When one time quantum expires and the next begins, the force magnitude may change to another level or remain at the old value. The time quantum remains the same for all writing speeds and sizes. One reason for this restriction is the generally accepted observation that writings of different sizes are all executed in the same time (see references); what must vary then are the force amplitudes rather than the durations. A second reason was a need for clear separation of acceleration from deceleration because of the disparate affect of sliding friction. A third reason for a fixed time quantum strategy is conceptual clarity and ease of planning, since distance varies linearly with acceleration but quadratically with time. The basic time quantum for the VICARM, representing a compromise among such factors as speed of response and jerkiness, was chosen as 24 msec.

■ Synchronous joint activation. Assuming equal time quanta for both joints, one has the choice of synchronizing the time quanta of the two joints or of offsetting one relative to the other. Synchronization was chosen for simplicity.

■ An underlying oscillation. The most important assumption in the simulation is a view of handwriting as a constrained modulation of an underlying oscillation pattern. The oscillation is fundamentally a down-up movement traveling from left to right. The vertical joint plays the role of oscillator: it drives the movement with rhythmic down-up movements. The horizontal joint acts as the shaping joint: by carrying the writing from left to right at different speeds and at different points in the vertical oscillation, it produces letter shapes.

This assumption departs from a view of handwriting as isolated letters hooked together, each letter with its own motor programs that sculpt the trajectories to some idealized internal representation of shape. The individual letter motor programs would not necessarily have any relations or commonalities among themselves. Under an oscillation strategy individual letter shapes are subjugated to the operation of the oscillation as a whole. There are no individual letters, only characteristic modulations of the oscillation train. Connective strokes are as important as strokes internal to the letters.

- A strict rhythmicity. A cycle of the oscillation will contain a certain number of time quanta; conceivably more time quanta could be required for tall letters than for short letters or for reasons of shape. Nevertheless I chose to impose strict rhythmicity on the oscillation; all cycles of the oscillation contain the same number of time quanta. Available experimental evidence indicated at the time a roughly constant cycle time; the invariance of writing time with size indicated that tall letters could be produced just as fast as short letters.

    Strict rhythmicity imposes time constraints on the action of the horizontal joint in shaping letters. The shape of a letter may need to be compromised for time considerations; the faster the handwriting, the fewer the number of time quanta in each cycle, and the less time there is for shaping letters. The effect of writing speed on style is discussed more thoroughly later.

- Constant force tendency. A cycle of an oscillation consists of a downstroke and an upstroke. Each of these strokes is made up of an acceleration period followed by a deceleration period; each period, moreover, is comprised of one or more time quanta. The force amplitude in an acceleration or deceleration period is required to stay the same for all the time quanta. For the vertical driving joint, the force magnitude in acceleration is also required to equal that in deceleration; the horizontal pattern is free from this restriction to allow latitude in shape production. A consequence of this last restriction is that acceleration and deceleration periods contain the same number of time quanta; to complete the symmetry, downstrokes and upstrokes also are required to contain the same number of quanta.

■   Factoring out friction. The construction of motor programs proceeds as if dealing with an idealized point mass in a frictionless environment. Before application of these motor programs to the actuators, frictional characteristics of the mechanical system are used to modify the idealized currents so that the actual movement is the desired one. In factoring out system characteristics in the planning stages the motor programs are more transparent and more readily synthesized. The only modification made to the idealized motor programs for the VICARM is a compensation for sliding friction arising from the torque motors and from the pressure of pen against paper. Viscous friction, centripetal forces, and moment of inertia changes are all negligible.

The choice of underlying oscillation pattern restricts the shapes the horizontal actuator can produce and is the primary factor influencing writing style. The fastest cycle consists of single quantum acceleration-deceleration bursts by the vertical actuator, resulting in a four quantum down-up cycle of 96 msec. When coupled with a horizontal pattern that rounds the bottoms of the oscillation, a smoothed sawtooth results (figure 1). Horizontal (H) and vertical (V) acceleration profiles corresponding to two cycles of 1a are indicated in 1b. The abscissa is marked off in single time quantum units. Simple amplitude modulation of the bursts in this pattern and a slight alteration to incorporate a left movement in the *l* produces the cursive rendering of *vial* in figure 2a; the acceleration profiles for the two cycles forming the *l* are shown in figure 2b.

Slower oscillation patterns allow the horizontal actuator

Figure 1. A smoothed sawtooth in 1b and its horizontal H and vertical V acceleration profiles in 1a. The ticks on the time axis t represent single time quanta of 24 msec. The horizontal and vertical time quanta are synchronized; acceleration may change only at single quantum intervals.

Figure 2. Amplitude modulation of the acceleration profiles of the smoothed sawtooth yields the cursive rendering of *vial* in 2b. A slight alteration to incorporate a leftward movement in the *l* is illustrated by the two cycles of the oscillation that form the *l* in 2a.

more time to shape letters, in particular more time to incorporate leftward movements. With an 8-quantum cycle, a garland chain with leftward movement and more rounded bottoms can be set up (figure 3a). When modified, the garland chain becomes the *vial* in figure 3b. A feature of this modification is hesitation at sharp corners such as the *i*, where the top loop of the garland is aborted. The hesitation is required to keep the writing in phase with the oscillation.

(a) *uuuu*   (b) *vial*

Figure 3. An 8-quantum cycle allows the production of a smooth garland chain in 3a, which when amplitude modified becomes the *vial* in 3b.

Corner Shape Vocabulary

The constraints on force patterns lead naturally to a vocabulary of corner shapes. The vocabulary applies only to patterns for the horizontal shaping joint, since the vertical joint is unalterably engaged in a rhythmic down-up motion. The three main descriptors of this vocabulary, outlined in table 1, are the symmetry of the pattern, the overlay of the horizontal pattern on the vertical corner, and the number of time quanta in the pattern. The symmetry descriptor assumes one of the values {S,L,R} depending on whether the pattern is symmetric with respect to acceleration-deceleration (S), unsymmetric with one more time quantum in acceleration than in deceleration (L), or unsymmetric with one more time quantum in deceleration than in acceleration (R).

Table 1

Corner Shape Vocabulary

1. Symmetry   S: symmetric
$$a^n(-a)^n$$
$$a^n 0(-a)^n$$
L: antisymmetric left
$$a^{n+1}b^n$$
$$a^{n+1}0b^n$$
R: antisymmetric right
$$a^n b^{n+1}$$
$$a^n 0 b^{n+1}$$

2. Overlay at corner
A: accelerating through
B: decelerating at
C: coasting at
D: decelerating through

3. Number of time quanta

The overlay descriptor refers to the disposition of the horizontal pattern with respect to the vertical corner, that is to say, the point where movement changes from down to up or from up to down. When the last horizontal acceleration time quantum begins at the vertical corner, the descriptor (A) is assigned. When the first deceleration time quantum begins at the vertical corner, the descriptor (B) is assigned. When the second deceleration time quantum begins at the vertical corner, the descriptor (D) is assigned. Lastly, when a coast quantum begins at the vertical corner, which is the only allowed position for a coast quantum, the descriptor (C) is assigned.

The third and final descriptor is the number of time

quanta in the horizontal pattern. Although the descriptors in table 1 represent only a fraction of the number of possible corner patterns, these are the only descriptors leading to useful corner shapes. Table 2 gives some examples of horizontal corner patterns and a rough description of the shapes produced.

Table 2

rounded:	$(2n+1)$S:C
	$(2n)$L:C
	$(2n)$R:C
one side straight:	$(2n)$S:A
	$(2n+1)$L:A
	$(2n+1)$R:D
sharp cornered:	$(2n)$S:B
	$(2n+1)$L:B
	$(2n+1)$R:B

Duplicating Human Handwriting

A natural question is whether the corner vocabulary and the aforementioned motor program strategies are rich enough to capture the complexity of human handwriting. As an illustration of sufficiency, an attempt was made to duplicate four a's as drawn by different human subjects, taken from Koster and Vredenbregt [1971]. These a's appear paired with their VICARM facsimilies in figure 4, the former the smaller writing on the left and the latter the larger writing to the right.

As is evident from the figure, the duplication is fairly good, especially considering the differences in mechanics. The

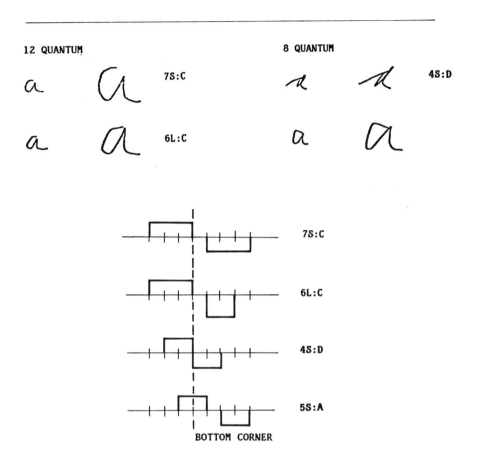

Figure 4. Four *a*'s produced by different human subjects (taken from Koster and Vredenbregt) in the left column appear paired with their VICARM duplications in the right column. The first two *a*'s are produced with a 12 quantum cycle, the second two with an 8 quantum cycle. The descriptor for the bottom corner of each *a* is shown to the right of the corresponding VICARM *a*'s; the horizontal acceleration profile for each bottom corner type is shown at the bottom.

process of manufacturing these shapes was accomplished first by choosing an appropriate oscillation speed and then selecting appropriate corner patterns. The first two *a*'s are rather rounded, and a relatively long 12 quantum cycle was required for correct shaping. The last two *a*'s are more angular, calling for a faster 8 quantum cycle. The selection of a corner pattern from the vocabulary was relatively straightforward; the patterns for the bottom corners of the *a* loops are indicated in the right column of the figure. The duplication was easily and quickly done with this paradigm of superimposed standard corner patterns on an underlying oscillation.

Even if human handwriting is executed under a different set of strategies than the VICARM writing, the VICARM results suggest a level of complexity for handwriting, namely that handwriting is an inherently simple task. Once a completely regular oscillation is set up, a limited number of corner types suffices to produce all letter shapes. A rough estimate places the number of required corner types in the vicinity of 20. The implication of this small number is that there is only limited control in handwriting in shaping letters. The number of necessary force levels is also small because writing naturally falls into letters of 3 or 4 different heights and perhaps 10 different widths. In a sense these strategies may be viewed as a trick to minimize the complexity of the motor task.

Measurements of Human Handwriting

Accelerometers mounted on a sliding X-Y rail system allow precise measurement of acceleration during handwriting (figure 5). A writing tablet in conjection with the accelerometer apparatus allows concurrent measurement of position, and hence of velocity. Extensive tests with this apparatus have demonstrated the integrity of the resultant data; inertia effects due to the housing mass, for example, were shown insignificant.

A shear transformation applied to the data is an important part of the analysis. The disposition of people's

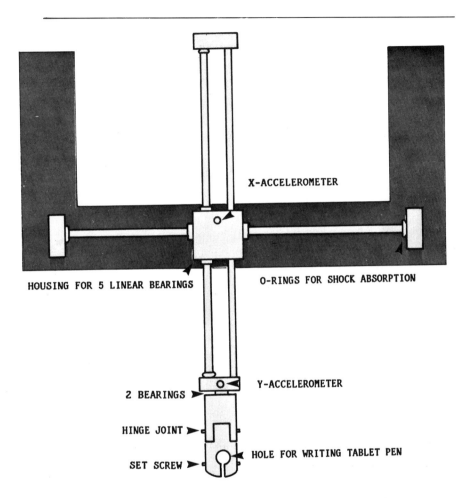

Figure 5. Handwriting measurement apparatus with accelerometers mounted on a sliding X-Y rail system. A writing tablet pen fits in the pen housing in order to provide position data.

DE0114 192.

SHEARED 70.
DE0114 192.
HORIZONTAL
ACCELERATION

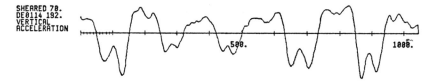

SHEARED 70.
DE0114 192.
VERTICAL
ACCELERATION

Figure 6. Horizontal and vertical acceleration profiles for one subject's writing of *hell*. The vertical profile is rhythmic and varies only slightly from letter to letter, while the horizontal profile shows great diversification.

writing joints is not usually orthogonal, but ranges anywhere from 50 to 90 degrees. Nonorthogonal disposition, and not any variations in the motor programs, is responsible for writing slant. To find the true movement produced by each joint, a shear transformation is applied to the orthogonally measured data.

The vertical acceleration profile in figure 6 reveals a rhythmic acceleration-deceleration pattern that varies only slightly from letter to letter. The horizontal acceleration profile on the other hand shows considerable diversification depending on the letter. This characterization is typical for the writing of most subjects, and bears out an assumption made in the simulation studies. There the two joints were assigned different roles. The vertical joint acted like an oscillator, driving the movement with a fairly unvarying down-up rhythm. The horizontal joint is the shaping joint, and varies its acceleration pattern according to the requirements of a particular letter.

An analysis of acceleration burst durations with different writing speeds by the same subject shows a continuous ability to vary the durations of bursts. Figure 7 shows a typical histogram from one subject of burst durations quantized at a level of 10 msecs. Thus the quantum assumption in the simulation studies is incorrect.

For a given writing speed the rhythmic bursts are also not exactly constant in duration, but vary essentially with the height of a letter. This dependence is not due to any inherent limitation in the power plant, but rather to a difference in strategy. Ordinarily large writing is just as fast as small writing, an accepted observation in the handwriting literature and one substantiated by my own measurements. A major tendency in modulating rhythmic constancy is the maintainance of constant acceleration levels throughout the duration of a burst. In the vertical acceleration plot of figure 6 a wide variation in the duration of bursts is evident. The longest burst is the 130 msec burst braking the downward movement from the top of the *e* and starting the upward movement to the top of the *l*. A relatively modest acceleration magnitude is required for the braking, but

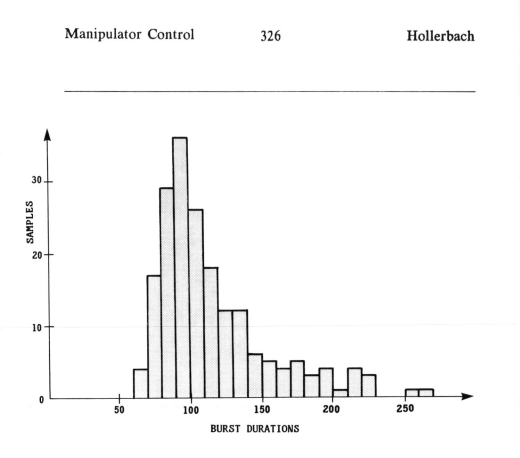

Figure 7. Histogram for one subject's negative and positive vertical acceleration burst durations quantized at a level of 10 msecs. A facility for continuously varying the burst durations is demonstrated.

this magnitude is maintained in forming the much larger *l*. Naturally more time is required than with a larger magnitude.

There are basically three different top corner types: the sharp top corners of letters such as *i*, *u*, and *w*; the rounded top corners such as *m*, *n*, and *h*; and loop top corners such as *e* and *l*; The horizontal and vertical velocity profiles illustrate the essential differences in their formation. In figure 8 three different writing samples are shown together with two plots: overplotted horizontal and vertical velocity, and overplotted

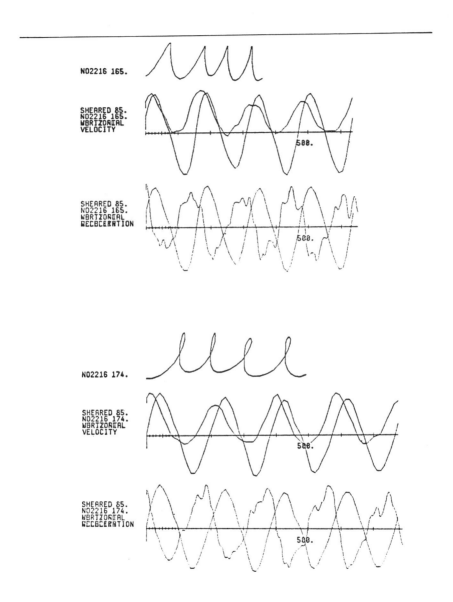

Figure 8. Three writing chains from one subject representing the top corner types loop, sharp, and rounded. Overlapped horizontal and vertical velocity plots and overlapped horizontal acceleration and vertical velocity plots are also shown for each chain.

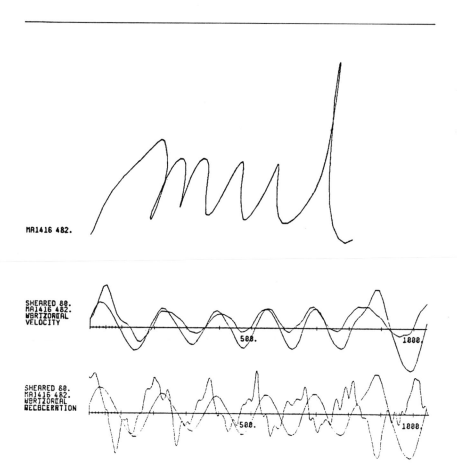

Figure 8 (continued). Three writing chains from one subject representing the top corner types loop, sharp, and rounded. Overlapped horizontal and vertical velocity plots and overlapped horizontal acceleration and vertical velocity plots are also shown for each chain.

vertical velocity and horizontal acceleration. For sharp corners the positive horizontal velocity goes to zero at the same time as the vertical velocity; for rounded corners the horizontal velocity trails the vertical velocity to zero; and for loop corners the horizontal velocity precedes the vertical velocity to zero.

The vertical acceleration profiles for these three corner types are similar, underlining once again the rhythmic rather than the shaping nature of this movement. The horizontal profiles show bursts not widely different in duration or amplitude among the corner types, but differing in synchronization with the vertical movement. For sharp corners the negative horizontal deceleration burst begins at or slightly before the point of maximum positive vertical velocity. The corresponding bursts for rounded corners begin somewhat right of this point, while bursts from loop corners begin to its left.

The shape of the bottom corners is affected by the requirements of the top corners. For sharp top corners the rightward acceleration begins relatively late to the bottom turning point, so that a fairly sharp bottom corner ensues. Continued rightward acceleration during the first part of the upstroke causes a rightward diagonaling stroke. For the same reason the angularity of the bottom corner is even more extreme when it follows a rounded corner. The loop top corners give rise to the most rounded bottom corners because the rightward positive acceleration bursts begin almost at the top corner and the negative deceleration bursts just after the bottom corner. Simulation of different corner types with the VICARM agrees with these observations. A rough alternation of horizontal acceleration/deceleration with vertical deceleration/acceleration as occurs with e bottom corners was found to yield the most rounded curves. When both joints are accelerating, as at the initial upstroke of a chain of u's, a straight line results.

A noteworthy feature of these corner patterns in human writing is that they take approximately the same time; e's are as fast as u's, and u's as fast as m's. The constant time feature arises from an ability to make fine adjustments in onset and

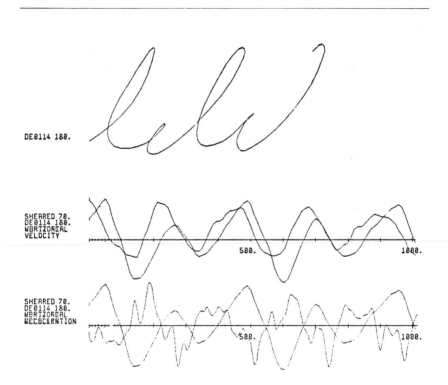

DE0114 180.

SHEARED 70.
DE0114 180.
HORIZONTAL
VELOCITY

SHEARED 70.
DE0114 180.
HORIZONTAL
ACCELERATION

Figure 9. The writing of *lele* illustrates a preference for regularity over exact shape control. While the vertical velocity bursts expand or contract between *l*'s and *e*'s, the horizontal acceleration bursts remain of constant duration throughout.

termination of horizontal acceleration bursts. By contrast the time quantum feature of the VICARM writing renders this impossible; the only way of changing the synchronization in a quasi-continuous fashion is to expand the number of time quanta in a stroke so that some quantum boundary approaches the desired relation to the vertical. For this reason it takes much longer to make an *e* than a *u* with the **VICARM**.

There is a transition problem in going from one top corner type to another. For the sample *mul* in figure 8 the subject had some difficulty in reigning in the horizontal velocity, since at the first sharp top corner of the *u* the horizontal velocity still lags the vertical. Not until the top loop of the *l* does the horizontal velocity catch up to the vertical. Evidently there is time and effort involved in shifting the horizontal acceleration bursts to produce a different corner pattern.

A different type of example of the perserverence of a horizontal acceleration pattern is provided by the *lele* in figure 9. Judging from the vertical velocity profile the *l*'s take much longer than the *e*'s measured bottom corner to bottom corner. The horizontal acceleration bursts maintain nearly a constant duration from one letter to the next, as if regularity were preferred over exact shape control. This is one example of modification of letter shape to suit requirements of the underlying oscillation.

References

Emilio Bizzi, Andres Polit, and Pietro Morasso, "Mechanisms Underlying Achievement of Final Head Position," *J. Neurophys.*, Vol. 39, pp. 435-444, 1976.

A. G. Feldman, "Control of Muscle Length," *Biofizika*, Vol. 19, pp. 534-538, 1974.

John M. Hollerbach, *The Minimum Energy Movement for a Spring Muscle Model*, MIT AI Laboratory Memo 424, 1977.

W. G. Koster and J. Vredenbregt, "Analysis and Synthesis of Handwriting," *Medicine and Sport, Vol. 6: Biomechanics II*, pp. 77-82, 1971.

D. G. Schultz and James L. Melsa, *State Functions and Linear*

Control Systems, McGraw-Hill, 1967.

COMPUTER DESIGN AND SYMBOL MANIPULATION

ALAN BAWDEN
RICHARD GREENBLATT
JACK HOLLOWAY
THOMAS KNIGHT
DAVID MOON
DANIEL WEINREB
HENRY BAKER
GUY STEELE
CARL HEWITT

Section Contents

There are two reasons why Artificial Intelligence creates a need for new computing ideas and better, cheaper computers: first, Artificial Intelligence involves large programs that humble the capabilities of commercially-available computers; and second, application opportunities are opportunities only if the costs are reasonable. The consequence of these considerations is the development of the LISP machine, one of two central subjects in this chapter:

■   *Greenblatt et al.* open the chapter with a description of the LISP machine itself. In their section, they detail the computer's organization and describe tests made with the prototype.

■   *Baker*, in his first section, discusses the tradeoff between the cost of function call and the cost of variable access, and then presents a method for determining the proper balance.

■   *Baker* then describes, in his second section, an elegant new algorithm for garbage collection that is to be used in the LISP machine. It enables storage reclaimation to be interleaved with storage consumption, thus avoiding the potentially dangerous garbage-collection phases used now in other LISP implementations.

The second central subject of this chapter is that of programming itself.

■   *Steele* shows how two powerful ideas contribute to compiler construction. One is the heavy use of macros to define constructs like WHILE, thus enabling the compiler writer to concentrate on a small number of primitives. The other is a restriction to lexically scoped

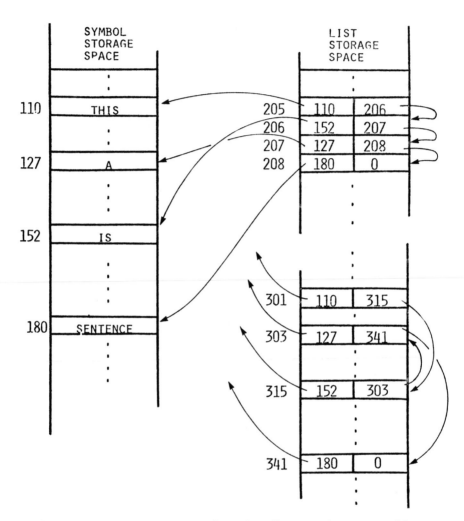

Figure 1. One simple way of storing lists requires two addresses to be stored in each word. For a simple list like (THIS IS A SENTENCE) there is no nesting. Consequently the first address in each word identifies a symbol in symbol storage space and the second gives the address of the next word in the list-storing chain. Thus the two chunks of memory at right both store the same list -- the first chunk happens to use consecutive words in memory while the second chunk does not.

variables, thus giving the compiler more complete knowledge of run-time environment, enabling optimizations that otherwise would be of questionable reliability.

■   *Hewitt* champions the idea that message passing should be the basic regime for procedural invocation, rather than the traditional call-save-return technique. This establishes a unified view encompassing both iteration and recursion.

Intelligent Information Processing Requires a New Machine

The section by Greenblatt *et al.* describes a computer designed specifically to run LISP. To deliver intelligent information processing, processors must be extremely good at executing LISP or a LISP-like language, for LISP is the *sine qua non* of intelligent information processing. This means the processor's design must exhibit a large number of features.

First the address space must be very large. The reason is that intelligent information processing at the lowest level has to do with representing symbol strings and symbol strings are represented by memory cells chained together after the fashion of the elementary scheme shown in figure 1. There, each memory cell holds two addresses: one is the address of a symbol stored in a portion of memory reserved for symbols; and the other is the address of the next memory cell in the chain. The second address is needed because it is not always possible to guarantee that consecutive cells will be called into service to represent a new string. There is no guarantee because new strings are constructed using the cells of old ones that are no longer needed. New strings are typically built out of cells drawn from all over the memory.

If a lot of information is to be stored, then, there will be a corollary need for a lot of addressable memory cells, each of which contains enough bits to completely specify the addresses of two other cells anywhere in the memory. The number of bits used to specify addresses determines the size of addressable memory, or to use the common term, the size of the address space. Note that this is not the same as the size of fast memory -- most of the addressable memory can reside on a disk.

The LISP machine devotes two 32-bit words to each cell. A full 24 bits in each 32-bit word is used to specify a single address. This makes its address space 64 times larger than the PDP-10's.

In addition to a large address space, there must be strong primitives for manipulating addresses. The need is clear: making new lists and tracing through existing ones call for strength in quickly isolating and dealing with the address portion of each word. The LISP machine's powerful microcode has the right design for manipulating addresses and facilitating the datatype checking of fetched pointers. (*Instructions* have to do with operations on and transfers between registers and memory locations. Typically, a high-level language statement requires many instructions. *Microinstructions* have to do with controlling the data paths. Instructions are implemented by combinations of microinstructions.)

Equally important, there must be fast function-call primitives. Intelligent programs tend to consist of subprograms that call each other a great deal. Each such call can require the execution of many instructions if there are many variables involved in the call, particularly if those variables are to be handled in some special way. The LISP machine is designed for fast, yet powerful function call. Simple cases are handled efficiently; more complicated function calls automatically invoke stronger mechanisms as required to handle the situation. Having the right microcode again is the key to flexibility.

Indeed, there must be a powerful microcode for many reasons. If instructions are to be powerful, if they are to be particularly adept at manipulating addresses, function call, and all the other things needed for symbol manipulations, then certainly the microcode they rest on must be powerful as well. A

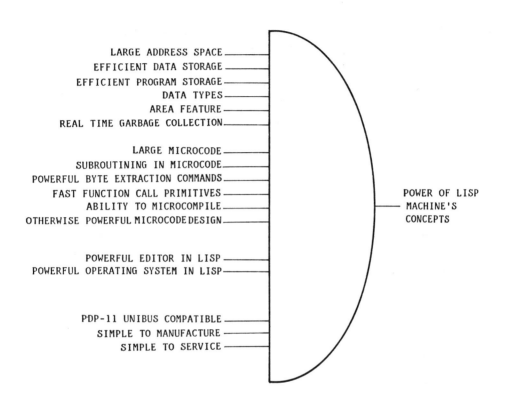

Figure 2. To make a powerful list-processing computer, many things must be done just right as suggested by this AND gate metaphor. The first group has to do with memory and memory management; the second, with microcode; the third, with using LISP as the sole implementation language above the microcode level; and the fourth, with general ease of deployment.

powerful microcode must have wide words so that data path control can be flexible and strong, and a powerful microcode memory must be large so that it can hold the necessary microcode programs for the key instructions.

The LISP machine has a wide, 48-bit microcode word size and a long, 16k word microcode memory size. The instruction and microcode instruction repertoire is oriented toward symbol manipulation, with many LISP instructions translating into single instructions that require a minimum number of microinstructions.

As suggested by figure 2, these are but a few of many things that must be right to have a viable processor for LISP. The diagram in the figure is meant to suggest an AND gate -- having most of the listed features does not do much good. Having all of them and having them properly brought together is the source of the LISP machine's revolutionary power.

We stress that these demands are not the idiosyncratic demands of a particular language. Rather, they are the demands always pressed by any language that supplies the data representation and manipulation features inherently required by intelligent information processing. We also stress that having these features does not make the LISP machine less capable at more traditional computing tasks. The demands of intelligent information processing are a superset of the demands of ordinary good computer design.

Garbage Collection must be Interleaved with other Processing

The process of deciding which memory cells may be reclaimed for use in building new lists is called garbage collection. One of the sections by Baker intoduces a new algorithm that interleaves a tiny amount of garbage collection with each primitive list-building operation. There is no danger that the machine will stop doing its job in a crisis. On the PDP-10, LISP programs drop dead periodically while the machine attends to this necessary custodial chore, examining all of memory for refuse.

THE
LISP
MACHINE

ALAN BAWDEN
RICHARD GREENBLATT
JACK HOLLOWAY
THOMAS KNIGHT
DAVID MOON
DANIEL WEINREB

For many years, the PDP-10 computer has been the workhorse of Artificial Intelligence. But many factors conspire to make serious researchers want more than PDP-10s can provide. The Artificial Intelligence Laboratory's LISP machine is the way to satisfy these wants. Among its advantages are a large address space, hardware data types, a general, large microcode that can be compiled into talented pointer-manipulating instructions, a real-time garbage collector, a powerful editor, LISP used as a system implementation language, reasonable speed, and perhaps most important, a low price. Some of the inspiration for the LISP Machine project comes from the pioneering research into personal computing and display-oriented systems done by Xerox's Palo Alto Research Center. For a time, the LISP machine work was a joint project between the Artificial Intelligence Laboratory and the Laboratory of Computer Science.

Background

The LISP Machine is a computer system designed to provide a high performance and economical implementation of the LISP programming language.

The LISP language is used widely in the Artificial Intelligence research community and is rapidly gaining adherents outside this group. Most serious LISP usage has historically been on the DEC PDP-10 computer, and both INTERLISP at BBN/XEROX and MACLISP at MIT were originally done on the PDP-10.

Over the years, dramatic changes have taken place in the MACLISP implementation. At a certain point, however, modification and reimplementation of a language on a given machine can no longer efficiently gloss over basic problems in the architecture of the computer system. This is now the case on the PDP-10 and similar timeshared computer systems.

Timesharing was introduced when it became apparent that computers are easier to use in an interactive fashion than in a batch system, and that during an interactive session a user typically uses only a small fraction of the processor and memory available; often the computer can be multiplexed among many users while giving each the impression that he is on his own machine.

However, in the LISP community there has been a strong trend towards programs that are very highly interactive, very large, and use a good deal of computer time; such programs include advanced editors and debuggers, the MACSYMA system for mathematical manipulation, and various programming assistants. When running programs such as these, that spend very significant amounts of time supporting user interactions, timesharing systems such as the PDP-10 run into increased difficulties. Not only is the processor incapable of providing either reasonable throughput or adequate response time for a reasonable number of users, but the competition for main memory results in large amounts of time being spent swapping pages in and out (a condition known as "thrashing"). Larger and larger processors and memory, and more and more complex operating systems are required, with more than proportionally higher cost, and still the competition for memory remains a bottleneck. The programs are sufficiently large, and the interactions sufficiently frequent, that the usual timesharing strategy of swapping a program out of memory while waiting for the user to interact, then swapping it back in when the user types something, cannot be successful because the swapping cannot happen fast enough.

The LISP Machine is a personal computer. Personal computing means that the processor and main memory are not time-division multiplexed; instead each person gets his own. The personal computation system consists of a pool of processors, each with its own main memory, and its own disk for swapping. When a user logs in, he is assigned a processor, and he has exclusive use of it for the duration of the session. When he logs out, the processor is returned to the pool, for the next person to use. This way, there is no competition from other users for memory; the pages the user is frequently referring to remain in core; and swapping overhead is considerably reduced. Thus the LISP Machine solves a basic problem of timesharing LISP systems.

The user also gets a much higher degree of service from a LISP machine than from a timesharing system because he can use the full throughput capacity of the processor and the disk. Although these are quite inexpensive compared to those used in PDP-10 timesharing systems, they are comparable in speed. In fact, since disk access times are mainly limited by physical considerations, it often turns out that the disk used in a personal computer system is less expensive simply because of its smaller size, and yet has fully comparable throughput charactistics to the larger disk used by a timesharing system.

In a single-user machine, there is no penalty for interactiveness, since there are no competing users to steal a program's memory while it is waiting for its user to type. Thus the LISP machine system, unlike time sharing systems, encourages highly interactive programs. It puts service to the user entirely ahead of efficiency considerations.

Another problem with the PDP-10 LISP implementations is the small address space of the PDP-10 processor. Many LISP systems, such as MACSYMA and Woods' LUNAR program, have difficulty running in an 18-bit address space. This problem is partly the result of inefficiency in the compiling of PDP-10 LISP code: compilers for the PDP-10 produce only a limited subset of the large instruction set made available by the hardware, and they usually make inefficient use of the addressing modes and fields provided. It is possible to design instruction sets that enable much more compact compilations. This is an important fact in view of the likelihood that future programs will be quite a bit bigger; intelligent systems with natural language front ends may well be five or ten times the size of a PDP-10 address space.

The LISP Machine has a 24-bit virtual address space and a compact instruction set. Thus much larger programs may be used, without running into address space limitations. Since the instruction set is designed specifically for the LISP language, the compiler is much simpler than the PDP-10 compiler, providing faster and more reliable compilation.

The LISP machine's compact size and simple hardware construction are likely to make it more reliable than other machines, such as the PDP-10; the prototype machine has had almost no hardware failures.

The LISP Machine Implementation

A LISP Machine user has a processor, a memory, a keyboard, a display, and a means of getting to the shared resources. Terminals, of course, are placed in offices and various rooms; ideally there would be one in every office. The processors, however, are all kept off in a machine room. Since they may need special environmental conditions, and often make noise and take up space, they are not welcome office companions. The number of processors is unrelated to the number of terminals, and may be much smaller depending on usage patterns and economic circumstance.

The key to the system is the microprogrammed CONS processor [Steele]. CONS is a very unspecialized machine with 32-bit data paths and 24-bit address paths. It has a large microcode memory (16K of 48-bit words) to accommodate the large amount of specialized microcode to support LISP. It has hardware for extracting and depositing arbitrary fields in arbitrary registers, which substitutes for the specialized data paths found in conventional microprocessors. It does not have a cache, but does have a "pdl buffer" (a memory with hardware push-down-list pointer), that acts as a kind of cache for the stack, which is where most of the memory references go in LISP.

Using a very unspecialized processor was found to be a good idea for several reasons. For one thing, it is faster, less expensive, and easier to debug. Moreover, it is much easier to microprogram, which facilitates writing and debugging the large amounts of microcode required to support a sophisticated LISP system with high efficiency. It also makes feasible a compiler that generates microcode, allowing users to microcompile some of their functions to increase performance.

The memory is typically 64k of core or semiconductor memory, and is expandable to about one million words. The full virtual address space is stored on a 16 million word disk and paged into core (or semiconductor) memory as required. A given virtual address is always located at the same place on the disk. The access time of the core memory is about one microsecond, and of the disk, about 25 milliseconds. Additionally, there is an internal 1k buffer used for holding the top of the stack (the PDL buffer) with a 200ns access time.

The display is a raster scan TV driven by a 1/4 Mbit memory. Since characters are drawn entirely by software, any type or size of font can be used. Indeed, one of the advantages of having an unspecialized microinstruction processor such as CONS is that one can implement a flexible terminal in software for less cost than an inflexible, hardwired conventional terminal. The TV system is easily expanded to support gray scale, high resolution, and color. It is therefore very useful for both character display and graphics.

The keyboard has several levels of control/shifting to facilitate easy single-keystroke commands to programs such as the editor. The keyboard is also equipped with a speaker for beeping and a pointing device.

The shared resources are accessed through a 10 million bit/sec packet switching network with completely distributed control. The shared resources are to include a highly reliable file system implemented on a dedicated computer equipped with state of the art disks and tapes, specialized I/O devices such as high-quality hardcopy output, special-purpose processors, and connections to the outside world (e.g. other computers in the building, and the ARPANET).

As in a time sharing system, the file system is shared between users. Time sharing has demonstrated many advantages of a shared file system, such as common access to files, easy interuser communication, centralized program maintenance, and centralized backup. There are no personal disk packs to be lost, dropped by users who are not competent as operators, or to be filled with copies of old, superseded software.

The complete LISP Machine, including processor, memory, disk, terminal, and connection to the shared file system, is packaged in a single 19" logic cabinet, except for the disk, which is free-standing. The complete machine would be likely to cost about $80,000 if commercially produced today. Since this is a complete, fully-capable system (for one user at a time), it can substantially lower the cost of entry by new organizations into serious Artificial Intelligence work.

LISP as a System Language

In the software of the LISP Machine system, code is written in only two languages (or "levels"): LISP, and CONS machine microcode. The intermediate macrocode level, corresponding to traditional assembly languages, is not used for hand-coding, since it corresponds so closely with LISP; anything one could write in macrocode could be more easily and clearly written in the corresponding LISP. The READ, EVAL, and PRINT functions are completely written in LISP, including their subfunctions (except that APPLY of compiled functions is in microcode). This illustrates the ability to write "system" functions in LISP.

In order to allow various low-level operations to be performed by LISP code, a set of "subprimitive" functions exist. Their names by convention begin with a "%," so as to point out that they are capable of performing operations that may result in meaningless pointers. These functions provide "machine level" capabilities, such as performing byte deposits into memory. The compiler converts calls to these subprimitives into single instructions rather than subroutine calls. Thus LISP-coded low-level operations are just as efficient as they would be in machine language on a conventional machine.

In addition to subprimitives, the ability to do system programming in LISP depends on the LISP machine's augmented array feature. There are several types of arrays, one of which is used to implement character strings. This makes it easy and efficient to manipulate strings either as a whole or character by character. An array can have a "leader," which is a little vector of extra information tacked on. The leader always contains LISP objects while the array often contains characters or small packed numbers. The leader facilititates the use of arrays to represent various kinds of abstract object types. The presence in the language of both arrays and lists gives the programmer more control over data representation.

A traditional weakness of LISP has to do with functions that should be allowed to have a variable number of arguments. Various implementors have added mechanisms that allow variable numbers of arguments; these, however, tend to slow down the function-calling mechanism, even when the feature is not used, or to force peculiar programming styles. LISP-machine LISP allows functions to have optional parameters with automatic, user-controlled defaulting to an arbitrary expression in the case where a corresponding argument is not supplied. It is also possible to have a "rest" parameter, which is bound to a list of the arguments not bound to previous parameters. This is frequently important to simplify system programs and their interfaces.

A similar problem with LISP function calling occurs when one wants to return more than one value. Traditionally one either returns a list or stores some of the values into global variables. In LISP Machine LISP, there is a multiple-value-return feature that allows multiple values to be returned without going through either of the above subterfuges.

LISP's functional orientation and encouragement of a programming style of small modules and uniform data structuring is appropriate for good system programming. The LISP machine's microcoded subroutine calling mechanism allows it to also be efficient.

Paging is handled entirely by the microcode, and is considered to be at a very low level (a lower level than any kind of scheduling). Making the details of the virtual memory invisible to all LISP code and most microcode helps keep things simple. It would not be practical in a time sharing system, but in a one-user machine it is reasonable to put paging at the lowest level and forget about it, accepting the fact that sometimes the machine will be tied up waiting for the disk and unable to run any LISP code.

Microcoded functions can be called by LISP code by the usual LISP calling mechanism, and provision is made for microcoded functions to call macrocoded functions. Thus there is a uniform calling convention throughout the entire system. This has the effect that uniform subroutine packages can be written, (for example the TV package, or the EDITOR package) that can be called by any other program. (A similar capability is provided by the Multics system, but not by ITS or TENEX).

Many of the capabilities that system programmers create

over and over again in an ad hoc way are built into the **LISP** language, and are sufficiently good in their **LISP**-provided form that it usually is not necessary to waste time worrying about how to implement better ones. These include symbol **tables, storage** management, both fixed and flexible data **structures,** function-calling, and an interactive user **interface.**

Representation of Data

A **LISP** object in MACLISP or INTERLISP is represented as an 18-bit pointer, and the datatype of the object is determined from the pointer: each page of memory can only contain objects of a single type. In the LISP Machine, LISP objects are represented by a 5-bit datatype field and a 24-bit pointer. (The LISP machine virtual address space is 24 bits).

　　　The LISP Machine data types are designed according to these criteria: there should be a wide variety of useful and flexible data types; some effort should be made to increase the bit efficiency of data representation, in order to improve performance; the programmer should be able to exercise control over the storage and representation of data, if he wishes; it must always be possible to take an anonymous piece of data and discover its type; and there should be much type-checking and error-checking.

　　　Symbols are stored as four consecutive words, each of which contains one object. The words are termed the **PRINT NAME** cell, the **VALUE** cell, the **FUNCTION** cell, and the **PROPERTY LIST** cell. The **PRINT NAME** cell holds a string object, which is the printed representation of the symbol. **The PROPERTY LIST** cell, of course, contains the property list, and the **VALUE CELL** contains the current value of the symbol (it is a so-called shallow-binding system). **The FUNCTION** cell replaces the EXPR, SUBR, FEXPR, MACRO, and similar properties in MACLISP. When a form such as (FOO ARG1 ARG2) is evaluated, the object in FOO's function cell is applied to the arguments. A symbol object has datatype **DTP-SYMBOL,** and the pointer is the address of these four words.

Storage of list structure is somewhat more complicated. Normally a "list object" has datatype DTP-LIST, and the pointer is the address of a two word block; the first word contains the CAR, and the second the CDR of the node.

However, note that since a LISP object is only 29 bits (24 bits of pointer and 5 bits of data-type), there are three remaining bits in each word. Two of these bits are termed the CDR-code field, and are used to compress the storage requirement of list structure. The four possible values of the CDR-code field are given the symbolic names CDR-NORMAL, CDR-ERROR, CDR-NEXT, and CDR-NIL. CDR-NORMAL indicates the two-word block described above. CDR-NEXT and CDR-NIL are used to represent a list as a vector, taking only half as much storage as usual. Only the CARs are stored; the CDR of each location is simply the next location, except for the last, whose CDR is NIL. The primitive functions that create lists (LIST, APPEND, etc.) create these compressed lists. If RPLACD is done on such a list, it is automatically changed back to the conventional two-word representation in a transparent way.

The idea is that in the first word of a list node the CAR is represented by 29 bits, and the CDR is represented by 2 bits. It is a compressed pointer that can take on only 3 legal values: to the symbol NIL, to the next location after the one it appears in, or indirect through the next location. CDR-ERROR is used for words whose address should not ever be in a list object; in a "full node," the first word is CDR-NORMAL, and the second is CDR-ERROR. It is important to note that the CDR-code portion of a word is used in a different way from the data-type and pointer portion; it is a property of the memory cell itself, not of the cell's contents. A "list object" which is represented in compressed form still has data type DTP-LIST, but the CDR-code of the word addressed by its pointer field is CDR-NEXT or CDR-NIL rather than CDR-NORMAL.

Number objects may have any of three datatypes: "fixnums," bit-arrays, and others. "FIXNUMs," which are 24-bit signed integers, are represented by objects of datatype DTP-FIX, whose "pointer" parts are actually the value of the number. Thus fixnums, unlike all other objects, do not require any "CONS"ed storage for their representation. This speeds up arithmetic programs when the numbers they work with are reasonably small. Other types of numbers, such as floating point, BIGNUMs (integers of arbitrarily big size), complex numbers, and so on, are represented by objects of the datatype DTP-EXTENDED-NUMBER that point to a block of storage containing the details of the number. The microcode automatically converts between the different number representations as necessary, without the need for explicit declarations on the programmer's part.

The most important other data type is the array. Some problems are best attacked using data structures organized in the list-processing style of LISP, and some are best attacked using the array-processing style of FORTRAN. The complete programming system needs both. LISP Machine arrays are augmented beyond traditional LISP arrays in several ways. First of all, we have the ordinary arrays of LISP objects, with one or more dimensions. Compact storage of positive integers, which may represent characters or other non-numeric entities, is afforded by arrays of 1-bit, 2-bit, 4-bit, 8-bit, or 16-bit elements.

For string-processing, there are string-arrays, which are usually one-dimensional and have 8-bit characters as elements. At the microcode level strings are treated the same as 8-bit arrays. However, strings are treated differently by READ, PRINT, EVAL, and many other system and user functions. For example, they print out as a sequence of characters enclosed in quotes. The characters in a character string can be accessed and modified with the same array-referencing functions as one uses for any other type of array. Unlike arrays in other LISP systems, LISP Machine arrays usually have only a single word of overhead, so the character strings are quite storage-efficient.

There are a number of specialized types of arrays that are used to implement other data types, such as stack groups, internal system tables, and, most importantly, the refresh memory of the TV display as a two-dimensional array of bits.

An important additional feature of LISP machine arrays is the "array leader." A leader is a vector of LISP objects, of user-specified size, that may be tacked on to an array. Leaders are a good place to remember miscellaneous extra information associated with an array. Many data structures consist of a combination of an array and a record; the array contains a number of objects all of the same conceptual type, while the record contains miscellaneous items all of different conceptual types. By storing the record in the leader of the array, the single conceptual data structure is represented by a single actual object. Many data structures in LISP Machine system programs work this way.

Another thing that leaders are used for is remembering the "current length" of a partially-populated array. By convention, array leader element number 0 is always used for this.

Many programs use data objects structured as "records;" that is, a compound object consisting of a fixed number of named subobjects. To facilitate the use of records, the LISP Machine system includes a standard set of macros for defining, creating, and accessing record structures. The user can choose whether the actual representation is to be a LISP list, an array, or an array-leader. Because this is done with macros, which translate record operations into the lower-level operations of basic LISP, no other part of the system needs to know about records.

Since the reader and printer are written in LISP and are user-modifiable, this record-structure feature could easily be expanded into a full-fledged user-defined data type facility by modifying read and print to support input and output of record types.

Representation of Programs

In the LISP Machine there are three representations for programs. Interpreted LISP code is the slowest, but the easiest for programs to understand and modify. It can be used for functions that are being debugged, for functions that need to be understood by other functions, and for functions that are not worth the bother of compiling. A few functions, notably EVAL, will not work interpreted.

Compiled LISP ("macrocode") is the main representation for programs. It consists of instructions in a somewhat conventional machine-language, whose unusual features will be described below. Unlike the case in many other LISP systems, macrocode programs still have full checking for unbound variables, data type errors, wrong number of arguments to a function, and so forth. Therefore it is not necessary to resort to interpreted code just to get extra checking to detect bugs. Often, after typing in a function to the editor, one skips the interpretation step and requests the editor to call the compiler on it, which only takes a few seconds since the compiler is always in the machine and only has to be paged in.

Compiled code on the LISP Machine is stored inside objects called (for historical reasons) Function Entry Frames (FEFs). For each function compiled, one FEF is created, and an object of type DTP-FEF-POINTER is stored in the function cell of the symbol that is the name of the function. A FEF consists of some header information, a description of the arguments accepted by the function, pointers to external LISP objects needed by the function (such as constants and special variables), and the macrocode that implements the function.

The third form of program representation is microcode. The system includes a good deal of hand-coded microcode that executes the macrocode instructions, implements the data types and the function-calling mechanism, maintains the paged virtual memory, does storage allocation and garbage collection, and performs similar systemic functions. The primitive operations on the basic data types, such as CAR and CDR for lists, arithmetic for numbers, reference and store for arrays, are implemented as microcode subroutines. In addition, a number of commonly-used LISP functions, for instance GET and ASSQ, are hand-coded in microcode for speed.

In addition to this system-supplied microcode, there is a feature called microcompilation. Because of the simplicity and generality of the CONS microprocessor, it is feasible to write a compiler to compile user-written LISP functions directly into microcode, eliminating the overhead of fetching and interpreting macroinstructions. This can be used to boost performance by microcompiling the most critical routines of a program. Because it is done by a compiler rather than a system programmer, this performance improvement is available to everyone. The amount of speedup to be expected depends on the operations used by the program: simple low-level operations such as data transmission, byte extraction, integer arithmetic, and simple branching benefit the most. Function calling, and operations that already spend most of their time in microcode, such as ASSQ, will benefit the least. In the best case one can achieve a factor of about 20; in the worst case, maybe no speedup at all.

Since the amount of control memory is limited, only a small number of microcompiled functions can be loaded in at one time. This means that programs have to be characterized by spending most of their time in a small inner kernel of functions in order to benefit from microcompilation; this is probably true of most programs. There will be metering facilities for identifying such critical functions.

In all three forms of program, the flexibility of function-calling is augmented with generalized LAMBDA lists. In order to provide a more general and flexible scheme to replace EXPRs, FEXPRs, and LEXPRs, a syntax borrowed from MUDDLE [Galley and Pfister 1975] and CONNIVER [Sussman and McDermott 1974] is used in LAMBDA lists. In the general case, there are an arbitrary number of required parameters, followed by an arbitrary number of optional parameters, possibly followed by one rest parameter. When a function is applied to its arguments, first the required formal parameters are paired off with arguments; if there are fewer arguments than required parameters, an error condition is caused. Then, any remaining arguments are paired off with the optional parameters; if there are more optional parameters than arguments remaining, then the rest of the optional parameters are initialized in a user-specified manner. The REST parameter is bound to a list, possibly NIL, of all arguments remaining after all OPTIONAL parameters are bound. It is also possible to control whether or not arguments are evaluated.

Normally, such a complicated calling sequence would require an unacceptable amount of overhead. Because this is all implemented by microcode, and because the simple, common cases are teated specially, these advanced features could be provided while retaining the efficiency needed in a practical system.

Each macroinstruction is 16 bits long; they are stored two per word. The instructions work in a stack-oriented machine. The stack is formatted into frames; each frame contains a bunch of arguments, a bunch of local variable value slots, a push-down stack for intermediate results, and a header that gives the function that owns the frame, links this frame to previous frames, remembers the program counter and flags when this frame is not executing, and may contain "additional information" used for certain esoteric purposes. Originally this was intended to be a spaghetti stack, but the invention of closures and stack-groups, combined with the extreme complexity of spaghetti stacks, made us decide to use a simple linear stack. The current frame is always held in the pdl buffer, so accesses to arguments and local variables do not require memory references, and do not have to make checks related to the garbage collector, which improves performance. Usually several other frames will also be in the pdl buffer.

The macroinstruction set is bit-compact. The stack organization and LISP's division of programs into small, separate functions means that address fields can be small. The use of tagged data types, powerful generic operations, and easily-called microcoded functions makes a single 16-bit macroinstruction do the work of several instructions on a conventional machine such as a PDP-10.

The primitive operations that are the compiler-generated instructions are higher-level than the instructions of a conventional machine. They all do data type checks; this provides more run-time error checking than in MACLISP, which increases reliability. It also eliminates much of the need to make declarations in order to get efficient code. Since a data type check is being made, the "primitive" operations can dynamically decide which specific routine is to be called. This means that they are all "generic;" that is, they work for all data types where they make sense.

The operations that are regarded as most important, and hence are easiest for macrocode to do, are data transmission, function-calling, conditional testing, and simple operations on primitive types. These include CAR, CDR, CADR, CDDR, RPLACA, and RPLACD, plus the usual arithmetic operations and comparisons. More complex operations are generally done by "miscellaneous" instructions, that call microcoded subroutines, passing arguments on the temporary-results stack.

There are three main kinds of addressing in macrocode. First, there is implicit addressing of the top of the stack. This is the usual way that operands get from one instruction to the next.

Second, there is the source field. The source can address any of the following: up to 64 arguments to the current function; up to 64 local variables of the current function; the last result, popped off the stack; one of several commonly-used constants (e.g. NIL) stored in a system-wide constants area; constants stored in the FEF of this function; and a value cell or a function cell of a symbol, referenced by means of an invisible pointer in the FEF -- this mode is used to reference special variables and to call other functions.

Third, there is the destination field, which specifies what

to do with the result of the instruction. The possibilities are: ignore it, except set the indicators used by conditional branches; push it on the stack; pass it as an argument; return it as the value of this function; and make a list.

There are five types of macroinstructions, which will be described. First, there are the data transmission instructions, that take the source and MOVE it to the destination, optionally taking CAR, CDR, CAAR, CADR, CDAR, or CDDR in the process. Because of the powerful operations that can be specified in the destination, these instructions also serve as argument-passing, function-exiting, and list-making instructions.

Next we have the function calling instructions. The simpler of the two is CALL0, call with no arguments. It calls the function indicated by its source, and when that function returns, the result is stored in the destination. The microcode takes care of identifying what type of function is being called, invoking it in the appropriate way, and saving the state of the current function. It traps to the interpreter if the called function is not compiled.

The more complex function call occurs when there are arguments to be passed. First, a CALL instruction is executed. The source operand is the function to be called. The beginnings of a new stack frame are constructed at the end of the current frame, and the function to be called is remembered. The destination of the CALL instruction specifies where the result of the function will be placed, and it is saved for later use when the function returns. Next, instructions are executed to compute the arguments and store them into the destination NEXT-ARGUMENT. This causes them to be added to the new stack frame. When the last argument is computed, it is stored into the destination LAST-ARGUMENT, that stores it in the new stack frame and then activates the call. The function to be called is analyzed, and the arguments are bound to the formal parameters (usually the arguments are already in the correct slots of the new stack frame). Because the computation of the arguments is introduced by a CALL instruction, it is easy to find out where the arguments are and how many there are. The new stack frame becomes current and that function begins execution. When it returns, the saved destination of the CALL instruction is retrieved and the result is stored. Note that by using a destination of NEXT-ARGUMENT or LAST-ARGUMENT function calls may be nested. By using a destination of RETURN the result of one function may become the result of its caller.

The third class of macro instructions consists of a number of common operations on primitive data types. These instructions do not have an explicit destination, in order to save bits, but implicitly push their result (if any) onto the stack. This sometimes necessitates the generation of an extra MOVE instruction to put the result where it was really wanted. These instructions include operations to store results from the pdl into the "source," the basic arithmetic and bitwise boolean operations, comparison operations, including EQ and arithmetic comparison, instructions that set the "source" operand to NIL or zero, iteration instructions that change the "source" operand using CDR, CDDR, 1+, or 1- (add or subtract one), binding instructions that lambda-bind the "source" operand, then optionally set it to NIL or to a value popped off the stack, and finally, an instruction to push its effective address onto the stack.

The fourth class of macro instructions are the branches, that serve mainly for compiling COND. Branches contain a self-relative address that is transferred to if a specified condition is satisfied. There are two indicators that tell if the last result was NIL, and if it was an atom. The state of these indicators can be branched on; there is also an unconditional branch, of course. For branches more than 256 half-words away, there is a double-length long-branch instruction. An interesting fact is that there are not really any indicators; it turns out to be faster just to save the last result in its entirety, and compare it against NIL or whatever when that is needed by a branch instruction. It only has to be saved from one instruction to the immediately following one.

The fifth class of macro instructions is the "miscellaneous function" category. This selects one of 512 microcoded functions to be called, with arguments taken from results previously pushed on the stack. A destination is specified to receive the result of the function. In addition to commonly-used functions such as GET, CONS, CDDDDR, REMAINDER, and ASSQ, miscellaneous functions include subprimitives (discussed above), and instructions that are not as commonly used as the first four classes, including operations such as array-accessing.

The way CONSing together is done is that one first does a miscellaneous function saying "make a list N long." One then executes N instructions with destination NEXT-LIST to supply the elements of the list. After the Nth such instruction, the list-object appears on the top of the stack.

Another type of "instruction set" used with macrocode is the Argument Description List, that is executed by a different microcoded interpreter at the time a function is entered. The ADL contains one entry for each argument that the function expects to be passed, and for each auxiliary variable. It contains all relevant information about the argument: whether it is required, optional, or rest, how to initialize it if it is not provided, whether it is local or special, datatype checking information, and so on. Sometimes the ADL can be dispensed with if the "fast argument option" can be used instead; this helps save time and memory for small, simple functions. The fast-argument option is used when the optional arguments and local variables are all to be initialized to NIL, there are not many of them, there is no data-type checking, and the usage of special variables is not complicated. The selection of the fast-argument option, if appropriate, is automatically made by the system, so the user need not be concerned with it.

Control Structures

Function calling is, of course, the basic main control structure in LISP. As mentioned above, LISP machine function calling is made fast through the use of microcode and augmented with optional arguments, rest arguments, multiple return values, and optional type-checking of arguments.

CATCH and THROW are a MACLISP control structure that will be mentioned here since they may be new to some readers. CATCH is a way of marking a particular point in the stack of recursive function invocations. THROW causes control to be unwound to the matching CATCH, automatically returning through the intervening function calls. They are used mainly for handling errors and unusual conditions. They are also useful for getting out of a piece of code when it discovered what value is to be returned; this applies particularly to nested loops.

The LISP Machine contains a data-type called "closure" that is used to implement "full funarging." By turning a function into a closure, it becomes possible to pass it as an argument with no worry about naming conflicts, and to return it as a value with exactly the minimum necessary amount of binding environment being retained, solving the classical "funarg problem." Closures are implemented in such a way that when they are not used the highly speed- and storage-efficient shallow binding variable scheme operates at full efficiency, and when they are used, things are slowed down only slightly. The way one creates a closure is with a form such as

```
(CLOSURE '(FOO-PARAM FOO-STATE)
         (FUNCTION FOO-BAR))
```

The function could also be written directly in place as a LAMBDA-expression, instead of referring to the externally defined FOO-BAR. The variables FOO-PARAM and FOO-STATE are those variables that are used free by FOO-BAR and are intended to be "closed." That is, these are the variables whose binding environment is to be fixed to that in effect at the time the closure is created. The explicit declaration of which variables are to be closed allows the implementation to have high efficiency since it does not need to save the whole variable-binding environment, almost all of which is useless. It also allows the programmer to explicitly choose for each variable whether it is to be dynamically bound (at the point of call) or statically bound (at the point of creation of the closure), a choice that is not conveniently available in other languages. In addition the program is clearer because the intended effect of the closure is made manifest by listing the variables to be affected.

Consider an example in which the closure feature is used to solve a problem presented in a paper by Steele [1977]. The problem is to write a function called

GENERATE-SQRT-OF-GIVEN-EXTRA-TOLERANCE,

which is to take as its single argument the factor by which the tolerance is to be increased, and to return a function that takes square roots with that much more tolerance than usual, whatever "usual" is later defined to be. The programmer is given a function SQRT that makes a free reference to EPSILON, which is the tolerance it demands of the trial solution. The reason this example presents difficulties to various languages is that the variable EPSILON must be bound at the point of call (i.e. dynamically scoped), while the variable FACTOR must be bound at the point of creation of the function (i.e. lexically scoped). Thus the programmer must have explicit control over how the variables are bound.

```
(DEFUN GENERATE-SQRT-OF-GIVEN-EXTRA-TOLERANCE (FACTOR)
    (CLOSURE '(FACTOR)
             (FUNCTION
             (LAMBDA (X)
               ((LAMBDA (EPSILON) (SQRT X))
                (* EPSILON FACTOR))))))
```

The function, when called, rebinds EPSILON to FACTOR times its current value, then calls SQRT. The value of FACTOR used is that in effect when the closure was created, that is, the argument to GENERATE-SQRT-OF-GIVEN-EXTRA-TOLERANCE.

The way closures are implemented is as follows. For each variable to be closed an "external value cell" is created, that is a CONSed up free-storage cell that contains the variable's value when it is at that level of binding. Because this cell is CONSed up, it can be retained as long as necessary, just like any other data, and unlike cells in a stack. Because it is a cell, if the variable is SETQed the new value is seen by all the closures that should see it. The association between the symbol that is the name of the variable and this value cell is of the shallow-binding type, for efficiency; an invisible pointer in the normal (internal) value cell supplies the connection, eliminating the overhead of searching stack frames or a-lists. If at the time the closure is created an external value cell already exists for a variable, that one is used instead of creating a new one. Thus all closures at the same "level of binding" use the same value cell, which is the desired semantics.

The CLOSURE function returns an object of type DTP-CLOSURE, that contains the function to be called and, for each variable closed over, locative pointers to its internal and external value cells.

When a closure is invoked as a function, the variables mentioned in the closure are bound to invisible pointers to their external value cells; this puts these variables into the proper binding environment. The function contained in the closure is then invoked in the normal way. When the closed variables happen to be referred to, the invisible pointers are automatically followed to the external value cells. If one of the closed variables is then bound by some other function, the external value cell pointer is saved away on the binding stack, like any saved variable value, and the variable reverts to normal nonclosed status. When the closed function returns, the bindings of the closed variables are restored just like any other variables bound by the function.

Note the economy of mechanism. Almost all of the system is completely unaffected by and unaware of the existence of closures; the invisible pointer mechanism takes care of things.

The retainable binding environments are allocated through the standard CONS operation. The switching of variables between normal and "closed" status is done through the standard binding operation. The operations used by a closed function to access the closed variables are the same as those used to access ordinary variables; closures are called in the same way as ordinary functions. Closures work just as well in the interpreter as in the compiler. An important thing to note is the minimality of CONSing in closures. When a closure is created, some CONSing is done; external value cells and the closure-object itself must be created, but there is no extra "overhead." When a closure is called, no CONSing happens.

The stack group is a type of LISP object useful for implementation of certain advanced control structures such as coroutines, asynchronous processes, and generators. A stack group is similar to a process (or fork or job or task or control-point) in a timesharing system; it contains such state information as the "regular" and "special" (binding) PDLs and various internal registers. At all times there is one stack group running on the machine.

Control may be passed between stack groups in several ways. A stack-group may be called like a function; when it wants to return it can do a %STACK-GROUP-RETURN which is different from an ordinary function return in that the state of the stack group remains unchanged; the next time it is called it picks up from where it left off. This is good for generator-like applications; each time %STACK-GROUP-RETURN is done, a value is emitted from the generator, and as a side-effect, execution is suspended until the next time the generator is called. %STACK-GROUP-RETURN is analogous to the ADIEU construct in CONNIVER.

Control can simply be passed explicitly from one stack group to another, coroutine-style. Alternatively, there can be a scheduler stack-group that invokes other stack groups when their requested scheduling conditions are satisfied.

Interrupts cause control of the machine to be transferred

to an interrupt-handler stack group. Essentially this is a forced stack group call like those calls described above. Similarly, when the microcode detects an error the current stack group is suspended and control is passed to an error-handling stack group. The state of the stack group that got the error is left exactly as it was when the error occurred, undisturbed by any error-handling operations. This facilitates error analysis and recovery.

Note that the same scheduler-driven stack-group switching mechanism can be used both for user programs which want to do parallel computations, and for system programming purposes such as the handling of network servers and peripheral handlers.

One important difference between stack groups and other means proposed to implement similar features is that the stack group scheme involves no loss of efficiency in normal computation. In fact, the compiler, the interpreter, and even the runtime function-calling mechanism are completely unaware of the existence of stack groups.

Storage Organization

The LISP machine will use a real-time, incremental, compacting garbage collector. Real-time means that CONS and related functions never delay LISP execution for more than a small, bounded amount of time. This is very important in a machine with a large address space, where a traditional garbage collection could bring everything to a halt for several minutes. The garbage collector compactifies in order to improve the paging characteristics.

The basic algorithm is described in a paper by Baker [1977]. It is much simpler than previous methods of incremental garbage collection in that only one process is needed; this avoids interlocking and synchronization problems that are often very difficult to debug.

Storage in the LISP machine is divided into "areas." Each area contains related objects of any type. Since we do not encode the data type in the address, we are free to use the address to encode the area. Areas are intended to give the user control over the paging behavior of his program, among other things. By putting related data together, locality can be greatly increased. Whenever a new object is created, for instance with CONS, the area to be used can optionally be specified. There is a default working storage area that collects those objects that the user has not chosen to control explicitly.

Areas also give the user a handle on the garbage collector. Some areas can be declared to be "static," which means that they change slowly and the garbage collector should not attempt to reclaim any space in them. This can eliminate a lot of useless copying. All pointers out of a static area can be collected into an "exit vector," eliminating any need for the garbage collector to look at that area. As an important example, an English-language dictionary can be kept inside the LISP without adversely affecting the speed of garbage collection. A "static" area can be explicitly garbage-collected at infrequent intervals when it is believed that that might be worthwhile.

Each area can potentially have a different storage discipline, a different paging algorithm, and even a different data representation. The microcode will dispatch on an attribute of the area at the appropriate times. The structure of the machine makes the performance cost of these features negligible; information about areas is stored in extra bits in the memory mapping hardware where it can be quickly dispatched on by the microcode. These dispatches usually have to be done anyway to make the garbage collector work, and to implement invisible pointers.

An invisible pointer is similar to an indirect address word on a conventional computer except the indirection is specified in the data instead of in the instruction. A reference to a memory location containing an invisible pointer is automatically altered to use the location pointed to by the invisible pointer. The term "invisible" refers to the fact that the presence of such pointers is not visible to most of the system, since they are handled by the lowest-level memory-referencing operations. The invisible pointer feature does not slow anything down much, because it is part of the data type checking that is done anyway (this is one of the benefits of a tagged architecture). A number of advanced features of the LISP machine depend upon invisible pointers for their efficient implementation.

Closures use invisible pointers to connect internal value cells to external value cells. This allows the variable binding scheme to be altered from normal shallow binding to allocated-value-cell shallow binding when closures are being used, without altering the normal operation of the machine when closures are not being used. At the same time the slow-down when closures are used amounts to only 2 microseconds per closed-variable reference, the time needed to detect and follow the invisible pointer.

Invisible pointers are necessary to the operation of the CDR-coded compressed list scheme. If RPLACD is done to a compressed list, the list can no longer be represented in the compressed form. It is necessary to allocate a full 2-word cons node and use that in its place. But, it is also necessary to preserve the identity (with respect to EQ) of the list. This is done by storing an invisible pointer in the original location of the compressed list, pointing to the uncompressed copy. Then the list is still represented by its original location, preserving EQness, but the CAR and CDR operations follow the invisible pointer to the new location and find the proper car and cdr.

This is a special case of the more general use of invisible pointers for "forwarding" references from an old representation of an object to a new one. For instance, there is a function to increase the size of an array. If it cannot do it in place, it makes a new copy and leaves behind an invisible pointer.

The exit-vector feature uses invisible pointers. One may set up an area to have the property that all references from inside that area to objects in other areas are collected into a single exit-vector. A location that would normally contain such a reference instead contains an invisible pointer to the appropriate slot in the exit vector. Operations on this area all work as before, except for a slight slow-down caused by the invisible pointer following. It is also desirable to have automatic checking to prevent the creation of new outside references; when an attempt is made to store an outside object into this area execution can trap to a routine that creates a new exit vector entry if necessary and stores an invisible pointer instead. The reason for exit vectors is to speed up garbage collection by eliminating the need to swap in all of the pages of the area in order to find and relocate all its references to outside objects.

Results

As a demonstration of the system, and a test of its capabilities, two large programs have been brought over from the PDP-10. William Woods's LUNAR English-language data-base query system was converted from INTERLISP to MACLISP, thence to LISP machine LISP. On the LISP machine it runs approximately 3 times as fast as in MACLISP on the KA-10, that in turn is 2 to 4 times as fast as in INTERLISP. Note that the LISP machine time is elapsed real time, while the PDP-10 times are virtual run times as given by the operating system and do not include the delays due to timesharing.

Most of the Macsyma symbolic algebraic system has been converted to the LISP machine; nearly all the source files were simply compiled without any modifications. Most of Macsyma works except for some things that require BIGNUMS. The preliminary speed is the same as on the KA-10, but a number of things have not been optimally converted. (This speed measurement is, again, elapsed time on the LISP machine version versus reported run time on the KA-10 time sharing system. Thus, paging and scheduling overhead in the KA-10 case are not counted in this measurement.)

LUNAR (including the dictionary) and MACSYMA can reside together in the LISP machine with plenty of room left over; either program alone will not entirely fit in a PDP-10 address space.

References

Guy L. Steele, *Cons,* not yet published (this is a revision of MIT AI Laboratory Working Paper 80, *CONS* by Thomas Knight).

Henry Baker, *List Processing in Real Time on a Serial Computer,* MIT AI Laboratory Working Paper 139, 1977.

Guy L. Steele, *LAMBDA - The Ultimate Imperative,* MIT AI Laboratory Memo 353, 1976.

Galley and Phister, *The MDL Language,* MIT Laboratory for Computer Science, 1975.

Gerald Sussman and Drew McDermott, *The CONNIVER Reference Manual,* MIT AI Laboratory Memo 259a, 1974.

SHALLOW BINDING IN LISP 1.5

HENRY G. BAKER, JR.

There are two processes which affect variable bindings in LISP. To find the current value of a variable, the current binding of that variable must be accessed. When the context changes (when a function returns to its caller, for example), then a different collection of bindings becomes "current." There is a trade-off in the amount of time taken by these two processes. In so-called deep binding systems like LISP 1.5, the access time is unbounded but the context switching time is constant. In MACLISP, access time is constant, while context switching time is unbounded. Henry Baker presents a technique which gives the programmer (or the system) continuous control over this trade-off.

How a Variable can be Bound

A severe problem in LISP 1.5 [McCarthy 1965] systems is the amount of time needed to access the value of a variable. This problem is compounded in LISP and APL by the "fluid" or "dynamic" binding of free variables; it is not so bad in ALGOL and PL/I, where free variables are "lexically" bound. Dynamic variable binding requires that free variables be looked up in the environment of the caller (dynamically embracing block) rather than that of the statically embracing block. This decision leads to environment trees which are "tall and thin" rather than "short and bushy." Since the length of time required to access the binding of a variable is proportional to the distance in the tree from the current environment to the place where that variable is bound, this time can be quite large with tall environment trees. For example, accessing a "global" variable at the bottom of a deep recursion can require time proportional to the depth of the recursion.

The MACLISP interpreter [Moon 1974] solves this problem through a scheme called "shallow binding." In this scheme, variables have "value cells" as well as bindings in the environment. The scheme always endeavors to keep the bindings associated with the current environment in the "value cells" so that they can be accessed without any search. Whenever a context change occurs, such as when calling or returning from a function, these "value cells" must be changed or restored. Since the changes in the environment structure mirror those in the return-point stack, MACLISP implements shallow binding by saving old bindings on a stack when calling and popping them off when returning. Thus, there is a trade-off between the time needed to access the binding of a variable and the time needed to switch contexts. In so-called deep binding systems like LISP 1.5, the access time is unbounded but the context switching time is constant. In MACLISP, access time is constant, while context switching time is unbounded.

The scheme used in MACLISP does not qualify as a

model for shallow-binding in LISP 1.5 because it does not handle function-producing functions, i.e. upward FUNARGs, correctly [Moses 1970]. No *stack* environment has that capability because conforming to stack discipline can lead to premature unbinding of variables. Our model for shallow binding keeps a *tree* environment and hence is capable of handling full FUNARGs.

Rerooting Environment Trees

In our model, we assign to each variable a *value cell*, which contains the default value of that variable, i.e. the value to be used if the variable is not bound in the path from the current environment to the root of the environment tree. The algorithm for accessing a variable is to search the environment tree from the current environment to the root and if the variable is found, use the associated value; or else use the value in the value cell. (This scheme is used in several LISP 1.5 systems where the default value is the global or top level value of the variable). So far, we have described a conventional deep binding interpreter. In order to convert this system into a *shallow* binding system, we need only make sure that the distance from the current environment to the root in the environment tree is *short*; that is, *make sure that the current environment is always the root.* In this case, the variable search is always trivial and is eliminated.

The way that we do this is to reroot the environment tree at each context-switch, so that the context following the switch becomes the new root. Consider the situation in which a function of one parameter, x, is called from the null environment. Suppose (see figure 1) that x is bound to 5 in the null environment e_0 (i.e. x has 5 in its value cell), and that x is to be bound to 6 in the body of the function. The function call creates a new environment e_1 which pairs x with 6 and has e_0 as its parent environment. A deep binding interpreter would set the current environment pointer to e_1 and all variable accesses would be done through e_1, thus lengthening the access time to all variables but x. A shallow binding call, on the other hand, transforms the environment tree in the following manner: 1) e_0 is changed to pair x with 5 and have e_1 as its parent; 2) e_1 is changed to a null environment; and 3) the value cell of x is set to 6. In this way, all variable access are shallow inside the function. Upon return from the function, the environment is rerooted back to e_0.

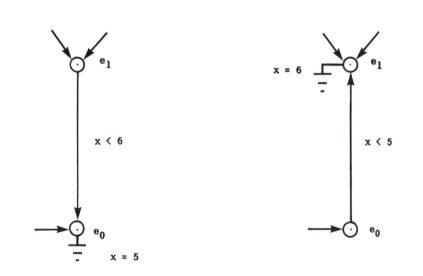

Figure 1. Environment transformations.

We outline a proof that (ASSOC X A) is left invariant under the rerooting transformation. There are only four basic cases: 1) (ASSOC X e_0); 2) (ASSOC y e_0); 3) (ASSOC X e_1); and 4) (ASSOC y e_1); y is any variable other than X. In each case, the reader can check that the expression is left invariant. By induction on the length of the search path, (ASSOC X A) and (ASSOC y A) are left invariant for all other environments A.

Finally, if the root can be moved by one step in the tree, it can be moved to any node in the tree by iterating the one step procedure. Thus, we have proved that rerooting to any node in the tree is possible while preserving (ASSOC X A), for all variables X and all environments A.

Code for ASSOC

We present a modified ASSOC function which gets a variable binding from its value cell and a modified APPLY function which reroots the environment tree whenever a context switch is made, that is, when a function is called or returned from. RE-ROOT allows rerooting to an environment more than one step from the old root essentially by iterating the process described above. These functions are intended to work with a LISP interpreter like that found in the LISP 1.5 Programmer's Manual [McCarthy 1965]. (Note, however, that boundary conditions require a null environment to bind NIL to NIL.) All variables are assumed to have *some* value in every environment; the more general case is left to the reader.

```
(DEFUN ASSOC (X A)
       (VCELL X))


(DEFUN APPLY (FN X A)
       (COND ((ATOM FN)
              (COND ((EQ FN 'CAR) (CAAR X))
                    ((EQ FN 'CDR) (CDAR X))
                    ((EQ FN 'CONS) (CONS (CAR X) (CADR X)))
                    ((EQ FN 'ATOM) (ATOM (CAR X)))
                    ((EQ FN 'EQ) (EQ (CAR X) (CADR X)))
                    (T (APPLY (EVAL FN A) X A))))
             ((EQ (CAR FN) 'LAMBDA)
              (PROG1 (EVAL (CADDR FN)
                          (RE-ROOT
                             (PAIRLIS (CADR FN) X A)))
                     (RE-ROOT A)))
             ((EQ (CAR FN) 'FUNARG)
              (PROG1 (APPLY (CADR FN) X (CADDR FN))
                     (RE-ROOT A)))))


(DEFUN RE-ROOT (A)
       (PROG (P Q)
             (SETQ Q (NREVERSE A))
             (SETQ P (CDR Q))
        LOOP (COND ((EQ Q A)
                    (RPLACA (CAR A) NIL)
                    (RPLACD (CAR A) NIL)
                    (RETURN A)))
             (RPLACA (CAR Q) (CAAR P))
             (RPLACD (CAR Q) (CDR (VCELL (CAAR P))))
             (RPLACD (VCELL (CAAR P)) (CDAR P))
             (SETQ Q P)
             (SETQ P (CDR P))
             (GO LOOP)))
```

(DEFUN f p b) defines a function f with parameters p and body b in the top-level environment.

(VCELL y) returns the value cell of variable y, which is a cons cell having the value as its CDR.

(NREVERSE x) reverses a list x destructively, by flipping the CDR pointers.

(PROG1 e1 e2 ...) evaluates e1, e2, ... in that order and returns the value of e1.

The Rerooting Algorithm

The rerooting algorithm is quite simple. Suppose that e is the current root of the environment tree and e' is any other node in the tree which we wish to become the new root. Now, since e is the current root of the tree, the "parent" path from every other node in the tree will terminate at e, and we have a directed path from e' to e. We make two passes over that path, one forwards and one backwards. On the first pass, we go from e' to e while reversing all of the parent pointers. On the second pass, we go from e back to e' while exchanging the values in the association pairs with those in the value cells. This has the effect of shifting the values in the path over by one occurrence and terminating with the proper values for e' in the value cells.

This algorithm has much in common with the Deutch-Waite-Schorr marking algorithm for LISP-style garbage collection [Knuth 1968] in that no additional storage is used, and pointers that previously pointed to a node's son are changed to point to that node's parent. Unlike that algorithm, the pointers are not changed back, unless of course the context is switched back to a previous environment.

The continuous shallow binding interpreter presented here is equivalent to the MACLISP interpreter for that class of LISP programs which do not have FUNARGs in the sense that the tree environment created will consist of a single filament which is isomorphic to the MACLISP specpdl (for *spec*ial variable *p*ush-*d*own *l*ist). However, our implementation of the model, being simple for pedagogic reasons, is not meant to be the most efficient way to perform shallow binding; storage reclamation, for example, is much less efficient than using a push-down stack.

Occasional Rerooting

Suppose now that we have a standard deep binding LISP 1.5 interpreter which has been augmented only by the (SHALLOW) primitive. When this primitive is invoked, the environment tree will be rerooted to the current environment. Rerooting transforms the environment tree in such a way that (ASSOC X A) is left invariant; therefore the interpretation proceeds correctly, but the length of the searches is changed. In other words, we can reroot at any point in the computation, not just during context-switching. Here is a sketch for an occasional shallow binding interpreter.

```
(DEFUN ASSOC (X A)
      (COND ((NULL A) (VCELL X))
            ((EQ (CAAR A) X) (CAR A))
            (T (ASSOC X (CDR A)))))

(DEFUN APPLY (FN X A)
      (COND ((ATOM FN)
             (COND ((EQ FN 'CAR) (CAAR X))
                   ((EQ FN 'CDR) (CDAR X))
                   ((EQ FN 'CONS) (CONS (CAR X) (CADR X)))
                   ((EQ FN 'ATOM) (ATOM (CAR X)))
                   ((EQ FN 'EQ) (EQ (CAR X) (CADR X)))
                   ((EQ FN 'SHALLOW) (PROG2 (RE-ROOT A) T))
                   (T (APPLY (EVAL FN A) X A))))
            ((EQ (CAR FN) 'LAMBDA)
             (EVAL (CADDR FN) (PAIRLIS (CADR FN) X A)))
            ((EQ (CAR FN) 'FUNARG)
             (APPLY (CADR FN) X (CADDR FN)))))
```

We see that rerooting is a transformation on the environment structure which preserves (ASSOC X A) and has nothing to do with how the structure was created. As a result, the interpreter could do either dynamic or lexical free variable binding and still be able to reroot. However, lexical binding interpreters may have nothing to gain from rerooting, since there exist schemes for them such as Dijkstra's display [Randell 1964] in which variable look-up time is bounded by a constant. A display cannot be used in LISP, though, because there it is impossible to tell *a priori* which variable occurrences are to refer to the same storage location.

Giving the programmer a choice as to which functions are to run shallow- or deep-bound can produce more efficient programs. For example, a tight loop may run faster when shallow-bound, while an interrupt handler might run better deep-bound, since rerooting can be time consuming.

LISP 1.5 can be augmented with primitives for

multiprocessing such as fork, p, and v. Several processes can be active in the environment tree in such a system without conflict because none of the processes changes the backbone of the tree. Since rerooting preserves the value of (ASSOC X A), executing (SHALLOW) in any process cannot affect the other processes so long as rerooting is indivisible. Of course, if more than one process tries to do continuous shallow binding, then we will get a form of thrashing in which the processor spends all of its time rerooting!

Our algorithm was discovered by pondering the Greenblatt LISP machine proposal [Greenblatt 1974] which includes a shallow scheme for handling general funargs. His scheme does not reverse any pointers, but appends an up/down bit to each node in the environment tree which keeps the information as to which pointers would be reversed in our scheme. His scheme *must* continuously shallow-bind because the pointers in the "down" path point in the wrong direction to be used by ASSOC. Our scheme both simplifies and generalizes his so that not only can shallow-binding be implemented more uniformly, but we also get the serendipidous benefit of being able to choose at any point between shallow and deep binding.

A Comparison to Cache Schemes

Our scheme can also be compared with the *cache scheme* developed by C. Hewitt, C. Reeve, and G. Sussman for the MDL language [Galley 1975]. Their scheme associates, in addition to the value cell, a cache cell with each variable which is a pair consisting of a value and a pointer to an environment in which that value is valid. To access the value of a variable, the current environment pointer is compared with that in the cache cell and if they are equal, the cache value is used; otherwise, a search is made in the environment. In either case, the cache cell is updated to reflect its value in the current environment. Here is a version of ASSOC that implements this approach.

```
(DEFUN ASSOC (X A)
        (PROG (V)
                (SETQ V (ASSOC1 X A))
                (RPLACA (CCELL X) V)
                (RPLACD (CCELL X) A)
                (RETURN V)))

(DEFUN ASSOC1 (X A)
        (COND ((EQ A (CDR (CCELL X)))
                (CAR (CCELL X)))
               ((NULL A) (VCELL X))
               ((EQ (CAAR A) X) (CAR A))
               (T (ASSOC1 X (CDR A)))))
```

(CCELL y) returns the cache cell of variable y, which is a cons cell having a value cell as its CAR and an environment as its CDR.

The cache scheme is independent of rerooting in the sense that one, the other, or both can be implemented together. (Of course, with *continuous* shallow-binding, the cache is superfluous.) We claim that cache and occasional rerooting are incomparable; i.e., complementary, in the sense that there exist programs that would run faster on a rerooting scheme than on a cache scheme and vice versa. On a major context-switch involving many variables, a cache will perform poorly because only one variable will be updated at a time and searches will have to be made for each different variable before the interpreter is running truly shallowly. Rerooting, on the other hand, will switch all of the deep variables to be shallow in one operation, thus economizing on searches. The cache will perform better in contexts where there are a large number of variables which could be accessed, but only a small fraction ever are. As our programs exhibit, both schemes are compatible, and together they can minimize variable access time.

References

S. Galley and G. Pfister, *The MDL Language*, MIT Laboratory for Computer Science, 1975.

R. Greenblatt, *The LISP Machine*, MIT AI Laboratory Working Paper 79, 1974.

D. Knuth, *The Art of Computer Programming, Vol 1, Fundamental Algorithms*, Addison-Wesley, 1968.

J. McCarthy, P. Abrahams, D. Edwards, T. Hart, and M. Levin, *LISP 1.5 Programmer's Manual*, MIT Press, 1965.

D. Moon, *MACLISP Reference Manual*, MIT Laboratory for Computer Science, 1974.

J. Moses, *The Function of FUNCTION in LISP*, MIT AI Laboratory Memo 9, 1970.

B. Randell and L. Russell, *ALGOL & Implementation*, Academic Press, 1964.

The complete version of this paper appears in *Communications of the ACM*, Volume 21, No. , July 1978, copyright 1978, Association for Computing Machinery, Inc.

OPTIMIZING ALLOCATION AND GARBAGE COLLECTION OF SPACES

HENRY G. BAKER, JR.

The version of LISP known as **MACLISP** allocates storage for different types of objects in noncontiguous areas called *spaces*. These spaces partition the active storage into disjoint areas, each of which holds a different type of object. If all data types are allocated from the same heap, there is no problem with varying demand for the different data types; all data types require storage from the same pool, so that only the total amount of storage is important. If different data types must be allocated from different spaces, however, the relative sizes of the spaces becomes important. Henry Baker presents a procedure that determines in what ratios the spaces should be allocated so that garbage collection is minimized.

Space Management Problems

MACLISP, unlike some other implementations of LISP, allocates storage for different types of objects in noncontiguous areas called *spaces*. These spaces partition the active storage into disjoint areas, each of which holds a different type of object. For example, *list cells* are stored in one space, *full-word integers* reside in another space, *full-word floating point numbers* in another, and so on.

Allocating space in this manner has several advantages. An object's type can easily be computed from a pointer to it, without any memory references to the object itself. Thus, the LISP primitive ATOM(x) can easily compute its result without even paging in x. Another advantage is that the type of an object does not require any storage within the object, so that arithmetic with hardware data types such as full-word integers can use hardware instructions directly.

There are problems associated with this method of storage and type management, however. When all data types are allocated from the same heap, there is no problem with varying demand for the different data types; all data types require storage from the same pool, so that only the total amount of storage is important. Once different data types must be allocated from different spaces, however, the relative sizes of the spaces becomes important.

We would like to find optimal policies for deciding in what ratios the spaces should be allocated so that garbage collection is minimized. Suppose, for example, that a program is in an equilibrium situation, where the rate of storage allocation for each data type is equal to the rate of garbage generation for that data type. Suppose further that the rate r_1 for data type 1 is twice the rate r_2 of data type 2, and that the number of free words in both spaces is the same. Then the program will continually run out of data type 1 before data type 2. Suppose now that we halve the free words in space 2. The user program will now run out of both kinds equally often. Furthermore, the timing and amount of garbage collection will be the same as before because the additional free words in space 2 were never used.

This analysis gives the key to optimal allocation for an equilibrium situation: balance the free storage for each data type against the rate of use of that data type. In other words, make all spaces run out of free words at the same time.

The calculation of optimal space size is now simple algebra. Let:

r_i be the rate of word usage for data type i;
F_i be the free words available for data type i;
F be the free words available to all data types.

Then for optimal allocation,

$$F_i = (r_i / \Sigma r_j)F$$

Intelligent Allocation

The question now is: "How can the rate of free storage usage for each data type be measured?" A "cons-counter" could be implemented for each data type, which would count the cells allocated for that data type, but in MACLISP this measurement is better made by the garbage collector. The gc-daemon interrupt, which is triggered by each garbage collection, invokes the gc-daemon with an argument which associates with each space four quantities: the number of words free and the size of that space, both before and after the garbage collection. This information, together with the information from the gc-daemon argument at the previous garbage collection, allows us to calculate the average rates of free storage usage for each space since the last garbage collection. This information allows us to use the ALLOC function to reallocate free storage to each space in proportion to its usage.

PDP-10 MACLISP presents another problem when reallocating. Since it does not use a compacting garbage collector, the spaces can be expanded, but never contracted. Therefore, the gc-daemon must be conservative in its reallocation strategy, because it can not back down on an allocation.

Suppose that we wish to achieve an overall garbage collection efficiency of m words allocated to each word traced. This means that if the total storage used by accessible structures consists of T words, then we wish to have $(1+m)T$ words allocated to the various spaces, in total. In other words, $F=mT$ words are free and should be divided among the spaces for their free areas. Now we have determined that the free storage for each space should be proportional to the rate of storage allocation in that space. Therefore,

$$F_i = (r_i/\Sigma r_j)mT$$

Now since spaces can be expanded but not contracted, we need only make sure that space i has *at least* F_i free words. This is achieved through the gcsize, gcmax, and gcmin parameters of ALLOC.

In MACLISP, one can communicate one's intentions with regard to the management of a space to the system by calling a function ALLOC with the space name and 3 parameters. The gcsize parameter specifies how large the space is allowed to grow before the garbage collector is called. Gcmax specifies the maximum size the space may grow to before triggering the gc-overflow interrupt. Finally, gcmin specifies how much of the space should be free after performing a garbage collection; if the free storage is less than gcmin, the garbage collector immediately allocates more storage to the space. (Gcmin may be specified as either an absolute number of words or a percentage).

We will make use in our gc-daemon of only the gcsize allocation parameters of each space. Gcmin will be set to 0 (or as small as possible), and gcmax will be set to infinity (or as large as possible). We ignore gcmin because the garbage collector uses it to to allocate space before the gc-daemon has had a chance to think things over. Setting gcmin instead of gcsize would mean that any decision by the daemon would not take effect until after the next garbage collection, which would greatly reduce the responsiveness of the gc-daemon to the current situation.

The Garbage Collection Deamon

The gc-daemon needs to be able to calculate two quantities for every space--the current number of accessible words and the gross number of words allocated since the last garbage collection. The current number of accessible words for a space can easily be calculated by subtracting the number of words free at the end of the current garbage collection from the size of the space at that time. The gross number of words allocated since the previous garbage collection can be calculated as the difference between the number in use at the beginning of the current garbage collection (size before minus free before) and the number accessible at the end of the previous garbage collection.

With these figures calculated for each space, it is easy to calculate the total number of accessible words and the differential rates of allocation. Taking the total free storage to be a percentage of the total accessible storage, we can divide up this free space among the spaces based on their differential rates of allocation. MACLISP is informed of this decision by setting the gcsize of each space to the sum of the accessible cells in that space plus the new free storage allotment just calculated. (We also round gcsize up to the next multiple of 512 because 512 words is the smallest unit of allocation in MACLISP).

The system could be improved by varying the allocate/mark ratio as the total number of accessible words grew. The idea is to garbage collect more to keep the working-set size small. However, since the paging depends so heavily on the current operating system load, one would need information from the operating system to make that decision properly.

The gc-daemon tries to divide up the free storage among the various spaces based on their relative allocation histories. This strategy hopes that the future will be like the near past (since the previous garbage collection). However, in practice, programs go through phases, with one phase requiring a drastically different mix of cell types than another. Therefore the gc-daemon can be wrong. Since the costs of misallocation are larger with the larger spaces, and since storage can never be retracted from a space once allocated, the gc-daemon may wish to hedge its bets by giving the larger spaces only partial allocations.

A gc-daemon having the characteristics described above is presented below in the CGOL input notation for LISP. This daemon stores all the information about a space on the property list of that space's name. For example, the normalized rate of list consing can be accessed by (GET 'LIST 'ALLOCRATE). Summary information is stored on the property list of TOTAL-STORAGE. The only user-settable parameter is the variable ALLOCMARKRATIO. This value must be a positive floating point number less than 5.0. It is set initially to 1.0. Making it smaller decreases working set size and increases garbage collection time.

```
define "GC-DAEMON" (spacelist);
   let totalaccessible = 0.0,
       totalconsed = 0.0;
   % Go through spaces and accumulate consed and accessible information.  %
   for element in spacelist        % Argument is "alist" of spaces. %
       do (let space = car(element),        % Give names to parameters.  %
               freebefore = cadr(element),
               freeafter = caddr(element),
               sizebefore = cadddr(element),
               sizeafter = car(cddddr(element));
           % Compute consed since last gc and accessible now for this space.  %
           consed ofq space := sizebefore-freebefore-accessible ofq space;
           totalconsed := totalconsed + consed ofq space;
           accessible ofq space := sizeafter-freeafter;
           totalaccessible := totalaccessible + accessible ofq space);
   % Store total consed, total accessible and compute total free.  %
   consed ofq "TOTAL-STORAGE" := totalconsed;
   accessible ofq "TOTAL-STORAGE" := totalaccessible;
   let totalfree = allocmarkratio * totalaccessible;
   free ofq "TOTAL-STORAGE" := totalfree;
   % Go through spaces and reallocate where necessary.  %
   for element in spacelist
       do (let space = car element;
           allocrate ofq space := consed ofq space / totalconsed;
           free ofq space := fix(totalfree * allocrate ofq space);
           let spcsize = accessible ofq space + free ofq space + 511.;
               if spcsize>511. then alloc([space,[spcsize,262143.,32.]]))
```

COMPILER OPTIMIZATION BASED ON VIEWING LAMBDA AS RENAME PLUS GOTO

GUY L. STEELE, JR.

In this section, Guy Steele describes a compiler for the lexically-scoped dialect of LISP known as SCHEME. The compiler knows relatively little about specific data manipulation primitives such as arithmetic operators, but concentrates on general issues of environment and control. Rather than having specialized knowledge about a large variety of control and environment constructs, the compiler handles only a small basis set that reflects the semantics of lambda calculus. All of the traditional imperative constructs, such as sequencing, assignment, looping, and GOTO, as well as many standard LISP constructs such as AND, OR, and COND, are expressed as macros in terms of the applicative basis set. A small number of optimization techniques, coupled with the treatment of function calls as GOTO statements, serves to produce code as good as that produced by more traditional compilers. The macro approach enables speedy implementation of new constructs without sacrificing efficiency in the generated code.

Lexically-scoped LISP

We have developed a compiler for the lexically-scoped dialect of LISP known as SCHEME. The compiler knows relatively little about specific data manipulation primitives such as arithmetic operators, but concentrates on general issues of environment and control. Rather than having specialized knowledge about a large variety of control and environment constructs, the compiler handles only a small basis set which reflects the semantics of lambda-calculus. All of the traditional imperative constructs, such as sequencing, assignment, looping, GOTO, as well as many standard LISP constructs such as AND, OR, and COND, are expressed as macros in terms of the applicative basis set. A small number of optimization techniques, coupled with the treatment of function calls as GOTO statements, serve to produce code as good as that produced by more traditional compilers. The macro approach enables speedy implementation of new constructs as desired without sacrificing efficiency in the generated code.

    A subset of SCHEME serves as the representation intermediate between the optimized SCHEME code and the final output code; code is expressed in this subset in the so-called continuation-passing style. As a subset of SCHEME, it enjoys the same theoretical properties; one could even apply the same optimizer used on the input code to the intermediate code. However, the subset is so chosen that all temporary quantities are made manifest as variables, and no control stack is needed to evaluate it. As a result, this apparently applicative representation admits an imperative interpretation which permits easy transcription to final imperative machine code.

Background

In 1975 Sussman and Steele reported on the implementation of SCHEME, a dialect of LISP with the properties of lexical scoping and tail-recursion; this implementation is embedded within MacLISP [Moon 1974], a version of LISP which does not have these properties. The property of lexical scoping (that a variable can be referenced only from points textually within the expression which binds it) is a consequence of the fact that all functions are closed in the "binding environment." [Moses 1970] That is, SCHEME is a "full-funarg" LISP dialect. The property of tail-recursion implies that loops written in an apparently recursive form will actually be executed in an iterative fashion. Intuitively, function calls do not "push control stack;" instead, it is argument evaluation which pushes control stack. The two properties of lexical scoping and tail-recursion are not independent. In most LISP systems [McCarthy 1962] [Moon 1974] [Teitelman 1975], which use dynamic scoping rather than lexical, tail-recursion is impossible because function calls must push control stack in order to be able to undo the dynamic bindings after the return of the function. On the other hand, it is possible to have a lexically scoped LISP which does not tail-recurse, but it is easily seen that such an implementation only wastes storage space needlessly compared to a tail-recursing implementation. Together, these two properties cause SCHEME to reflect lambda-calculus semantics much more closely than dynamically scoped LISP systems. SCHEME also permits the treatments of functions as full-fledged data objects; they may be passed as arguments, returned as values, made part of composite data structures, and notated as independent, unnamed ("anonymous") entities. (Compare this with most ALGOL-like languages, in which a function can be written only by declaring it and giving it a name; then imagine being able to use an integer value only by giving it a name in a declaration!) The property of lexical scoping allows this to be done in a consistent manner without the possibility of identifier conflicts (that is, SCHEME "solves the FUNARG problem"). Also of interest is the technique of "continuation-passing style," a way of writing programs in SCHEME such that no function ever returns a value.

Since the first appearance of SCHEME we have continued

to explore the properties of lexical scoping and tail-recursion, and various coding styles. These properties and styles of coding may be exploited to implement most traditional programming constructs, such as assignment, looping, and call-by-name, in terms of function application. Such applicative (lambda-calculus) models of programming language constructs are well-known to theoreticians (see [Stoy 1974], for example), but have not been used in a practical programming system. All of these constructs are actually made available in SCHEME by macros which expand into these applicative definitions. This technique has permitted the speedy implementation of a rich user-level language in terms of a very small, easy-to-implement basis set of primitive constructs. The escape operator CATCH is easily modelled by transforming a program into the continuation-passing style. Transforming a program into this style enforces a particular order of argument evaluation, and makes all intermediate computational quantities manifest as variables.

Examination of the properties of tail-recursion shows that the usual view of function calls as pushing a return address must lead to an either inefficient or inconsistent implementation, while the tail-recursive approach of SCHEME leads to a uniform discipline in which function calls are treated as GOTO statements which also pass arguments. A consequence of lexical scoping is that the only code which can reference the value of a variable is in a given environment is code which is closed in that environment or which received the value as an argument; this in turn implies that a compiler can structure a run-time environment in any arbitrary fashion, because it will compile all the code which can reference that environment, and so can arrange for that code to reference it in the appropriate manner. Such references do not require any kind of search (as is commonly and incorrectly believed in the LISP community because of early experience with LISP interpreters which search a-lists) because the compiler can determine the precise location of each variable in an environment at compile time. It is not necessary to use a standard format, because neither interpreted code nor other compiled code can refer to that environment.

Transforming a program into the continuation-passing style elucidates traditional compilation issues such as register allocation because user variables and intermediate quantities alike are made manifest as variables on an equal footing. We have exhibited an algorithm for converting any SCHEME program (not containing ASET) to continuation-passing style.

We have implemented two compilers for the language SCHEME. The purpose was to explore compilation techniques for a language modelled on lambda-calculus, using lambda-calculus-style models of imperative programming constructs. Both compilers use the strategy of converting the source program to continuation-passing style.

The first compiler was a throw-away version which, while usable, was written only to clear up some technical points of implementation. The second compiler, with which we are primarily concerned here, is known as RABBIT. It, like the first, is written almost entirely in SCHEME (with minor exceptions due only to problems in interfacing with certain MacLISP I/O facilities). However, it is much more clever. It is intended to demonstrate a number of optimization techniques related to lexical environment and tail-recursive control structures.

The Thesis

■ Function calls are not expensive when compiled correctly; they should be thought of as GOTO statements that pass arguments.

■ The combination of cheap function calls, lexical scoping, tail-recursion, and anonymous notation of functions permits the definition of a wide variety of "imperative" constructs in applicative terms. Because these properties result from adhering to the principles of the well-known lambda-calculus, such definitions can be lifted intact from existing literature and used directly.

■ A macro facility (the ability to specify syntactic transformations) makes it practical use these as the only definitions of imperative constructs in a programming system. Such a facility makes it extremely easy to define new constructs.

■ A few well-chosen optimization strategies enable the compilation of these applicative definitions into the imperative low-level code which one would expect from a traditional compiler.

■ The macro facility and the optimization techniques used by the compiler can be conceptually unified. The same properties which make it easy to write the macros make it easy to define optimizations correctly. Just as many programming constructs are defined in terms of a small, well-chosen basis set, so a large number of traditional optimization techniques fall out as special cases of the few used in RABBIT. This is no accident. The separate treatment of a large and diverse set of constructs necessitates separate optimization techniques for each. As the basis set of constructs is reduced, so is the set of interesting transformations.

■ The technique of compiling by converting to continuation-passing style elucidates some important compilation issues in a natural way. Intermediate quantities are made manifest; so is the precise order of evaluation. Moreover, this is all expressed in a language isomorphic to a subset of the source language SCHEME; as a result the continuation-passing style version of a program inherits many of the phisophical and practical advantages. For example, the same optimization techniques can be applied at this level as at the original source level. While the use of continuation-passing style may not make the decisions any easier, it provides an effective and natural way to express the results of those decisions.

■ Continuation-passing style, while apparently applicative in nature, admits a peculiarly imperative interpretation as a consequence of the facts that it requires no control stack to be evaluated and that no functions ever return values. As a result, it is easily converted to an imperative machine language.

■ A SCHEME compiler should ideally be a designer of good data structures, since it may choose any representation whatsoever for environments. RABBIT has a rudimentary design knowledge, involving primarily the preferral of registers to heap-allocated storage. However, there is room for knowledge of "bit-diddling" representations.

■ We suggest that those who have tried to design useful UNCOL's (UNiversal Computer-Oriented Languages) [Sammet 1969] [Coleman 1974] have perhaps been thinking too imperatively, and worrying more about data manipulation primitives than about environment and control issues. As a result, proposed UNCOLs have been little more than generalizations of contemporary machine languages. We suggest that SCHEME makes an ideal UNCOL at two levels. The first level is the fully applicative level, to which most source-language constructs are easily reduced; the second is the continuation-passing style level, which is easily reduced to machine language. We envision building a compiler in three stages: reduction of a user language to basic SCHEME, whether by macros, a parser of algebraic syntax, or some other means; transformation to continuation-passing style; and generation of code for a particular machine. RABBIT addresses itself to the middle stage. Data manipulation primitives are completely ignored at this stage, and are just passed along from input to output. These primitives, whether integer arithmetic, string concatenation and parsing, or list structure manipulators, are chosen as a function of a particular source language and a particular target machine. RABBIT deals only with fundamental environment and control issues common to any mode of algorithmic expression.

■   While most syntactic issues tend to be rather superficial, we point out that algebraic syntax tends to obscure the fundamental nature of function calling and tail-recursion by arbitrarily dividing functions into syntactic classes such as "operators" and "functions." ([Standish 1976], for example, uses much space to exhibit each conceptually singular transformation in a multiplicity of syntactic manifestations.) The lack of an "anonymous" notation for functions in most algebraic languages, and the inability to treat functions as data objects, is a distinct disadvantage. The uniformity of LISP syntax makes these issues easier to deal with.

To the LISP community in particular we address these additional points:

■   Lexical scoping need not be as expensive as is commonly thought. Experience with lexically-scoped *interpreters* is misleading. Lexical scoping is not inherently slower than dynamic scoping. While some implementations may entail access through multiple levels of structure, this occurs only under circumstances (accessing of variables through multiple levels of closure) which could not even be expressed in a dynamically scoped language! Unlike deep-bound dynamic variables, lexical access requires no search; unlike shallow-bound dynamic variables, lexical binding does not require that values be put in a canonical value cell. The compiler has complete discretion over the manipulation of environments and variable values.

■	Lexical scoping does not necessarily make LISP programming unduly difficult. The very existence of RABBIT, a working compiler some fifty pages in length written in SCHEME, implemented in about a month, part-time, substantiates this claim (which is, however, admitted to be mostly a matter of taste and experience). SCHEME has also been used to implement several AI problem-solving languages, including AMORD [Doyle 1977].

The Source Language - SCHEME

The basic language processed by RABBIT is a subset of the SCHEME language as described in [Sussman 1975], the primary restrictions being that the first argument to ASET must be quoted and that the multiprocessing primitives are not permitted. This subset is summarized here.

SCHEME is essentially a lexically scoped ("full funarg") dialect of LISP. Interpreted programs are represented by S-expressions in the usual manner. Numbers represent themselves. Atomic symbols are used as identifiers (with the conventional exception of T and NIL, which are conceptually treated as constants). All other constructs are represented as lists.

In order to distinguish the various other constructs, SCHEME follows the usual convention that a list whose car is one of a set of distinguished atomic symbols is treated as directed by a rule conceptually associated with that symbol. All other lists (those with non-atomic cars, or with undistinguished atoms in their cars) are <u>combinations</u>, or function calls. All subforms of the list are uniformly evaluated in an unspecified order, and then the value of the first (the function) is applied to the values of all the others (the arguments). Notice that the function position is evaluated in the same way as the argument positions (unlike most other LISP systems).

The atomic symbols which distinguish special constructs are as follows:

LAMBDA This denotes a function. A form (LAMBDA (var1 var2 ... varn) body) will evaluate to a function of n arguments. The <u>parameters</u> vari are identifiers (atomic symbols) which may be used in the body to refer to the respective <u>arguments</u> when the function is invoked. Note that a LAMBDA-expression is not a function, but <u>evaluates</u> to one, a crucial distinction.

IF This denotes a conditional form. (IF a b c) evaluates the <u>predicate</u> a, producing a value x; if x is non-NIL, then the <u>consequent</u> b is evaluated, and otherwise the <u>alternative</u> c. If c is omitted, NIL is assumed.

QUOTE As in all LISP systems, this provides a way to specify any S-expression as a constant. (QUOTE x) evaluates to the S-expression x. This may be abbreviated to 'x, thanks to the MacLISP read-macro-character feature.

LABELS This primitive permits the local definition of one or more mutually recursive functions. The format is:

```
(LABELS ((name1 (LAMBDA ...))
         (name2 (LAMBDA ...))
         ...
         (namen (LAMBDA ...)))
 body)
```

This evaluates the body in an environment in which the names refer to the respective functions, which are themselves closed in that same environment. Thus references to these names in the bodies of the LAMBDA-expressions will refer to the labelled functions.

ASET This is the primitive side-effect on variables. (ASET' var body) evaluates the body, assigns the resulting value to the variable var, and returns that value. Note the use of "'" to quote the variable name. The SCHEME interpreter permits one to compute the name of the variable, but for technical and philosophical reasons RABBIT forbids this.

CATCH This provides an escape operator facility. [Landin 1965] [Reynolds 1972] (CATCH var body) evaluates the body, which may refer to the variable var, which will denote an "escape function" of one argument which, when called, will return from the CATCH-form with the given argument as the value of the CATCH-form.

Macros Any atomic symbol which has been defined in one of various ways to be a macro distinguishes a special construct whose meaning is determined by a macro function. This function has the responsibility of rewriting the form and returning a new form to be evaluated in place of the old one. In this way complex syntactic constructs can be expressed in terms of simpler ones.

The Target Language

The "target language" is a highly restricted subset of MacLISP, rather than any particular machine language for an actual hardware machine such as the PDP-10. RABBIT produces MacLISP function definitions which are then compiled by the standard MacLISP compiler. In this way we do not need to deal with the uninteresting vagaries of a particular piece of hardware, nor with the peculiarities of the many and various data-manipulation primitives (CAR, RPLACA, +, etc.). We allow the MacLISP compiler to deal with them, and concentrate on the issues of environment and control which are unique to SCHEME. While for production use this is mildly inconvenient (since the code must be passed through two compilers before use), for research purposes it has saved the wasteful re-implementation of much knowledge already contained in the MacLISP compiler.

On the other hand, the use of MacLISP as a target language does not by any means trivialize the task of RABBIT. The MacLISP function-calling mechanism cannot be used as a target construct for the SCHEME function call, because MacLISP's function calls are not guaranteed to behave tail-recursively. Since tail-recursion is a most crucial characteristic distinguishing SCHEME from most LISP systems, we must implement SCHEME function calls by more primitive methods. Similarly, since SCHEME is a full-funarg dialect of LISP while MacLISP is not, we cannot in general use MacLISP's variable-binding mechanisms to implement those of SCHEME. On the other hand, it is a perfectly legitimate optimization to use MacLISP mechanisms in those limited situations where they are applicable.

Language Design Considerations

We divide the definition of the SCHEME language into two parts: the environment and control constructs, and the data manipulation primitives. Examples of the former are LAMBDA-expressions, combinations, and IF; examples of the latter are CONS, CAR, EQ, and PLUS. Note that we can conceive of a version of SCHEME which did not have CONS, for example, and more generally did not have S-expressions in its data domain. Such a version would still have the same environment and control constructs, and so would hold the same theoretical interest for our purposes here. (Such a version, however, would be less convenient for purposes of writing a meta-circular description of the language, however!)

SCHEME is an applicative language which conforms to the essential properties of the axioms obeyed by lambda-calculus [Church 1965] expressions. Among these are the rules of alpha-conversion and beta-conversion. The first intuitively implies that we can uniformly rename a function parameter and all references to it without altering the meaning of the function. An important corollary to this is that we can effectively locate all the references. The second implies that in a situation where a known function is being called with known argument expressions, we may substitute an argument expression for a parameter reference within the body of the function (provided no naming conflicts result). Both of these operations are of importance to an optimizing compiler. Another property which follows indirectly is that of tail-recursion. This property is exploited in expressing iteration in terms of applicative constructs.

There are those to whom lexical scoping is nothing new, for example the ALGOL community. For this audience, however, we should draw attention to another important feature of SCHEME, which is that functions are first-class data objects. They may be assigned or bound to variables, returned as values of other functions, placed in arrays, and in general treated as any other data object. Just as numbers have certain operations defined on them, such as addition, so functions have an important operation defined on them, namely invocation.

The ability to treat functions as objects is not at all the same as the ability to treat *representations* of functions as objects. It is the latter ability that is traditionally associated with LISP; functions can be represented as S-expressions. In a version of SCHEME which had no S-expression primitives, however, one could still deal with functions (i.e. closures) as such, for that ability is part of the fundamental environment and control facilities. Conversely, in a SCHEME which does have CONS, CAR, and CDR, there is no defined way to use CONS by itself to construct a function (although a primitive ENCLOSE is now provided which converts an S-expression representation of a function into a function), and the CAR or CDR of a function is in general undefined. The only defined operation on a function is invocation.

We draw this sharp distinction between environment and control constructs on the one hand and data manipulation primitives on the other because only the former are treated in any depth by RABBIT, whereas much of the knowledge of a "real" compiler deals with the latter. A PL/I compiler must have much specific knowledge about numbers, arrays, strings, and so on. We have no new ideas to present here on such issues, and so have avoided this entire area. RABBIT itself knows nothing about data manipulation primitives beyond being able to recognize them and pass them along to the output code, which is a small subset of MacLISP. In this way RABBIT can concentrate on the interesting issues of environment and control, and exploit the expert knowledge of data manipulation primitives already built into the MacLISP compiler.

The Use of Macros

An important characteristic of the SCHEME language is that its set of primitive constructs is quite small. This set is not always convenient for expressing programs, however, and so a macro facility is provided for extending the expressive power of the language. A macro is best thought of as a <u>syntax rewrite rule</u>. As a simple example, suppose we have a primitive GCD which takes only two arguments, and we wish to be able to write an invocation of a GCD function with any number of arguments. We might then define (in a production-rule style) the conditional rule:

```
(XGCD)            =>  0
(XGCD x)          =>  x
(XGCD x . rest)   =>  (GCD x (XGCD . rest))
```

(Notice the use of LISP dots to refer to the rest of a list.) This is not considered to be a definition of a function XGCD, but a purely syntactic transformation. In principle all such transformations could be performed before executing the program. In fact, RABBIT does exactly this, although the SCHEME interpreter naturally does it incrementally, as each macro call is encountered.

Rather than use a separate production rule and pattern-matching language, in practice SCHEME macros are defined as transformation functions from macro-call expressions to resulting S-expressions, just as they are in MacLISP. (Here, however, we shall continue to use production rules for purposes of exposition.) It is important to note that macros need not be written in the language for which they express rewrite rules; rather, they should be considered an adjunct to the interpreter, and written in the same language as the interpreter (or the compiler). To see this more clearly, consider again a version of SCHEME which does not have S-expressions in its data domain. If programs in this language are represented as S-expressions, then the interpreter for that language cannot be written in that language, but in another meta-language which does deal with S-expressions. Macros, which transform one S-expression (representing a macro call) to another (the replacement form, or the interpretation of the call), clearly should be expressed in this meta-language also. The fact that in most LISP systems the language and the meta-language appear to coincide is a source of both power and confusion.

Let us consider some typical macros used in SCHEME. The BLOCK macro is similar to the MacLISP PROGN; it evaluates all its arguments and returns the value of the last one. One critical characteristic is that the last argument is evaluated "tail-recursively" (quotation marks are used because normally we speak of invocation, not evaluation, as being tail-recursive). An expansion rule is given for this in [Steele 1976A] equivalent to:

```
(BLOCK x)        => x
(BLOCK x . rest) => ((LAMBDA (DUMMY) (BLOCK . rest)) x)
```

This definition exploits the fact that SCHEME is evaluated in applicative order, and so will evaluate all arguments before applying a function to them. Thus, in the second subrule, x must be evaluated, and then the block of all the rest is. It is then clear from the first subrule that the last argument is evaluated "tail-recursively."

One problem with this definition is the occurrence of the variable DUMMY, which must be chosen so as not to conflict with any variable used by the user. This we refer to as the "GENSYM problem," in honor of the traditional LISP function which creates a "fresh" symbol. It would be nicer to write the macro in such a way that no conflict could arise no matter what names were used by the user. There is indeed a way, which ALGOL programmers will recognize as equivalent to the use of "thunks," or call-by-name parameters:

```
(BLOCK x)          => x
(BLOCK x . rest)   => ((LAMBDA (A B) (B))
                         x
                       (LAMBDA () (BLOCK . rest))))
```

This is a technique which should be understood quite thoroughly, since it is the key to writing correct macro rules without any possibility of conflicts between names used by the user and those needed by the macro. As another example, let us consider the AND and OR constructs as used by most LISP systems. OR evaluates its arguments one by one, in order, returning the first non-NIL value obtained (without evaluating any of the following arguments), or NIL if all arguments produce NIL. AND is the dual to this; it returns NIL if any argument does, and otherwise the value of the last argument. A simple-minded approach to OR would be:

```
(OR)             => 'NIL
(OR x . rest)    => (IF x x (OR . rest))
```

There is an objection to this, which is that the code for x is duplicated. Not only does this consume extra space, but it can execute erroneously if x has any side-effects. We must arrange to evaluate x only once, and then test its value:

```
(OR)              =>  'NIL
(OR x . rest)  =>  ((LAMBDA (V) (IF V V (OR . rest))) x)
```

This certainly evaluates x only once, but admits a possible naming conflict between the variable V and any variables used by rest. This is avoided by the same technique used for BLOCK:

```
(OR)              =>  'NIL
(OR x . rest)  =>  ((LAMBDA (V R) (IF V V (R)))
                     x
                     (LAMBDA () (OR . rest)))
```

Let us now consider a rule for the more complicated COND construct:

```
(COND)  =>  'NIL
(COND (x) . rest)  =>  (OR x (COND . rest))
(COND (x . r) . rest)  =>  (IF x (BLOCK . r) (COND . rest))
```

This defines the "extended" COND of modern LISP systems, which produces NIL if no clauses succeed, which returns the value of the predicate in the case of a singleton clause, and which allows more than one consequent in a clause. An important point here is that one can write these rules in terms of other macro constructs such as OR and BLOCK.

SCHEME also provides macros for such constructs as DO and PROG, all of which expand into similar kinds of code using LAMBDA, IF, and LABELS (see below). In particular, PROG permits the use of GO and RETURN in the usual manner. In this way all the traditional imperative constructs are expressed in an applicative style.

None of this is particularly new; theoreticians have modelled imperative constructs in these terms for years. What is new, we think, is the serious proposal that a practical interpreter and compiler can be designed for a language in which such models serve as the sole definitions of these imperative constructs. This approach has both advantages and disadvantages.

One advantage is that the base language is small. A simple-minded interpreter or compiler can be written in a few hours. (We have re-implemented the SCHEME interpreter from scratch a half-dozen times or more to test various representation strategies; this was practical only because of the small size of the language.) Once the basic interpreter is written, the macro definitions for all the complex constructs can be used without revision. Moreover, the same macro definitions can be used by both interpreter and compiler (or by several versions of interpreter and compiler!). It is not necessary to "implement a construct twice," once each in interpreter and compiler.

Another advantage is that new macros are very easy to write (using facilities provided in SCHEME). One could easily invent a new kind of DO loop, for example, and implement it in SCHEME for both interpreter and all compilers in less than five minutes.

A third advantage is that the attention of the compiler can be focused on the basic constructs. Rather than having specialized code for two dozen different constructs, the compiler can have much deeper knowledge about each of a few basic constructs. One might object that this "deeper knowledge" consists of recognizing the two dozen special cases represented by the separate constructs of the former case. This is true to some extent. It is also true, however, that in the latter case such deep knowledge will carry over to any new constructs which are invented and represented as macros.

Among the disadvantages of the macro approach are lack of speed and the discarding of information. Many people have objected that macros are of necessity slower than, say. the FSUBR implementation used by most LISP systems. This is true in many current interpretive implementations, but need not be true of compilers or more cleverly designed interpreters. Moreover, the FSUBR implementation is not general; it is very hard for a user to write a meaningful FSUBR and then describe to the compiler the best way to compile it. The macro approach handles this difficulty automatically. We do not object to the use of the FSUBR mechanism as a special-case "speed hack" to improve the performance of an interpreter, but we insist on recognizing the fact that it is not as generally useful as the macro approach.

Another objection relating to speed is that the macros produce convoluted code involving the temporary creation and subsequent invocation of many closures. We feel, first of all, that the macro writer should concern himself more with producing correct code than fast code. Furthermore, convolutedness can be eliminated by a few simple optimization techniques in the compiler, to be discussed below. Finally, function calls need not be as expensive as is popularly supposed. [Steele 1977A]

Information is discarded by macros in the situation, for example, where a DO macro expands into a large mess that is not obviously a simple loop; later compiler analysis must recover this information. This is indeed a problem. We feel that the compiler is probably better off having to recover the information anyway, since a deep analysis allows it to catch other loops which the user did not use DO to express for one reason or another. Another is the possibility that DO could leave clues around in the form of declarations if desired.

The Imperative Treatment of Applicative Constructs

Given the characteristics of lexical scoping and tail-recursive invocations, it is possible to assign a peculiarly imperative interpretation to the applicative constructs of SCHEME, which consists primarily of treating a function call as a GOTO. More generally, a function call is a GOTO that can pass one or more items to its target; the special case of passing no arguments is precisely a GOTO. It is never necessary for a function call to save a return address of any kind. It is true that return addresses are generated, but we adopt one of two other points of view, depending on context. One is that the return address, plus any other data needed to carry on the computation after the called function has returned (such as previously computed intermediate values and other return addresses) are considered to be packaged up into an additional argument (the continuation) which is passed to the target. This lends itself to a non-functional interpretation of LAMBDA, and a method of expressing programs called the continuation-passing style, to be discussed further below. The other view, more intuitive in terms of the traditional stack implementation, is that the return address should be pushed before evaluating arguments rather than before calling a function. This view leads to a more uniform function-calling discipline, and is discussed in [Steele 1976B].

We are led by this point of view to consider a compilation strategy in which function calling is to be considered very cheap (unlike the situation with PL/I and ALGOL, where programmers avoid procedure calls like the plague -- see [Steele 1977A] for a discussion of this). In this light the code produced by the sample macros above does not seem inefficient, or even particularly convoluted. Consider the expansion of (OR a b c):

```
((LAMBDA (V R) (IF V V (R)))
   a
   (LAMBDA () ((LAMBDA (V R) (IF V V (R)))
                b
                (LAMBDA () ((LAMBDA (V R) (IF V V (R)))
                             c
                             (LAMBDA () 'NIL))))))
```

Then we might imagine the following (slightly contrived) compilation scenario. First, for expository purposes, we shall rename the variables in order to be able to distinguish them.

```
((LAMBDA (V1 R1) (IF V1 V1 (R1)))
   a
 (LAMBDA () ((LAMBDA (V2 R2) (IF V2 V2 (R2)))
             b
           (LAMBDA () ((LAMBDA (V3 R3) (IF V3 V3 (R3)))
                        c
                      (LAMBDA () 'NIL))))))
```

We shall assign a generated name to each LAMBDA-expression, which we shall notate by writing the name after the word LAMBDA. These names will be used as tags in the output code.

```
((LAMBDA name1 (V1 R1) (IF V1 V1 (R1)))
   a
 (LAMBDA name2 () ((LAMBDA name3 (V2 R2) (IF V2 V2 (R2)))
             b
           (LAMBDA name4 () ((LAMBDA name5 (V3 R3)
                                        (IF V3 V3 (R3)))
                        c
                      (LAMBDA name6 () 'NIL))))))
```

Next, a simple analysis shows that the variables R1, R2, and R3 always denote the LAMBDA-expressions named name2, name4, and name6, respectively. Now an optimizer might simply have substituted these values into the bodies of name1, name3, and name5 using the rule of beta-conversion, but we shall not apply that technique here. Instead we shall compile the six functions in a straightforward manner. We make use of the additional fact that all six functions are closed in identical environments (we count two environments as identical if they involve the same variable bindings, regardless of the number of "frames" involved; that is, the environment is the same inside and outside a (LAMBDA () ...)). Assume a simple target machine with argument registers called reg1, reg2, etc.

```
main:   <code for a>            ;result in reg1
        LOAD reg2,[name2]       ;[name2] is the closure for name2
        CALL-FUNCTION 2,[name1] ;call name1 with 2 arguments

name1:  JUMP-IF-NIL reg1,name1a
        RETURN                  ;return the value in reg1
name1a: CALL-FUNCTION 0,reg2    ;call function in reg2, 0 arguments

name2:  <code for b>            ;result in reg1
        LOAD reg2,[name4]       ;[name4] is the closure for name4
        CALL-FUNCTION 2,[name3] ;call name3 with 2 arguments

name3:  JUMP-IF-NIL reg1,name3a
        RETURN                  ;return the value in reg1
name3a: CALL-FUNCTION 0,reg2    ;call function in reg2, 0 arguments

name4:  <code for c>            ;result in reg1
        LOAD reg2,[name6]       ;[name6] is the closure for name6
        CALL-FUNCTION 2,[name5] ;call name5 with 2 arguments

name5:  JUMP-IF-NIL reg1,name5a
        RETURN                  ;return the value in reg1
name5a: CALL-FUNCTION 0,reg2    ;call function in reg2, 0 arguments

name6:  LOAD reg1,'NIL          ;constant NIL in reg1
        RETURN
```

Now we make use of our knowledge that certain variables always denote certain functions, and convert CALL-FUNCTION of a known function to a simple GOTO. (We have actually done things backwards here; in practice this knowledge is used before generating any code. We have fudged over this issue here, but will return to it later. Our purpose here is merely to demonstrate the treatment of function calls as GOTOs.)

```
main:    <code for a>            ;result in reg1
         LOAD reg2,[name2]       ;[name2] is the closure for name2
         GOTO name1

name1:   JUMP-IF-NIL reg1,name1a
         RETURN                  ;return the value in reg1
name1a:  GOTO name2

name2:   <code for b>            ;result in reg1
         LOAD reg2,[name4]       ;[name4] is the closure for name4
         GOTO name3

name3:   JUMP-IF-NIL reg1,name3a
         RETURN                  ;return the value in reg1
name3a:  GOTO name4

name4:   <code for c>            ;result in reg1
         LOAD reg2,[name6]       ;[name6] is the closure for name6
         GOTO name5

name5:   JUMP-IF-NIL reg1,name5a
         RETURN                  ;return the value in reg1
name5a:  GOTO name6

name6:   LOAD reg1,'NIL          ;constant NIL in reg1
         RETURN
```

The construction indicates the creation of a closure for foo in the current environment. This will actually require additional instructions, but we shall ignore the mechanics of this for now since analysis will remove the need for the construction in this case. The fact that the only references to the variables R1, R2, and R3 are function calls can be detected and the unnecessary LOAD instructions eliminated. (Once again, this would actually be determined ahead of time, and no LOAD instructions would be generated in the first place. All of this is determined by a

general pre-analysis, rather than a peephole post-pass.)
Moreover, a GOTO to a tag which immediately follows the
GOTO can be eliminated.

```
main:   <code for a>            ;result in reg1
name1:  JUMP-IF-NIL reg1,name1a
        RETURN                  ;return the value in reg1
name1a:
name2:  <code for b>            ;result in reg1
name3:  JUMP-IF-NIL reg1,name3a
        RETURN                  ;return the value in reg1
name3a:
name4:  <code for c>            ;result in reg1
name5:  JUMP-IF-NIL reg1,name5a
        RETURN                  ;return the value in reg1
name5a:
name6:  LOAD reg1,'NIL          ;constant NIL in reg1
        RETURN
```

This code is in fact about what one would expect out of an
ordinary LISP compiler. (There is admittedly room for a little
more improvement.) RABBIT indeed produces code of
essentially this form, by the method of analysis outlined here.

Similar considerations hold for the BLOCK macro.
Consider the expression (BLOCK a b c); conceptually this
should perform a, b, and c sequentially. In fact, the code
produced by the same methods used for OR above is:

```
main:   <code for a>
name1:
name2:  <code for b>
name3:
name4:  <code for c>
        RETURN
```

which is precisely what is desired.

Notice that this has fallen out of a general strategy involving only an approach to compiling function calls, and has involved no special knowledge of OR or BLOCK not encoded in the macro rules. The cases shown so far are actually special cases of a more general approach, special in that all the conceptual closures involved are closed in the same environment, and called from places that have not disturbed that environment, but only used "registers." In the more general case, the environments of caller and called function will be different. This divides into two subcases, corresponding to whether the closure was created by a simple LAMBDA or by a LABELS construction. The latter involves circular references, and so is somewhat more complicated; but it is easy to show that in the former case the environment of the caller must be that of the (known) called function, possibly with additional values added on. This is a consequence of lexical scoping. As a result, the function call can be compiled as a GOTO preceded by an environment adjustment which consists merely of lopping off some leading portion of the current one (intuitively, one simply "pops the unnecessary crud off the stack"). LABELS-closed functions also can be treated in this way, if one closes all the functions in the same way (but this is not always desirable). If one does, then it is easy to see the effect of expanding a PROG into a giant LABELS as outlined in [Steele 1976A] and elsewhere: normally, a GOTO to a tag at the same level of PROG will involve no adjustment of environment, and so compile into a simple GOTO instruction, whereas a GOTO to a tag at an outer level of PROG probably will involve adjusting the environment from that of the inner PROG to that of the outer. All of this falls out of the proper imperative treatment of function calls.

Optimization

The previous section, in order to elucidate the issue of tail-recursion, showed optimizations as if they were performed at the target-language level. In fact, the necessary optimizations are performed at the source level. Once one realizes that there is a direct correspondence between function calls and "goto" statements, there is no problem with representing arbitrarily complex control structures at the source level.

RABBIT uses only about a half dozen types of source-to-source transformations. Some of these are fairly obvious:

```
((LAMBDA () body))  =>  body
```

Others are well-known transformations, such as substituting arguments for formal parameters in LAMBDA-expressions, or eliminating unreferenced parameters, or dead code elimination. The one interesting and not-widely-known transformation involves nested IF expressions. The basic idea is:

```
(IF (IF a b c) d e)  =>  (IF a (IF b d e) (IF c d e))
```

One problem with this is that the code for d and e is duplicated. This can be avoided by the use of LAMBDA-expressions:

```
((LAMBDA (Q1 Q2)
        (IF a
            (IF b (Q1) (Q2))
            (IF c (Q1) (Q2))))
  (LAMBDA () d)
  (LAMBDA () e))
```

While this code may appear unnecessarily complex, the calls to the functions Q1 and Q2 will, as shown above, be compiled as simple GOTO's. As an example, consider the expression:

```
(IF (AND PRED1 PRED2) (PRINT 'WIN) (ERROR 'LOSE))
```

Expansion of the AND macro will result in an IF expression. Applying the transformation above and then simplifying produces:

```
((LAMBDA (Q2)
        (IF PRED1
            (IF PRED2 (PRINT 'WIN) (Q2))
            (Q2)))
    (LAMBDA () (ERROR 'LOSE)))
```

Recalling that (Q2) is, in effect, a GOTO branching to the common piece of code, and that by virtue of later analysis no actual closure will be created for either LAMBDA-expression, this result is quite reasonable. It does not evaluate the second predicate if the first results in NIL (false). The optimization on nested IF expressions has resulted in a simple source-level implementation of the optimization known as "anchor pointing" or "evaluation for control." (In most compilers this is handled at the code generation level by routines that pass around tags to jump to on success or failure of a predicate.)

This is a phenomenon we have noticed several times in RABBIT: because the many control constructs have been expressed in terms of only a few, only a few general and powerful optimizations techniques are needed, which tend to combine to produce more traditional techniques as special cases. (Another example of this phenomenon is that loop unrolling falls out as a special case of parameter substitution in LABELS statements.)

Environment and Closure Analysis

Just before the code generation stage, RABBIT determines for each LAMBDA-expression whether a closure will be needed for it at run time. The idea is that in many situations (particularly those generated as expansions of macros) one can determine at compile time precisely which function will be invoked by a combination, and perhaps also what its expected environment will be. There are three possibilities:
(1) If the function denoted by the LAMBDA-expression is bound to some variable, and that variable is referenced other than in

function position, then the closure is being treated as data, and must be a full (standard CBETA format) closure. If the function itself occurs in non-function position other than in a LAMBDA-combination, it must be fully closed.

(2) If the closure is bound to some variable, and that variable is referenced only in function position, but some of these references occur within other partially or fully closed functions, then this function must be partially closed. By this we mean that the environment for the closure must be "consed up," but no pointer to the code need be added on as for a full closure. This function will always be called from places that know the name of the function and so can just perform a GO to the code, but those such places which are within closures must have a complete copy of the necessary environment.

(3) In other cases (functions bound to variables referenced only in function position and never within a closed function, or functions occurring in function position of LAMBDA-combinations), the function need not be closed. This is because the environment can always be fully recovered from the environment at the point of call. The typical case of this is LABELS functions, which are seldom passed as parameters and which are all defined in the same environment. Because no run-time closures are needed for them, there is no run-time cost associated with entering or leaving a LABELS expression; because they are defined in the same environment, there is usually no environment adjustment needed for one to call another. Using LABELS functions to express GOTO or iteration entails no unexpected overhead.

In order to determine the closure information, it is necessary to determine, for each node, the set of variables referred to from within closed functions at or below that node. Thus this process and the process of determining which functions to close are highly interdependent, and so is accomplished in a single pass.

Conclusions

Lexical scoping, tail-recursion, the conceptual treatment of functions (as opposed to representations thereof) as data objects, and the ability to notate "anonymous" functions make SCHEME an excellent language in which to express program transformations and optimizations. Imperative constructs are easily modelled by applicative definitions. Anonymous functions make it easy to avoid needless duplication of code and conflict of variable names. A language with these properties is useful not only at the preliminary optimization level, but for expressing the results of decisions about order of evaluation and storage of temporary quantities. These properties make SCHEME as good a candidate as any for an UNCOL. The proper treatment of functions and function calls leads to generation of excellent imperative low-level code.

We have emphasized the ability to treat functions as data objects. We should point out that one might want to have a very simple run-time environment which did not support complex environment structures, or even stacks. Such an end environment does not preclude the use of the techniques described here. Many optimizations result in the elimination of LAMBDA-expressions; post CPS-conversion analysis eliminates the need to close many of the remaining LAMBDA-expressions. One could use the macros and internal representations of RABBIT to <u>describe</u> intermediate code transformations, and require that the final code not actually create any closures. As a concrete example, imagine writing an operating system in SCHEME, with machine words as the data domain (and functions excluded from the run-time data domain). We could still meaningfully write, for example:

```
(IF (OR (STOPPED (PROCESS I))
        (AWAITING-INPUT (PROCESS I)))
    (SCHEDULE-LOOP (+ I 1))
    (SCHEDULE-PROCESS I))
```

While the intermediate expansion of this code would conceptually involve the use of functions as data objects, optimizations would reduce the final code to a form which did not require closures.

References

Frances E. Allen and John Cocke, "A Catalogue of Optimizing Transformations," in Randall Rustin (ed.), *Design and Optimization of Compilers*, Proc. Courant Comp. Sci. Symp. 5, Prentice-Hall, 1972.

Daniel G. Bobrow and Ben Wegbreit, "A Model and Stack Implementation of Multiple Environments," *CACM* Vol. 16, No. 10, 1973.

Alonzo Church, *The Calculi of Lambda Conversion*, Annals of Mathematics Studies Number 6, Princeton University Press, 1941, Reprinted by Klaus Reprint Corp., 1965.

Samuel S. Coleman, *JANUS: A Universal Intermediate Language*, PhD thesis, University of Colorado, 1974.

Edsger W. Dijkstra, *A Discipline of Programming*, Prentice-Hall, 1976.

Jon Doyle, Johan de Kleer, Gerald Jay Sussman, and Guy L. Steele Jr., "AMORD: Explicit Control of Reasoning," Proc. AI and Programming Languages Conf., SIGPLAN Notices 12, 8, SIGART Newsletter 64, 1977.

Charles M. Geschke, *Global Program Optimizations*, PhD thesis, Carnegie-Mellon University, 1972.

David Gries, *Compiler Construction for Digital Computers*, John Wiley and Sons, 1971.

Peter J. Landin, "A Correspondence between ALGOL 60 and Church's Lambda-Notation," *CACM* Vol. 8, No. 2-3, 1965.

John McCarthy *et al.*, *LISP 1.5 Programmer's Manual*, The MIT Press, 1962.

David A. Moon, *MACLISP Reference Manual, Revision 0*, MIT Laboratory for Computer Science, 1974.

Joel Moses, *The Function of FUNCTION in LISP*, MIT AI Laboratory Memo 9, 1970.

John C. Reynolds, "Definitional Interpreters for Higher Order Programming Languages," *ACM Conference Proceedings*, 1972.

Jean E. Sammet, *Programming Languages: History and Fundamentals*, Prentice-Hall, 1969.

T. A. Standish *et al.*, *The Irvine Program Transformation Catalogue*, University of California, 1976.

Guy L. Steele Jr., "Debunking the 'Expensive Procedure Call' Myth," submitted to the 77 ACM National Conference, 1977A.

Guy Lewis Steele Jr., *Compiler Optimization Based on Viewing LAMBDA as RENAME Plus GOTO*, SM Thesis, MIT, 1977B.

Guy Lewis Steele Jr. and Gerald Jay Sussman, *LAMBDA: The Ultimate Imperative*, MIT AI Laboratory Memo 353, 1976A.

Guy Lewis Steele Jr., *LAMBDA: The Ultimate Declarative*, MIT AI Laboratory Memo 379, 1976B.

Joseph Stoy, *The Scott-Strachey Approach to the Mathematical Semantics of Programming Languages*, MIT Laboratory for Computer Science, 1974.

Warren Teitelman, *InterLISP Reference Manual* Revised edition, Xerox Palo Alto Research Center, 1975.

Mitchell Wand, and Daniel P. Friedman, *Compiling Lambda Expressions Using Continuations*, Technical Report 55, Indiana University, 1976.

William A. Wulf, et al., *The Design of an Optimizing Compiler*, American Elsevier, 1975.

CONTROL STRUCTURE AS PATTERNS OF PASSING MESSAGES

CARL HEWITT

Carl Hewitt presents an approach to modelling intelligence in terms of communicating knowledge-based problem-solving experts. Each of the experts can be viewed as a society that can be further decomposed until the primitive actors of the system are reached. This section investigates the nature of the <u>communication mechanisms</u> needed for effective problem solving by a society of experts and the conventions of discourse that make this possible. The ability to analyze or synthesize any kind of control structure as a pattern of passing messages among the members of a society provides an important tool for understanding control structures.

The Actor Programming Methodology

We are developing methods to specify the behavior of actors (objects) in terms that are natural to the semantics of the causal and incidental relationships among the objects. Causal relationships are determined by physical causation in activating computational events whereas incidental relationships are determined by the local order of arrival of messages at their destinations. That is, we are attempting to develop a transparent medium for constructing models in which the control structure emerges *as a pattern of passing messages among the objects being modeled. Towards that end, we are developing a programming methodology consisting of the following activities:*

- Deciding on the natural kinds of actors (objects) to have in the system to be constructed.

- Deciding for each kind of actor what kind of messages it should receive.

- Deciding for each kind of actor what it should do when it receives each kind of message.

Making the above decisions *should constitute* the design of an implementation. Thus the data structures and control structures of the implementation *should be determined by these decisions* instead of being determined by the limitations of the programming language being used. This is not to say that the resulting implementation should be unstructured. Rather the structure of the implementation should develop naturally from the structure of the system being modeled working within the conventions of discourse among actors.

Actors are a local model of computation. There is no such thing as "action at a distance" nor is there any "global state" of all actors in the universe. Actors interact on a purely local way by sending messages to one another.

Actors

The basic construct of our computation model is the *ACTOR*. The *BEHAVIOR* of each actor is *DEFINED* by the relationships among the events which are caused by the actor.

At a more superficial and imprecise level, each actor may be thought of as having two aspects which together realize the behavior which it manifests:

- the ACTION it should take when it is sent a message

- its ACQUAINTANCES which is the finite collection of actors that it directly KNOWS ABOUT.

We first discuss actors in terms of their physical arrangement because it makes the discussion more concrete and familiar to most readers. Gradually the emphasis will change to a discussion of the behaviors realized by actors.

Diagramatically we will represent a situation in which an actor A knows about an actor B by drawing a directed arc (which may be labeled for the convenience of the reader) from A to B.

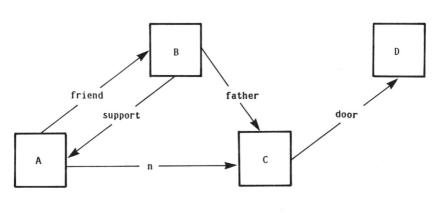

A directly knows about B as "friend"
B directly knows about A as "support"
A directly knows about C as "n"
B directly knows about C as "father"
C directly knows about D as "door"

The notation (acquaintances x) will be used to denote the immediate acquaintances of an actor x. For example

(acquaintances A) = {C B}
(acquaintances B) = {A C}
(acquaintances C) = {D}
(acquaintances D) = {}

Note that the KNOWS ABOUT relationship is asymmetric; i.e. it is possible for an actor A to know about another actor C without C also knowing about A. Should it happen that A and B know about each other then we will say that they are MUTUAL ACQUAINTANCES.

The acquaintances of an actor are an abstraction of its physical representation. Consider for example a list L with first element x and rest y The actual physical representation of L could be in terms of a linked list, a vector of storage, or even a hash table:

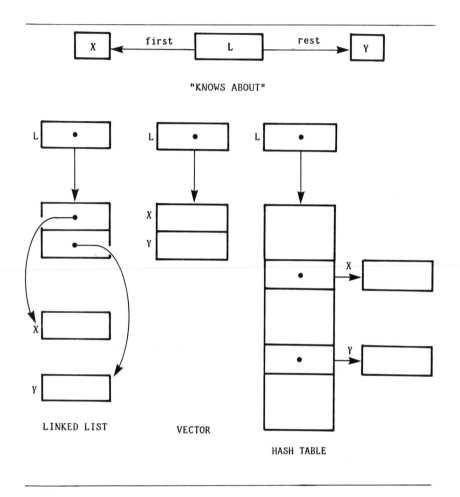

"KNOWS ABOUT"

LINKED LIST   VECTOR

HASH TABLE

Actors are straightforward to implement on conventional machines. We will mention a couple of ways to do this in order to add concreteness to our discussion. Practical implementations are particularly easy to construct using list-processing languages and micro-processors. Our implementation of actors in LISP uses one cons pair for every actor. One component of the pair is a LISP procedure which provides an entry point into the machine code necessary to implement the behavior of the actor when it is sent a message. The other component of the pair is an ordered list of the acquaintances of the actor. A similar representation could be used on a micro-processor (such as the CONS micro-processor of Knight et. al.). A reference to an actor on a micro-processor would in general require one word of memory which consisted of two sub-fields. One field would be used as an index into the micro-code and the other field would be used to point to a vector of the acquaintances of the actor.

The reader should keep in mind that within the actor model of computation there is no way to decompose an actor into its parts. An actor is defined by its behavior; not by its physical representation!

Components of the Actor Model

The actor message-passing model is being developed as four tightly related and mutually supportive components: 1: A method for the *rigorous specification of behaviors* from various perspectives. An important degree of flexibility available in actor semantics involves the ability to carefully control the articulation of detail to be included in specifications. That is, the constraints on the behavior of a system of actors can be specified in as much or as little detail as is germane. Too much detail is distracting and impractical. Too little detail fails to specify important aspects of the desired behavior. The wrong kind of detail deflects attention down fruitless paths. Often the specifications need to be very highly articulated for some crucial aspects of the desired behavior and less so for other aspects. We are developing a methodology through which the desired behavior of a system can be specified by axioms which characterize the relationships among the events which must constitute the behavior of the system. At the highest level these axioms are specifications of *what* is to be done rather than *how.* As more detailed constraints of the allowable events are gradually imposed, the possible behaviors which will realize these constraints become more restricted until one is uniquely determined. Conversely, in order to demonstrate that a set of specifications is satisfied by a particular actor, one examines the behaviors of the component actors and demonstrates that the connection of these behaviors realizes the behavior that is required. 2: A system (called PLASMA for PLANNER-like System Modeled on Actors) implemented in terms of actor message passing that is convenient for the interactive construction of scenarios, scripts, and justifications. A *SCRIPT* is a PLASMA program which can be used to specify the action that an actor will take when it receives a message. In our research we have attempted to investigate semantic instead of syntactic issues. We have designed PLASMA to be a *transparent medium* for expressing the underlying semantics of actor message-passing. For example the semantics of the "knows-about" relationship for actors dictates that PLASMA must use a particular syntactic rule (lexical binding) for the referents of identifiers. The semantic model specifies that acquaintances of an actor must be specified when the actor is created. PLASMA satisfies this semantic constraint by using the values of the identifers at at the time of creation for the free identifiers in the script of a newly created actor since these are the only actors available to be used as acquaintances. 3: A *mathematical theory of computation* which can represent any kind of discrete behavior that can be physically realized. Our goal is to have a *robust* theory whose theorems are not sensitive to arbitrary conventions and definitions. A theory which will be widely applicable as a mathematical tool is needed for formalizing and investigating properties of procedures. Currently our theory takes the form of a set of laws that any physically realizable actor system must satisfy together with a set of axioms that characterize the behavior of a powerful modular set of physically realizable actors (the primitives of PLASMA) which embody *conventions for discourse* among actors. 4: The *Event Diagrams* presented in this paper are a further development of a graphical notation used by Richard Steiger in his masters thesis for displaying relationships among the events of an actor computation. In this paper we use them to show the causal and knowledge relationships that characterize simple control structures such as iteration and recursion as patterns of passing messages. Given an outline of important hypothesized events and causal relations among the events of a particular computation (i.e. a *SCENARIO* of the intended behavior of the system), event diagrams aid in abstracting scripts of modules that are capable of realizing this behavior. For example we plan to explore the abstraction of the scripts of actors for simple procedures for data structures from scenarios of their intended use. Conversely, they aid in the analysis of an existing system by graphically displaying the relationships among the events occuring in the system for particular cases of behavior. Using the displays available on our time-sharing system, we would like to automate the construction and analysis of event diagrams that have been done by hand in this paper. We would like to investigate the construction of an *"eclectic magnifying glass"* which provides flexible ways to specify which events and relationships in the history of a computation are to be be displayed.

Introduction to Event Diagrams

From a strictly input-output point of view there is no difference between iterative and non-iterative implementations of a module. In order to rigorously analyze control structures it is necessary to have a model of computation that is capable of displaying the *internal structure of computations.*

We shall use <u>event diagrams</u> to display the internal structure of computations. Such diagrams can be used to display many of the significant internal structural relations in a computation.

the box represents the actor A

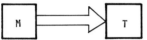

x *knows about* y as "helper"

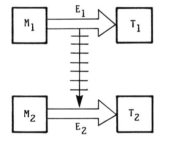

the double line represents the EVENT which consists of <u>sending</u> the messenger M to the target T

the "railroad tracks" are used to indicate that the occurrence of event E_1 results in the occurrence of the event E_2 and thus E_1 must precede E_2 in time. The event E_1 has messenger M_1 and target T_1 whereas the event E_2 has messenger M_2 and target T_2.

Actor Transmission

Actors make use of one universal communication mechanism called *ACTOR TRANSMISSION* which consists of sending one actor (called the *MESSENGER* of the transmission) to another actor (called the *TARGET* of the transmission). Each actor transmission defines an EVENT in which the MESSENGER arrives at the TARGET. The target and messenger are the immediate *PARTICIPANTS* in the event, i.e. if E is an event with messenger actor M and target actor T then

$$(\text{participants } E) = \{M\ T\}$$

Actor transmission enables the knowledge in the local context of the target actor T to be integrated with the information of the messenger actor M since the acquaintances of both the messenger and target are available for use when the messenger arrives at the target. Furthermore this constitutes the only information available at the instant of computation defined by the event!

Actor transmission is used to provide the necessary communication between actors to accomplish the following kinds of actions:

- calling a procedure

- obtaining an element from a data structure

- invoking a co-routine

- modifying a data-structure

- returning a value

- synchronization of communicating parallel processes

The actor transmission communication mechanism enforces the modularity and protection of actor systems. It provides the basis for constructing actor systems with explicit modular interfaces such that user of a module (actor) can only depend of the behavior of the actor. The hardware enforces the constraint that the user of a module cannot depend on its current physical representation.

Messengers

In order to have a useful model of a message-passing system, the problem of infinite regress must be explicitly addressed. The actor message passing model provides for primitive actors to deal with this problem. When a primitive actor receives a request, it is unnecessary for the primitive to send any further messages in order to properly respond to the request. In particular this means that a primitive actor must be able to obtain some of the acquaintances of a messenger which it receives without having to send any messages. Packagers provide the primitive mechanism needed in PLASMA for transmitting messengers between actors.

Once an actor, m, (serving as messenger) is transmitted to another actor (serving as the target), t, the computation proceeds by following the script of t using information from m. For this to be of any use as a model of communication, it must be that m obeys some fairly standard conventions. These provide the basis for meaningful discourse between actors. We will adopt the convention that all of the messengers constructed by the PLASMA system are packagers of the following form:

(messenger: (agent: a) (envelope: e) (banker: b))

where a is an actor representing the agent responsible for the computation, e is the envelope of the transmission, and b is the banker funding the computation. The explanation of bankers and agents is outside the scope of this paper so we shall say no more about them.

Envelopes

In many cases the envelope of a messenger will simply contain a message. A response to a request is either a REPLY envelope with a reply message to the request packaged as

(reply: the-message)

or a COMPLAIN envelope with a complaint message packaged as

(complain: the-message)

which explains why the request could not be honored.

Often the envelope of a messenger is a REQUEST which in addition to a request message contains an actor c to which a reply to the request should be sent. Such an envelope is packaged as follows:

(request: the-message (reply-to: c))

The ACTOR c is closely related to the continuation FUNCTIONS used by Morris, Wadsworth, Reynolds, and Strachey.

An ordinary functional call to a function f with arguments arg_1, ..., through arg_k is implemented in PLASMA by passing to f a request envelope with a message consisting of the tuple [arg_1, ..., arg_k] of arguments and a continuation actor to which the value of f should be sent.

Request and Reply

Perhaps the simplest control structure is the ordinary request and reply pattern of activity that is implemented in most programming languages as a procedure call and return. None of the internal structure of the actor being invoked is shown. Instead the description articulates only the input-output behavior of the actor.

Consider the example of a request being sent to an actor factorial to compute its value for the argument tuple [3] and send the answer to the actor c. The diagram shows the two events consisting of the above REQUEST (i.e. factorial is sent a messenger M_1 with message [3] and continuation c) and the REPLY in which c is sent a newly created messenger M_2 with message 6:

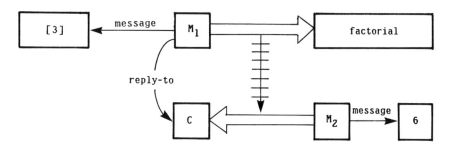

The above event diagram treats factorial as a "black box" with none of the internal events shown. Notice that the computational process follows the "railroad" tracks from the first event to the second event. We will now proceed to examine the computation more closely. This is an application of the idea of using an *eclectic magnifying glass* to articulate the description of a behavior in greater detail. What is seen depends on how factorial is implemented as well as the focus of the magnifying glass. When we look into the implementation of factorial, we will see a number of events that occur between the two which are diagrammed above.

Note that the value 6 which is constructed by the actor factorial is <u>not</u> an acquaintance of factorial. Instead it is the "reply" acquaintance of the messenger M_2 which is sent to the continuation c.

Scripts for a Non-Iterative Factorial

Suppose we have a non-iterative implementation of factorial. A script written in PLASMA for such an implementation is given below.

```
(factorial ≡ ;;factorial is defined to be
    (≡> [=n]  ;;receive a message with one element which will be called n
        (rules n ;;the rules for n are
            (≡> 1 ;;if it is 1
                1) ;;then return 1
            (≡> (> 1) ;;else if it is greater than 1 then
                (n * (factorial (n - 1))))))))) ;;return n times factorial
                                            ;; of n minus 1
```

We are interested in looking more deeply into the control structure of recursive procedures. To this end we take the above non-iterative implementation of factorial as a concrete example to be studied. When factorial receives the message [3] it is not able to reply immediately since it does not directly know what (factorial 3) is. Below is an event diagram of the computation that results from sending factorial a messenger M_1 with message [3] and continuation c up to the point of the first recursive call in which factorial is sent a newly created messenger M_2 with message [2] and continuation c' where c' is a newly created actor that knows about n and c. The script of c' is such that whenever it is sent a message y, it sends c the message (3 * y).

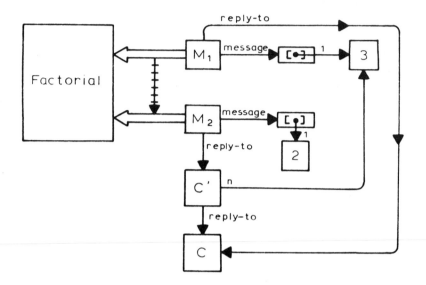

     Below we present a snapshot of the storage at the instant factorial receives the message [1]. The rule for computing the amount of storage being used at the instant of any particular event is very simple: Merely count all the actors that are in the transitive closure of the acquaintances of the participants involved in the event. Recall that the participants of an event are the actors immediately involved (i.e. the target and messenger).

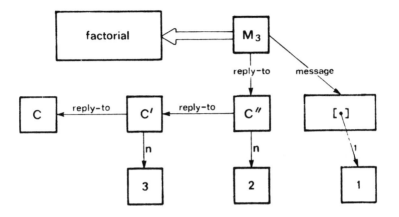

The above event diagram exhibits the characteristic structure of a recursive computation. This pattern is familiar to users of ALGOL, LISP 1.5, and PL/1 and other programming languages that make use of a pushdown stack to implement recursion. In such languages the amount of stack used by the implementation grows monotonically until factorial is called with the argument 1 and then monotonically decreases as the stack is popped.

Characterization of Recursion as a Pattern of Passing Messages

Recursion can be characterized as a pattern of passing messages using event diagrams. The characteristic feature is the build up of a chain of continuation actors each one of which knows only about the next and which eventually replies to the next with the answer. Notice that this characterization of recursion in terms of relations between events is independent of the syntax of the language for scripts which gives rise to the behavior. For example the same characterization would hold for a recursive implementation of factorial in ALGOL. The semantics of ALGOL can be defined using relations among events in a manner similar to the way in which the semantics of PLASMA is defined.

The existence of the actors labeled c' and c'' in the above diagram and the events in which they are the target are difficult to explain in terms of the above PLASMA script for factorial. In order to explain the origin of these actors and events, we need to explain more of the underlying implementation of PLASMA.

Envelope Level Scripts

Thus far in our PLASMA scripts we have examined information communicated in the messages of envelopes. At this point we would like to introduce the *envelope level* which allows access to other information in the messengers of actor transmissions. Every messenger always contains (among other things) an actor which serves as the ENVELOPE. In turn every envelope always contains an actor which serves as the MESSAGE. Additionally REQUEST envelopes contain actors called CONTINUATIONS to which replies to the messages should be sent.

The reason that it is useful to introduce the envelope level transmitters and receivers into scripts is that otherwise much of the control structure (pattern of passing messages) has to remain implicit in something like an evaluator or a compiler. Envelope receivers and transmitters provide the mechanism for expressing more explicit scripts so that none of the processing or allocation of storage is going on behind the scenes.

Envelope receivers and transmitters are analogous to ordinary receivers and transmitters in many respects. They are intended to be used as a notation for writing scripts in which all the computational events and actors are explicitly shown. In this way the structure of simple control structures such as iteration and recursion can be explicitly characterized as patterns of passing messages.

PLASMA uses the syntactic convention of using the number of shafts on the transmitter and receive arrows to reflect the level at which the transmission is being referenced; one shaft meaning ordinary message level, and two shafts meaning envelope level. Thus:

<= is an (ordinary) message-level-transmitter, and
<== is a envelope-level-transmitter.

Similarly,

≡> is an (ordinary) message-level-receiver, and
≡≡> is an envelope-level-receiver.

Below we use this notation to make the message-passing underlying the implementation of PLASMA more explicit.
    For example an ordinary message receiver which receives one argument n and replies with the value (n + 1) written as

```
(≡> [=n]
    (n + 1))
```

can be written at the envelope level as follows:

```
(≡≡> (request: [=n] (reply-to: =c))
     (c <== (reply: (n + 1))))
```

The = sign above is a prefix character used to indicate that matching should be used to bind the identifier which follows.

A More Explicit Script for the Non-Iterative Factorial

The correspondence between the event diagram for the non-iterative implementation of factorial and its script can be made more apparent by using envelope transmitters and receivers to make the underlying implementation explicit. *The script presented below is intended to explicate how the implementation of*

PLASMA actually works.

```
(factorial ≡ ;;factorial is defined to be
    (≡≡> (request: [=n] (reply-to: =c)) ;;receive a request to
                              ;; compute the value of factorial for
                              ;;an argument tuple whose only element is n
                              ;;and send the reply to the actor c
         (rules n ;;the rules for n are
             (≡> 1 ;;if it is 1 then
                 (c <== (reply: 1))) ;;send c a reply envelope with message 1
             (≡> (> 1) ;;else if it is greater than 1
                 (factorial <== ;;send factorial a request
                     (request: [(n - 1)] ;;with message (n - 1) and
                         (reply-to: ;;continuation the following actor
                             (≡≡> (reply: =y) ;;if a reply envelope
                                       ;;with message y is received
                                 (c <== (reply: (y * n))))))))))))) ;then send
                                                  ;; c a reply
                                                  ;;envelope with
                                                  ;; message (y * n)
```

Notice that the above script specifies that before recursively calling factorial (in the case where n≠1), a new actor is created as the reply-to: component of the envelope sent to factorial. This new actor is created with ACQUAINTANCES n and c and has the following SCRIPT:

```
(≡≡> (reply: =y)
    (c <== (reply: (y * n))))
```

Operationally, the script says "for each reply y that is received, multiply it by n and send the resulting product as a reply to c."

Iteration

It is well known that another, more efficient implementation of factorial uses iterative control structure. Event diagrams will be used as a tool to illustrate the behavior of this more efficient implementation of factorial. One idea for an iterative implementation is to gradually build up the product while counting down the argument --doing one multiply for each iteration. So we define an actor called loop which should be sent both the current accumulation (which is initially 1) and the current count (which is initially the input n) on each iteration. The obvious way to do this is to repeatedly send loop a sequence of the form [accumulation count].

A Script for an Iterative Implementation of Factorial

```
(factorial ≡ ;;factorial is defined to be
    (≡> [=n] ;;receive one argument and call it n
        ([1 n] => ;;send a 2-tuple with elements 1 and n to
            (loop ≡ ;;a newly created actor named loop which
                (≡> [=accumulation =count] ;;receive a 2-tuple
                    (rules count ;;the rules for the count are
                        (≡> 1 ;:if it is 1 then
                            accumulation) ;;return the accumulation
                        (≡> (> 1) ;;else if it is greater than 1
                            (loop ;;send loop
                                (accumulation * count)
                                    ;;the accumulation times the count
                                (count - 1)))))))))
                                    ;;and the count minus one
```

Notice that the argument n is <u>not</u> an acquaintance of the actor loop in the iterative implementation of factorial. The rule for calculating the acquaintances <u>from the script</u> of an actor defined in PLASMA is very simple: the acquaintances of a newly created actor are the actors named by the free identifiers in the script at the time the actor is created. Instead of being an acquaintance, the actor n is <u>sent</u> to loop as the second element of the two tuple [1 n].

The script given above will exhibit the behavior diagramed below when factorial is sent the message [3]. This is an illustration of iteration as a pattern of passing messages. Note the repeated use of the actor c as a continuation in the envelopes used in the iterative implementation of factorial.

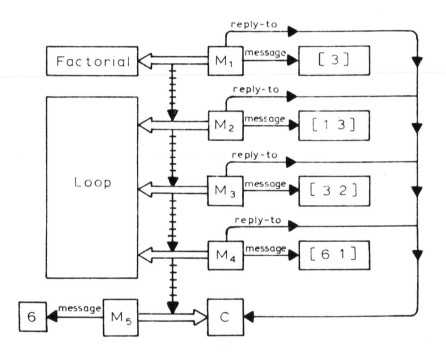

A More Explicit Script for Iterative Factorial

Notice that the above implementation of factorial definitely uses iterative (finite-state) control structure in the sense that it does not need any more memory than that needed for the values of count and accumulation. We now incorporate envelope transmitters and receivers to make the script of the iterative implementation of factorial more explicit. In this way the correspondence between the event diagram for the iterative implementation and its script becomes more apparent.

```
(factorial ≡ ;;factorial is defined to be

   (≡≡> (request: [=n] ;;receive a request with argument tuple [n]
          (reply-to: =c)) ;;and continuation c
      ((request: [1 n] (reply-to: c)) ==> ;;send a request with argument
                                          ;; tuple [1 n] and
                       ;;continuation c to the following newly created actor
          (loop ≡ ;;named loop
             (≡≡> (request: [=accumulation =count] (reply-to: =d))
                  ;;such that if a request is received with
                  ;;message containing the accumulation and count
                  ;;and continuation d
                (rules count ;;checks the count
                   (≡> 1 ;;to see if it is 1
                       (d <== (reply: accumulation)))
                                   ;;if so it sends the
                                   ;;accumulation as a reply to d
                   (≡> (> 1) ;;else if it is greater than 1 then
                       (loop <== ;;send loop a request with
                          (request: [(accumulation * count) (count - 1)]
                             ;;the appropriate message
                          (reply-to: d)))))))))))
                             ;;and the continuation
```

The reason that this is iterative is that loop always passes along the <u>same</u> continuation actor that it receives with the message. The only continuation it needs, and therefore the only one that it holds onto, is the one contained in the original envelope that was sent to factorial. The loop sends its answer to that continuation directly when it is done. Thus no extra storage is needed going around the loop. Furthermore, in this implementation of iteration there are no side effects which change the behavior of any actor. If the user wants, she can keep a complete history of all the events in her computation and be confident that no information has been lost. Actor semantics account for the iterative behavior of the above implementation of factorial without having to appeal to external implicit mechanism such as an interpreter or any kind of external storage mechanism such as activation records. All the behavior of the system is accounted for by the behavior of actors when they are sent messages. Furthermore all of the storage is accounted for by the actors shown in the event diagrams. *Event diagrams show how PLASMA is actually implemented using actors.* The actor model provides a complete self-contained rigorous theory of iteration as a pattern of passing messages. It provides an explanation for the semantics behind the optimization rule used by many compilers that all "tail recursive" self-referential definitions can be compiled using special iteration primitives such as "while" loops, "do" loops, etc.

Meaning of "Recursion"

The term RECURSIVE has come to have at least three different meanings in computer science:

> 1: Effectively computable as in "recursive function theory"
> 2: Self-referential as in "factorial can be defined recursively in terms of itself"
> 3: Non-iterative as in "recursive functions use up more push-down stack when they call each other whereas iterative loops do not."

Both the iterative and non-iterative definitions for factorial which we have presented are self-referential. However, only the non-iterative implementation is "recursive" in the third sense of the word.

Using factorial as a simple example, we have shown how the actor message passing model can be used to give additional precision to fundamental concepts in computer science.

Comparison of Recursion and Iteration

Below we present abstracted versions of the event diagrams for the iterative and non-iterative implementations of factorial when called with 3 as an argument. In the diagrams below the message is shown inside the messenger in order to more strongly bring out the pattern of message passing.

RECURSION

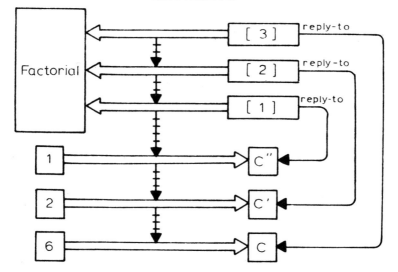

ITERATION

Generators

In knowledge based systems, it is unreasonable to store all the implications of the knowledge available at a given time. Explicitly storing the answers to all possible questions instead of incrementally generating them as they are needed is not only extremely inefficient since most of them may never be needed, but may in fact be impossible. For example expanding out all the possible games of chess before making the first move is clearly infeasible. Therefore it must be possible to incrementally generate implications as needed in order to answer questions.

In order to deal with this problem Newell, Shaw, Simon introduced a form of *generators* into their Information Processing Language. Since that time, the concept has undergone considerable further development. In terms of actors the idea is to construct a sequence s which <u>behaves</u> like a sequence of the possible answers to some question. The trick is that s does not physically contain all the answers but rather generates them incrementally as needed. To make this discussion more concrete we present a simple problem that illustrates how generators can be conveniently implemented in PLASMA.

We will assume that we have some actors called trees such that each tree is either of the form (terminal: T) where T is

the terminal symbol, or of the form (non-terminal: L R) where L
and R are left and right sub-trees.

For example the tree

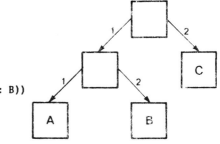

(non-terminal:

     (non-terminal: (terminal: A)

                   (terminal: B))

     (terminal: C))

has the fringe (sequence of terminals in left to right order)
[A B C] as does the following tree:

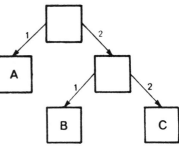

(non-terminal:

     (terminal: A)

     (non-terminal: (terminal: B)

   (terminal: C)))

whereas the following tree

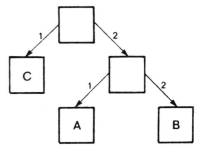

(non-terminal:

     (terminal: C)

     (non-terminal: (terminal: A)

               (terminal: B)))

has [C A B] as its fringe.

The problem is to define the actor fringe so that for any
tree T, (fringe T) behaves like a sequence of the terminal elements
of T. There are two important properties that characterize the
behavior of fringe. First, fringe of a terminal node must behave
like a sequence with one element

```
            (fringe (terminal: T))    α    [T]
```

The symbol α is used to denote behavioral equivalence of actors. Second, fringe of a non-terminal node must <u>behave</u> like the sequence produced by concatenating the fringe of the left sub-node and the fringe of the right subnode:

```
     (fringe (non-terminal: L R))    α    [!(fringe L) !(fringe R)]
```

The above specification makes use of the unpack operator ! of PLASMA.

A High-Level Implementation

From the above behavioral specifications we can immediately derive the following implementation of fringe:

```
(fringe ≡ ;;the behavior of fringe is defined to be
    (≡> [=the-tree] ;;whenever it receives a tree
        (rules the-tree ;;the rules for the tree are
            (≡> (terminal: =T) ;;if is a terminal T
                [T]) ;;then the fringe is a sequence whose
                        ;;only element is T
            (≡> (non-terminal: =L =R)
                        ;;else the tree must be a non-terminal
                [!(fringe L) !(fringe R)])))) ;;and the fringe of the
                ;; tree is the fringe of its left sub-tree
                ;; concatenated with the fringe of its
                ;; right sub-tree
```

Unfortunately, the above implementation is not incremental because it immediately looks at all the nodes of the tree and thus is exponentially inefficient. The above definition of fringe is still very much a specification of *what* fringe is supposed to do as opposed to a detailed specification of *how* to efficiently accomplish the task. This lack of concern with the details of implementation is the chief advantage (and at the same time the chief disadvantage) of high-level implementations.

An Incremental Implementation

Incremental generation amounts to adopting a "wait and see" approach as to whether the rest of the elements will be needed. The above implementation of fringe can be refined to be incremental by use of the delay operator.

```
(fringe ≡ ;;the behavior of fringe is defined to be
    (≡> [=the-tree] ;;whenever it receives a tree
        (rules the-tree ;;the rules for the tree are
            (≡> (terminal: =T) ;;if is a terminal T
                [T]) ;;then the fringe is a sequence
                    ;; whose only element is T
            (≡> (non-terminal: =L =R) ;;else the tree must be a non-terminal
                [!(delay (fringe L)) !(delay (fringe R))]))))) ;;and the
                    ;;tree fringe is the fringe of its left sub-tree
                    ;; concatenated with the fringe of its
                    ;; right sub-tree
```

The "wait and see" approach is not always the most efficient implementation for every problem. In particular often there is a space-time trade-off in the use of the delay operator. In many cases it is more efficient to simply compute an expression E immediately than to wait by the use of (delay E) since the latter can cause the retention of extra unnecessary storage. For example consider the following definition:

```
(f ≡
    (≡> [=x =h]
        (rules x
            (≡> (< 3)
                0)
            (else
                h))))
```

Notice that the expression (f 2 HUGE) immediately evaluates to 0 whereas the expression (delay (f 2 HUGE)) is an arbitrarily large amount of storage which will eventually evaluate to 0. The reader might consider how the efficiency of the implementation of the delay operator can be improved using partial evaluation.

Incremental Perpetual Development

The development of any large system (viewed as a society) having a long useful life must be viewed as an *incremental* and *evolutionary* process. Development begins with specifications, plans, domain dependent knowledge, and scenarios for a large task. Attempts to use this information to create an implementation have the effect of causing revisions: additions, deletions, modifications, specializations, generalizations, etc. At all times in the perpetual development of the system the programmers are confronted with

- A progression of more refined plans (programs, implementations, etc.) which partially accomplish some of the tasks specified.

- Partial specifications (contracts, intentions, constraints, etc.) for some of the subtasks which are to be accomplished.

- Partial justifications (proofs, demonstrations, analysis of dependencies) regarding how some of the plans satisfy some of their specifications.

■   Partial descriptions of some of the background knowledge
      (mathematical facts, physical laws, questions of interactive
      users, government regulations, etc.) of the environment
      in which the system will operate.

■   A collection of scenarios (at various articulations of
      detail) demonstrating how the system is supposed to work
      in concrete instances.

The success of an evolutionary behavioral modeling
methodology is highly dependent on the development of
competent Programming Apprentices [Hewitt and Smith 1975],
[Rich and Shrobe 1974], [Yonezawa 1975] that help keep the
above potentially disparate descriptions of a system coherently
organized. The primary benefit of maintaining this coherence is
not to prove once and for all that the implementation is CORRECT
in any absolute sense. Changes in the environment external to
the system will require that the system must either adapt its
behavior to the changed circumstances or be supplanted. *Rather
the chief benefit of demonstrating the coherence of multiple descriptions
of a system is to make the dependencies among the parts explicit so that
the system can be readily adapted to the perpetually changing external
environment.* Already for many systems considerably more money
is spent on modification and enhancement than on initial design
and implementation.

The Actor Problem-Solving Metaphor

The actor metaphor for problem solving is a large human
scientific society: each actor is a scientist. Each has her own
duties, specialties, and contracts. Control is decentralized among
the actors. Communication is highly stylized and formal using
messages that are sent to individual actors.
      Problem solving proceeds by the attempts of experts to

guess, or to conjecture, a plan for a solution followed by attempts to criticize the usually somewhat faulty initial plan. Plans for action are put forward for trial, to be eliminated or modified if not germane to the problem at hand. Tentative acceptance of a proposed plan must be combined with an ability to revise it if it is demonstrated to be infeasible. We make it our task to construct expert problem-solving modules to live in a world characterized by incomplete knowledge; to adjust themselves to it as well as they can; to take advantage of the opportunities they can find in it; and to solve the problem, if possible (they need not assume that it is), with the help of the knowledge available. If this is the task, then there is no more rational procedure than the method of *planning, refining, and criticizing*: of proposing new plans; progressively refining these plans to incorporate knowledge relevant to their execution, criticizing these refinements to expose their deficiencies; and of tentatively following them if they survive.

Newell [1962] points out two potential difficulties which must be dealt with by systems which adopt the actor problem solving methodology. First, the messages (carried by the messengers) must sometimes contain strategies, not just facts. They must be in the form of partial information that can be combined with other information available to the target actor. A good formal language must be developed for this kind of communication. The second potential difficulty is that a society operating in this fashion must not become a bureaucracy bogged down in sending messages back and forth without making any progress. We propose to rely on the critical nature of actors which are delegated subtasks to help control aimless thrashing.

We would like to emphasize that in the current state of the art only a small part of this metaphor can be realized in practice. At this point in time the metaphor serves mainly to provide suggestions of directions in which to work. Perhaps in the very far future it will be possible to construct computer systems which have a significant fraction of the expertise and communication ability of a small scientific subfield.

References

Carl Hewitt and Brian Smith, "Towards a Programming Apprentice" *IEEE Transactions on Software Engineering*, SE-1,1 1975.

A.   Newell, *Some Problems of Basic Organization in Problem-Solving Programs*, Rand Corporation Memorandum RM-3283-PR, 1962.

C.   Rich and H. Shrobe, *Understanding LISP Programs: Towards a Programmer's Apprentice*, MIT AI Laboratory Working Paper 82, 1974.

A.   Yonezawa, *Symbolic Evaluation of Programs as an Aid to Program Construction*, MIT AI Laboratory Working Paper, 1975.

This paper was previously published in *Artificial Intelligence*, Vol. 8, pp. 323-363, 1977.

THE
INDEX

destination frame, I-354
determination hypothesis, I-196
determined, I-52
Deutch-Waite-Schorr marking algorithm, II-382
developmental processes, I-428
difference, II-147
differentiation, I-430
diffuser, II-136
diode model, exponential, I-61
dipole statics, II-25
disambiguation, I-448
disambiguation, reference, I-233
disconnected discourse, I-240
discourse purposes, I-243
discourse, disconnected, I-240
discourse, I-235
discrimination, texture, II-24
domain specific heuristics, I-113
domain-specific meta-knowledge, I-460
doubly curved, II-174
dynamic binding, II-377
dynamic model, I-289
dynamic scoping, II-402
dynamically scoped, II-366
dynamics, II-276, II-287, II-299

E

eclectic magnifying glass, II-446
elementary rotations, II-304
emitter-coupled-pair, I-60
equivalences, I-63
error prediction, II-253
evolutionary process, II-462
EXEMPLAR, I-389
explanatory theory, I-198

W-X-Y-Z